GENERATION Rx

GENERATION RX

A STORY OF DOPE, DEATH, AND AMERICA'S OPIATE CRISIS

ERIN MARIE DALY

COUNTERPOINT

BERKELEY

Library of Congress Cataloging-in-Publication Data

Daly, Erin Marie.
  Generation Rx : a story of dope, death, and America's opiate crisis / Erin Marie Daly.
  Includes bibliographical references.
  ISBN 978-1-61902-291-1
  1. Youth—Drug use—United States. 2. Drug abuse—United States. 3. Substance abuse—United States. I. Title.
  HV5825.D354 2014
  362.29'30973—dc23
  2014014412

Cover design by Natalya Balnova
Interior design by Megan Jones Design

COUNTERPOINT
www.counterpointpress.com

Printed in the United States of America
Distributed by Publishers Group West

10 9 8 7 6 5 4 3 2 1

FOR ALL WHOSE LIVES HAVE BEEN AFFECTED BY OPIATE ADDICTION

and

FOR PAT

CONTENTS

PART V: ACCEPTANCE

AMERICA'S EPIDEMIC OF PRESCRIPTION PAINKILLER AND HEROIN ABUSE:

A NATIONAL TIMELINE

1898

✖ The Bayer Company releases heroin as a cough suppressant. It is legally sold over the counter in both pill and elixir forms.[1]

✖ Bayer touts the drug as having a low risk of causing addiction, but there is an explosion of heroin-related admissions at hospitals, and cities begin to report a substantial population of recreational users. Some of these users support their habits by collecting and selling scrap metal, hence the term *junkie*.[2]

1900

✖ The number of morphine addicts in the United States reaches an estimated three hundred thousand, including many Civil War veterans who were exposed to the painkiller for treatment of their war injuries.[3]

1911

✖ Bayer pulls heroin from the market due to widespread concerns about its addictive properties.[4]

1919

✖ The U.S. Supreme Court issues an opinion that interprets the Harrison Act of 1914—the nation's first drug law—as banning the prescribing of narcotics to those addicted to them. Tens of thousands of doctors are charged with offenses related to the law, leading many medical professionals to become hesitant to prescribe morphine for the treatment of pain, even when it is warranted.[5]

EARLY 1990S

✖ The purity of heroin on U.S. streets dramatically increases. In the 1970s and 1980s, purity levels had been about 3 to 10 percent; by 1991 heroin is about 27 percent pure. By 1994 it is about 40 percent pure.[6] Because heroin is so pure, it can be snorted rather than injected, increasing its popularity.

MID- TO LATE 1990S

✖ Two major groups representing doctors specializing in pain treatment, the American Pain Society and the American Academy of Pain Management, declare that U.S. doctors are not adequately treating pain and are underprescribing opioid pain medications due to a misguided fear of causing addiction.[7] The result is a national push to treat pain more aggressively.

✖ The two groups issue a landmark 1996 consensus statement claiming that there is little risk of addiction or overdose among pain patients. They cite a statistic that less than 1 percent of opioid users become addicted, a figure that comes from a single-paragraph report in the New England Journal of Medicine in 1980 describing hospitalized patients briefly given opioids.[8]

✖ The pharmaceutical industry begins to promote opioids as safe for the long-term treatment of chronic pain. Among the most widely used opioids are hydrocodone, which is used in Vicodin, and oxycodone, found in OxyContin and Percocet. Other potent opioids include fentanyl and methadone.[9]

✖ Many small-town family practice and general medicine doctors are relatively inexperienced in the treatment of either pain or addiction, but they begin prescribing large amounts of painkillers due to marketing efforts of pain-management specialists, who are often paid speakers for the companies that produce painkillers.[10]

✖ Chronic pain patients begin getting hooked on medications that were prescribed to them, a situation known as iatrogenic addiction.[11]

1997-2006

✖ The number of prescriptions for opioid pain pills increases dramatically: prescription sales of hydrocodone go up 244 percent, while oxycodone sales rise 732 percent.[12]

✖ Many parts of the United States, particularly rural areas, begin to see sky-rocketing rates of addiction and crime related to the use of painkillers, including pharmacy thefts.[13]

✖ In 2001 a study shows that between 18 and 45 percent of patients who take opioids for more than three months will develop true addiction, not mere physical dependency—far greater than the 1 percent incidence previously estimated.[14]

✖ OxyContin becomes the most commonly prescribed brand of opioid medication for moderate to severe pain, netting sales of over $1 billion per year.[15]

✖ The pharmaceutical industry becomes flush with cash: from 1995 to 2002, drug manufacturers are the nation's most profitable industry. These companies employ a large legion of lobbyists, with more than two for each member of Congress by 2004, allowing them to quell attempts to regulate their prices and promotional practices.[16]

✖ The increased amount of painkillers being prescribed means there are more pills available to be diverted to the black market. By 2006 the going rate on the street for OxyContin is about $1 per milligram, or up to $80 per pill.[17]

MAY 2007

✖ Purdue Pharma, the maker of OxyContin, pays a $634.5 million fine for misleading doctors and patients about the drug's risk of addiction. Three of its top executives plead guilty, but none serve jail time.[18]

DECEMBER 2007

✖ The insurance industry estimates that diversion of prescription medication to addicts and abusers costs medical insurers up to $72.5 billion per year.[19]

2008

✖ Florida becomes the nation's hotbed for prescription drugs. The state doesn't regulate the operation of pain-management clinics, and there is no tracking system to prevent patients from getting multiple pill prescriptions at once. People come from all over the Southeast to visit the state's pill mills. A drug pipeline is established from Florida to Massachusetts, as well as from Florida to the Appalachian states.[20]

✖ Prescription drug abuse continues its crawl from the rural eastern and southern demographic into middle-class areas, spreading westward across the nation.[21]

2009

✖ In many areas, painkiller addicts start turning to heroin to achieve the same high, because heroin is cheaper than pills. The trend starts to pop up in areas where heroin has a historic stronghold, including Boston, Philadelphia, and Los Angeles. Then it starts to spread to other areas where heroin has never been seen before: suburban middle- and upper-class areas where painkiller addiction is rampant.[22]

MARCH 2010

✖ The U.S. Department of Justice finds that heroin deaths rose 18.2 percent from 2007 to 2008 and 20.3 percent from 2006 to 2008.[23]

APRIL 2010

✖ Purdue reformulates OxyContin to include a tamper-resistant feature designed to thwart efforts to crush, split, grind, or dissolve the tablets—though users report that there are still ways to tamper with pills. Oxy becomes harder to get on the black market, causing other opioid painkillers, such as Opana, to rise in popularity. There is also a surge in heroin abuse.[24]

APRIL 2011

✖ The White House officially recognizes the national prescription drug addiction epidemic, unveiling an action plan that includes support for the expansion of state-based prescription drug monitoring programs.[25]

SEPTEMBER 2011

✖ Florida passes legislation implementing a state monitoring system and cracking down on doctors' and pain clinics' prescribing practices.[26] Law enforcement officials report an increase in heroin sales. Meanwhile, heroin use increases in areas of the country formerly supplied by pills from Florida.

✖ An analysis of federal data by the *Los Angeles Times* reveals that drugs have exceeded motor vehicle accidents as a cause of death, killing at least 37,485 people nationwide in 2009.[27] Fueling the trend is the increase in prescription painkiller overdoses.

NOVEMBER 2011

✖ The U.S. Centers for Disease Control and Prevention finds that painkillers were involved in 14,800 overdose deaths in 2008 and were responsible for more than 475,000 emergency department visits in 2009—a number that has nearly doubled in just five years. In 2010, 16,651 people died of overdoses involving painkillers, the agency says.[28]

MAY 2012

✖ A study published in the *Journal of the American Medical Association* finds that the incidence of babies being born addicted to opiates has nearly tripled in the past decade due to the rampant abuse of prescription drugs. The number of pregnant women who were dependent on or using opiates when they delivered increased from 4,839 in 2000 to 23,009 in 2009. As a result, in 2009 neonatal abstinence syndrome was diagnosed in newborns at a rate of 3.4 per 1,000 hospital births per year, up from 1.2 diagnoses per 1,000 births per year in 2000.[29]

SEPTEMBER 2012

✖ The 2011 National Survey on Drug Use and Health finds that the number of people who reported heroin use in the past year rose from 373,000 in 2007 to 620,000 in 2011.[30]

DECEMBER 2012

✖ Dr. Russell Portenoy, a prominent pain-care specialist who drove the movement in the 1990s to help people with chronic pain, says he was wrong to have used the 1 percent addiction-risk figure in lectures because it wasn't relevant for patients with chronic noncancer pain. "Data about the effectiveness of opioids does not exist," he tells *The Wall Street Journal*.[31]

FEBRUARY 2013

✖ Every nineteen minutes, on average, one person dies from prescription drug abuse, the CDC finds.[32]

APRIL 2013

✖ The U.S. Food and Drug Administration issues a decision banning generic drugmakers from producing versions of OxyContin that do not include tamper-resistant features. The move comes on the same day that Purdue's patent on the original OxyContin expires, which normally opens the door for generic drugmakers to launch their own, cheaper versions; the decision forces these companies to develop their own abuse-deterrent designs, preserving Purdue's monopoly on the OxyContin market for the time being.[33]

MAY 2013

✖ The FDA issues a decision allowing generic companies to continue to produce forms of an older version of the painkiller Opana, which was reformulated in 2012. According to the agency, the new version doesn't thwart drug abuse significantly better than earlier versions that aren't abuse-deterrent.[34]

✖ Despite the nationwide epidemic of addiction and deaths, prescription painkiller sales show no signs of slowing; they are on track to increase by 15 percent and hit $8.4 billion by 2017.[35]

JULY 2013

✖ Driven by the painkiller addiction epidemic, deaths due to heroin overdoses are on the rise across the nation. In West Virginia, for example, heroin overdose deaths in 2012 tripled compared to 2007;[36] in Maryland fatal overdoses from heroin rose by 54 percent from 2011 to 2012;[37] and in Oregon heroin deaths reached a record high in 2012, accounting for 65 percent of the state's illegal drug deaths.[38]

OCTOBER 2013

✖ Federal data from 2011 reveal that nearly 80 percent of people who had used heroin in the previous year also had a history of abusing prescription painkillers.[39]

✖ The FDA recommends tighter controls on how doctors prescribe hydrocodone-containing medications, which are among the most widely abused opioids; about 131 million prescriptions for such drugs were written for about 47 million patients in 2011.[40]

✖ The day after that decision, the FDA approves Zohydro, a powerful hydrocodone product that lacks an abuse-deterrent feature.[41] Addiction experts fear the approval will spark a wave of abuse much like that seen with OxyContin.[42]

INTRODUCTION

GEORGE, A FUNERAL home director in Brockton, Massachusetts, watched as the formaldehyde pulsed its way into the body lying before him on the porcelain embalming table. It was a task that was normally just part of a day's work, but today George was overwhelmed by emotion. He slid down to the floor, sobbing, and gripped the hand of the body on the table, willing it to come back to life.

The hand belonged to his twenty-two-year-old son, Lance.

The night before, just after the Boston Red Sox lost to the New York Yankees, George had climbed the stairs to Lance's bedroom in the home that also houses George's funeral business. Lance was kneeling on the floor against a chair, with his head slumped forward onto his chest. It looked like he was praying. But he was stiff and unnaturally still. A needle lay by his feet. Heroin had stopped his heart.

It was a twisted ending for the son of a funeral director, but unfortunately, it was hardly surprising. As with many young adults in the working-class Boston suburb, Lance's heroin addiction began when he became hooked on the powerful prescription painkiller OxyContin. An opioid medication originally developed to treat patients suffering from debilitating pain, the drug has become popular among local kids, who crush the pills and snort, smoke, or even inject them for a heroin-like high. When the pills become too expensive, kids increasingly turn to heroin itself.

George, for his part, had seen dozens of such cases come across his embalming table in recent years—the sons and daughters of good parents who thought that heroin was something only "junkies" did. And even though he was well aware of Lance's years-long struggle with opiate addiction—at one especially exasperated moment telling his son that he was saving a casket for him—a junkie's death wasn't what he had in mind for Lance.

Despite years of addiction and lies and close calls, he never thought it would be his son.

I MET GEORGE in the summer of 2010, after reading his story in a newspaper. I had traveled across the country from California with a story of my own: my youngest brother, Pat, was also addicted to OxyContin and had died of a heroin overdose in February 2009, six months shy of his twenty-first birthday. I was seeking answers as a sister and as a journalist. Shortly after Pat's death, I had started researching prescription painkiller addiction and had started blogging about my findings. Privately, I also began researching my brother's life, trying to piece together his downfall in an effort to understand where he went wrong.

Pat was my baby. I was ten years old when he was born, and he was the perfect addition to the pretend scenarios for which I had already bossily recruited my other younger brother and my younger sister. And as babies are, he was incontrovertibly lovable. Even as he grew older— even as he fell into painkiller and heroin addiction—he could charm anyone with his laugh and gaping grin. He told silly jokes and poured sugar on everything and did ollies on his skateboard and played the guitar while wearing our sister's leopard-printed slippers. He was goofy and sweet and random and endearing. He was the kind of person you always wanted to be around.

Yet, as much as I loved my brother, I could not understand his obsession with OxyContin. Nor did I know that it had put him straight on the path to heroin. I learned of the extent of his struggle too late. Also too late, I learned about the disease of addiction and about the particular insidiousness of narcotic painkillers, all of which provide a heroin-like high when abused—not just OxyContin but Vicodin, Opana, Darvocet, fentanyl, Percocet, Dilaudid, Lortab, and Roxicodone, to name just a few. (Central nervous system depressants like Xanax, Ativan, Valium, and Klonopin are also often abused due to their tranquilizing properties.) I learned that Pat wasn't a special case, that kids just like him, all over the country, were falling victim to these pills: in 2010 almost three thousand young adults age eighteen to twenty-five died of prescription drug overdoses —eight deaths per day.[43] Like Pat, many ended up turning to heroin after their pills became too expensive or scarce; in 2011, 4.2 million Americans age twelve or older reported using heroin at least once in their lives, and nearly half of young IV heroin users reported that they abused prescription opioids first.[44] Like these kids, my brother was the last person you'd picture with a needle in his arm; yet they were all dying as heroin addicts: between 2006 and 2010, heroin overdose deaths increased by a staggering 45 percent.[45] I wanted to understand why this was happening, so I quit my job as a legal journalist and began traveling around the country in the hopes that chronicling the experiences of other families affected by the trend would offer some answers.

George was one of the first people I encountered. He told me the story about embalming his son as we sat in the receiving room of his funeral home, surrounded by the proverbial mementos of death: prayer cards, dried floral arrangements, a casket stuffed with billowy waves of satin. He choked up as he talked about Lance, and I choked up too, unable to maintain my reporter's distance. It was my brother's story all over again.

A familiar refrain: *He was a good kid. We tried to save him. We loved him so much, but he loved the drugs more.*

And: *I never thought it would happen to our family.*

Embedded in these sentiments was an element of denial, and it fascinated me. How did we allow ourselves to believe that it would never come to this? Like George, I knew rationally that my brother was on a terribly dangerous path: a fatal overdose was practically inevitable in the course of repeatedly ingesting highly potent synthetic opiates and, later, shooting heroin. My family and I did everything in our power—or thought we did—to help Pat. And yet, while I feared the worst on a conscious level, subconsciously I really didn't think he would die. In the handful of Nar-Anon meetings I attended, I tried on the phrase like a too-small shoe: "My brother is a heroin addict." But in my heart, I didn't believe it. If someone had pressed me on the issue at the time, I probably would have said that Pat was going through a bad phase. I believed he would pull through.

I went on to meet many others like George. Always the same story: *My son was kind, athletic, popular. My daughter was beautiful, intelligent, loving.* How did they end up on this brutal path, and why weren't we able to stop them?

I turned to the experts. There is nothing new about opiates, which—in one form or another—have wreaked havoc on societies for centuries. But in drug treatment centers across the nation, substance abuse counselors and medical officials described the latest wave of destruction, fueled by the rise in popularity of prescription painkillers. Their facilities are inundated with opiate addicts—mostly young heroin abusers whose addiction began with pills. Often, they relapse within weeks, if not days, of their release from rehab, because the drugs create such agonizing cravings that even if the body doesn't physically need another hit, the mind does. I was repeatedly told that the long-term success rate for young opiate addicts is extremely dim. When I asked one inpatient program director about his facility's statistics, he simply gestured to the dorm rooms surrounding him.

"Why do you think you don't see any fifty-year-old opiate addicts here?" he said. "They all die."

It was a harsh prognosis, but the statistics back up his claim: nearly forty Americans die per day—about fifteen thousand per year—from painkiller overdoses, representing a threefold increase over the past decade.[46] This unprecedented rise in overdose deaths in the United States parallels a 300 percent increase since 1999 in the sale of opioid medications.[47] And as painkiller abuse has skyrocketed, so has heroin addiction: in many areas of the nation, efforts to crack down on the abuse of prescription medications have had the unintended effect of driving opiate addicts to heroin for a cheaper, widely available high.

I found further evidence of the far-reaching scope of the pills-to-heroin epidemic in stories of the devastated families who had begun contacting me through my blog, wanting to share their stories of addiction and, all too often, death. They talked of the code of silence that surrounds addiction, the distaste of society toward addicts like their sons and daughters, who were written off as weak-minded, self-indulgent, and aimless because of their drug abuse. And although I have always considered myself a fairly compassionate person, I began to realize that I had been guilty of that mind-set as well, before addiction happened to someone I loved.

Ask the average person to describe a heroin addict, and they're likely to use words like *Dirty. Desperate. Diseased. Needle users. Crazy. Homeless. Scum. Junkies.* They are not likely to describe their next-door neighbor's son, their sister's daughter, their student, their own child. But the stories of those who have been swept up in the current opiate addiction epidemic illustrate a different truth.

Take my own family: my siblings and I were raised in a suburban, middle-class town where the streets were named after trees and doors were left unlocked. We were neither rich nor poor. We rode our bikes to the ice cream store and played soccer in the grassy fields by the park. We had sleepovers with friends and built secret forts and begged our parents in vain for a dog every year for Christmas. We were typical American kids living in a typical American town. Growing up in the 1990s, we were educated in school on the dangers of illicit drugs like cocaine, methamphetamine, and even heroin. But we never learned anything about prescription drugs—they never registered on the radar as something dangerous. Medications like Ritalin and Adderall were being increasingly prescribed to children and teens, who developed an easy familiarity with pill bottles. Meanwhile, our parents' medicine cabinets were filling up with all the medications being pushed by direct-to-consumer advertising on television—everything from antidepressants like Prozac to erectile dysfunction treatments like Viagra to sleep aids like Ambien—making prescription medications seem like an innocuous part of everyday life. Indeed, while Americans constitute only 4.6 percent of the world's population, we consume 80 percent of the global opioid supply and 99 percent of the global hydrocodone supply.[48]

Against this backdrop, our generation grew up to become the new face of opiate addiction. Today's typical opiate addicts are likely to be young—under the age of thirty, a substantial proportion in their teens. They come from suburban and working-class homes. They are educated. They are involved in organized sports, student government, and extracurricular activities. Usually, they begin abusing prescription drugs in high school and are often addicted to heroin by the time they hit their twenties. Many times—as in Pat's case—their families have no idea they are using opiates, or to what extent, until it's too late. Many families, including ours, are shocked to learn that heroin is involved.

I sought out young addicts to hear their side of the story—what it was like to first become addicted to painkillers and then heroin. I asked them the questions I wish I could have asked my brother. They helped guide me to a profound revelation: by the time Pat died, he wasn't even trying to get high anymore—he was just trying to feed his body's craving. The perception that addicts are worthless, selfish junkies who don't care about anything but getting loaded—and the notion that they are having fun doing it—is a common one. But it could not be further from the truth. Not one addict I interviewed mentioned the word *fun* in connection with his or her addiction. By contrast, they knew they were hurting everyone around them, and they hated themselves for it. They lived a tortured existence that paired this horrible realization with a physical dependence on a drug that would send them into excruciating fits of withdrawal if they failed to get their next dose. Sadly, their loved ones sometimes berated them for their "choice" to do drugs—as I did on several occasions with Pat. But while individual choice is certainly an element of one's drug abuse, it does not account for the complexity of the disease of addiction.

Addiction is literally a disease of the brain. The National Institute on Drug Abuse defines addiction as "a chronic, relapsing brain disease that is characterized by compulsive drug seeking and use, despite harmful consequences." While the initial decision to use drugs may be voluntary, over time, drug abuse causes structural and functional changes to the brain that are critical to judgment, decision making, learning and memory, and behavior control. These changes can lead to the compulsive and destructive behaviors exhibited by those with the disease of addiction (which is not the same group as all those who try drugs).[49] As David Sheff puts it in his book *Clean*, "People aren't choosing to use. Using is a symptom of their disease."[50] Thus it is reprehensible that we, as a society, view addiction as a moral failing that deserves punishment rather than as a chronic, progressive illness of the brain that requires treatment.

I can say this now, but I so wish I'd understood this when my brother was still alive. I never had the chance to show Pat compassion, because I was too scared, ashamed, and uneducated about the reality of his addiction. Too often, I reacted to his addiction with anger, and while it was an anger that stemmed from love, it was unhelpful, and likely hurtful. I wrote this book in an effort to help others who are like Pat. In sharing my journey to understand Pat's addiction, and in sharing some of the stories of those I met along the way, I hope more people will be willing to face the truth about opiate addiction—especially if it is happening to someone they love. I do not know if Pat would have wanted to have his life immortalized in this way, but I hope he would understand that in this case, silence equals death. To find meaningful solutions to a problem, the problem must first be recognized. Speaking the truth about what happened to Pat, and what is happening to so many others, is the first step.

This is a work of nonfiction, and the events and experiences documented in the following pages are, to the best of my knowledge, true. I have taken some creative liberties in terms of the timing of events, but my intention has been to remain as faithful as possible to the essence of these events as they actually happened. When I describe the thoughts of individuals, those thoughts have been related to me directly by those individuals in repeated conversations and interviews. Regarding my retelling of Pat's story, I have done my best to piece together the truth based on my own perception and that of my family members and Pat's friends, as well as the documents and other evidence he left behind. Attributions and other information as to my methodology can be found in the "Notes" section at the end of the book.

The reader should also know that I have changed certain names and details where revealing them might have been disadvantageous or harmful to those involved. This is a controversial practice in the field of journalism, but without it, the shame of addiction and the fear of social repercussions would have prevented some of my sources from sharing their stories—stories that I believe contribute to a better understanding of the scope of this epidemic.

My brother died alone in a bedroom, slumped over a needle, steeped in secrets I wish I had known. I cannot go back in time and fix my failings, but I can try to give him a legacy. In Pat's short life, he showed great compassion toward those who were viewed as different, and he—like all addicts—deserves the same.

ERIN MARIE DALY
SAN FRANCISCO, JANUARY 15, 2014

PART I
DENIAL

I HAVE BEEN SO TRAUMATIZED BY HIS ADDICTION THAT THE SURREAL AND THE REAL HAVE BECOME ONE AND THE SAME. I CAN'T DISTINGUISH THE NORMAL FROM THE OUTRAGEOUS ANYMORE. I AM SO GOOD AT RATIONALIZING AND DENYING THAT I CANNOT TELL WHERE ONE ENDS AND THE OTHER BEGINS.

—DAVID SHEFF, *BEAUTIFUL BOY*

1 | WAITING

IT IS THAT time of year when days are short and nights are long, but on this particular day, the moon refuses to rise. I beg the sun to stop dragging its feet, so I can climb upstairs to my childhood bedroom and leave behind the madness. So I can shut the door and lock it. So I can fall into a dreamless sleep where things are as they should be, and my brother Pat is still alive.

The sun will not listen.

The sky is bitter and luminous through the muslin veils and wire mesh of the living room windows. My other brother, Brian, sits on the porch steps, waiting, and pulls his hoodie over his head. He is a statue, unmoving, protective. He faces the cold in silence as my sister Caitlin and I watch him from the inner folds of the house on Cedar Street. Cars trundle down the street, but not the one we are looking for. The house waits too.

We are waiting to tell our mother that Pat is dead.

I bite my nails and pace from the living room through the foyer to the dining room, where the windows look out onto the driveway. My car is there, and Mom will know when she sees it that something is wrong, because it's the middle of the day in the middle of the week. Brian is the messenger because with our father and Pat gone, he is the only man left in the family, and because he is brave. Shuttered in the house, we regard the back of his head, sheathed in his sweatshirt. From behind he looks like Pat, but taller.

Even before today, our childhood home felt ghostly to me. There were too many memories that floated through the hallways, tapping me on the shoulder. As children, we spent most of our time in the backyard. Back then, it was a gaping field of sour grass framed by a cottonwood tree that shed sticky pods in the springtime. There was a tiny playhouse painted beige and white, built by my father under a tree that produced a fruit too pungent to eat, the misguided marriage of orange and grapefruit. A rosebush on the side of the house, where my sister and I collected petals that we mixed with water and crushed into old mayonnaise jars to give to our mother as "perfume." And a rope swing on which Pat—the most athletic and also the most fearless of the four of us siblings—spent most of his time, using the high fence as a jumping-off point from which to hurl into the sky, grinning.

Today the vacant rope hangs from the tree in a manner so cruel that I want to strangle someone with it. But whom? Pat, whose addiction has consumed our lives these past few months? The psychiatrists and rehab counselors who failed to fix him? The kid who offered him his first cigarette back in fifth grade, which led to alcohol, which led to pot, which lead to cocaine, which led to prescription painkillers, which led to heroin?

In the end I settle on myself. I'll slip through the sliding glass door—it makes just a tiny squeak if you open it past the middle—and tiptoe up the little brick stairs, overgrown now with weeds. The sticky pods are just beginning to drop from the cottonwood tree; I'll have to tread carefully across the lawn because they smell like rotting herbs if you step on them. But I'll make it to the rope, and it will be rough and warm in my hands. The ladder Pat used to climb to get to the top of the fence still leans there. I'll climb up on it and loop the noose. Swallow one last time. Then go. To him. Away from this. Away from my homecoming mother, whose screams will soon fill the eerie absence of sound in a suburb in the cold springtime at noon.

✖

BRIAN CALLS ME while I'm in a cab driving through San Francisco. When he tells me Pat has overdosed again, my first reaction is to curse.

My initial anger fades into a familiar mixture of fear and adrenaline. There is also a dull ache that settles brick-like in my innards, lower than my heart but higher than my stomach. It feels like homesickness, like missing something precious and far away.

Less than two months ago, there was a similar call from Brian telling me of an overdose so severe that Pat had nearly died. I was walking the dog in the windswept hills near the park by my apartment and had hung up the phone, trembling. Looking toward the bay, I saw freight ships cutting lines through the opalescent waters. Looking toward the park, I saw a homeless man. He lurched toward the bushes on the other side of the street and vomited. I turned away, envying him. If only I could have expunged that ache. Pat nearly died.

Today's phone call brings on the same ache. As furious as I have been with Pat, I love him and can imagine nothing worse than losing him.

As the taxi picks up speed, it occurs to me that Brian is telling me gently—with just the slightest bit of hesitation in his voice, as if maybe it weren't quite true—that this time Pat is dead. He doesn't say that exactly, but rather that the paramedics are at the scene, and they are prepared to pronounce that Pat is unable to be resuscitated. The ache explodes, choking me with shards of terror. I say it first.

Pat is dead?

Pat is dead.

The world stops.

Everything goes black. I am nowhere. There is nothing. The spongy cushions cradle me, and though they are musty and smell of sweat, I want to wrap them around me. I lean my head between my knees and whisper to myself. It is not true. We have not lost Pat.

Suddenly I am home, back at the apartment I share with my fiancé, Ben. I hand money to the driver without asking for change and stumble up the creaky Victorian steps to our third-floor flat. The dog assails me at the door, jumping nearly sideways in his excitement. I sink to the floor. He licks my face wildly. I cannot move.

After a few minutes, panic sets in. Frenzied, I call Ben's cell phone: no answer. I call again. I call twenty times. I finally call the switchboard operator of the hospital where he works and ask her to page him. Doubting the operator's competence, I call a friend who works with Ben. The sound of her voice—a familiar voice, the comforting voice of someone who knows me—sends me into hysterics. I scream that my brother is dead. I need Ben. Through the buzzing in my ears, I hear her say that she will find him.

Feeling as though I am moving through water, I dial my sister's number. She lives just a few minutes away, but I don't want her driving once she hears the news: I will call a cab or have Ben bring her to me. This urge not to have her drive suddenly feels like the most crucial order I have ever been given. As the oldest sister, I should be calm and in control; I should protect her. I *must* protect her. But when she answers, the innocence in her voice—the slightly surprised *hey* of a random weekday morning phone call, the normalcy of her world about to be shattered—makes me lose my grasp again. My words come out in a high-pitched gasp, somewhere between a shriek and a moan, and she cries out in shock.

Pat is dead?

Pat is dead.

I lurch into the bathroom, grabbing onto the side of the claw-foot tub. The porcelain gape of the toilet bowl is cold and hard against my forehead. I vomit. The ache won't come up. I curl up on the floor and stare at the dog, who is standing in the doorway, dejected and confused. His tail wags slowly, hopefully, but he keeps his distance. Dogs can smell fear; I wonder if he can smell the ache that has lodged itself inside of me. My eyes close.

✖

MY SISTER IS on the bed. We hold each other, our arms trembling, our fingers clutching. We are crying and we cannot stop. Her blue eyes are pinched at the edges, her eyebrows arched upward in disbelief. Our tears and snot drip down into our laps. We look at each other and I want to say something to make it better or maybe I will just scream instead because I cannot fix this, I cannot bring him back, we have lost our baby brother and now what?

✖

BEN IS DRIVING the car, hastily packed with overnight bags stuffed with mismatched outfits and toothbrushes. In the backseat, I lean my head on my sister's shoulder and wish for Ben's strength, watching the slope of his neck as we head toward our family home in San Carlos, about half an hour away from San Francisco. Brian and his girlfriend, Elise, are meeting us there, along with our mom's friends Betty and Tom. Mom is still at the preschool where she works; we want her to hear the news at home, surrounded by us.

All these months, Mom was at the eye of the storm with Pat. Parenting him was always a challenge—he was headstrong, wildly energetic, the only one to struggle in school—but never more so than recently. His addiction complicated their ability to communicate, and her efforts to intervene often ended in fights, including three weeks ago when he graduated from his court-ordered outpatient rehab program and refused to move back in with her. He had left straight from the graduation ceremony to board a train to Los Angeles, where his girl-friend—with whom he frequently did drugs—was living with her mother and stepfather. Mom had pleaded with the rest of us to try and convince him of what he would not believe coming from her: if he moved back to southern California, where he had been living for most of his addiction, she feared he would not return.

Was it mother's instinct, something animalistic and unmistakable that none of the rest of us could sense? Will she know, when she sees all our cars in her driveway on a random Tuesday at midday, that he is gone?

The Cedar Street house is drafty and sickeningly silent when we all arrive. We hug numbly. Pat's sudden absence is garish, wrong. Elise lights a fire. Betty and Tom rub our backs and retreat into the back of the house to give us space, knowing we need to face our mother alone.

✖

WHEN HER CAR finally pulls up, Brian rises from the porch and walks quickly across the manicured lawn. From the house, my sister and I cannot hear what he says, but her throat makes a sound loud enough to pierce the walls. We run outside as she crumples into Brian's arms. Her eyes are wide and wild; though she's tiny, it takes all three of us to carry her back to the house.

Inside, we lay her down and surround her. I cradle her in my arms from behind, brushing the damp blond wisps from her forehead and feeling the shudders of her sobs through my body like a series of volcanic explosions.

She screams for what seems like hours.

Pat is dead.

2 | JUST LET ME FORGET

LUKE TELLS ME it is the rush that draws you in. It makes you forget the darkness.

He flicks a lighter under a spoonful of syrupy brown liquid and says he is ready to die. Fumes rise from the potion, filling the room with the scent of vinegar. It is sickly and sweet at the same time.

We are sitting side by side, Luke and I, on his unmade bed in a sober living house in San Juan Capistrano, a seaside town in southern California where I am reporting a story on the epidemic of pill and heroin abuse. We have just met, but he lets me in, lets me close to the poison that has taken over his life since he became hooked on prescription painkillers eleven years ago, at age fourteen. And he's right: there is a rush. There is something exhilarating about the poison in his hands, just in its presence, the way that it swirls and bubbles in the spoon. I wonder about the strange seduction of these little bits of crystallized black tar swimming around in circles. I wonder what my brother felt like as he stared down at them three years ago.

Since Pat's death, I am like a madwoman crazed with the silence he has left behind, the questions I should have asked of him years ago. I now seek those answers from others like Pat. But not the Pat I knew—a different Pat, a stranger, someone compelled by the darkness and at the same time repelled by it, but unable to leave it behind. Someone like Luke.

Luke binds his arm with a belt and cinches the noose with his teeth before plunging the fluid into his vein. It is his own form of death, a temporary suicide he commits every few hours.

Nothing will steal your soul like heroin, he tells me.

"Heroin will take your heart," he says. "It will take your looks first, it'll take your possessions, it'll take the people around you that you love, and after it can't take anything else, it'll take your life, man. It'll fucking take your life."

Luke says this as he releases the belt. His eyes roll back in his head and he flops backward onto the sheets beside me, nodding off. The palm trees outside his window nestle their leaves against the panes of glass, making a swishing sound that lulls him to sleep, riding the waves of morphine, escaping from the light. I sit motionless, a sanctioned spy, but wanting so badly to have sat like this with my brother. If he had let me in like Luke, perhaps I could have changed the outcome, spoken the magic words that would have reversed fate.

When Luke wakes up a few minutes later, he tells me again that he is ready to die. He's not suicidal exactly, but when you've been doing heroin for so long, you're ready, he says.

The only fun time is when you're about to get high, he adds, but then he takes it back.

"No man, it's just not fun anymore," he says, slurring heavily. "It's just to get well. It's just not to feel the feelings that you feel, because they suck, man. The feelings suck."

I ask him if he really wants to die, and he blinks hard and rapidly, as if trying to understand.

"No, I don't want to die, no," he says.

"Let's just put it this way," he says. "If I had a chain on, a gold chain on, and someone put a gun to my head and said give me the chain or else

I'm going to pull the trigger, honest to God I'd be saying do it, you'll be doing me a fucking favor. Fucking shoot me."

The afternoon light wanes as Luke lights a cigarette, filling the small room with smoke that now smells oddly dry and crisp after the pungent sweetness. He falls back against the pillows again, inhaling and exhaling sluggishly, like a marionette in slow motion. His friend Anna is coming over, and he needs to be coherent enough to convince her that he's all right: she got clean a few months ago, and she hates it when he's high. She worries about him. But she gets mad too, and when she's mad, she doesn't want to be around Luke, and right now he needs someone to be around him, or the loneliness will kill him.

He tells me he feels beaten down. He wants to stop doing it, but he can't. He does it because he doesn't want to feel.

The first time he got high on pills, he thought, *This is what's going to help me not think about everything that has happened.*

The feelings are what make you want to start. The feelings are what make you want to forget.

✖

WE GO TO sit outside at a patio table under the palm trees that frame Luke's window. The house manager waves as he gets out of his car but doesn't come over. Luke tells me his name is Jack and he used to be a doctor, before he lost his medical license.

"He sold pills," he says quietly, so Jack can't hear.

I've heard of sober houses that aren't really sober; this is clearly one of them, and the reporter in me has the urge to dig. But right now I'm more interested in Luke, the way his fingers tap on his knees, a thin line of grime tracing the half-moons of his uncut fingernails. He has a baby daughter, and though he rarely sees her since his ex-girlfriend moved to the East Coast, his arms are fatherly: strong and protective. He faces me head-on, resolute, with eyes deadened and pupils as small as pinpoints.

I ask him if he feels desperate, if he's anxious about getting his next fix.

"What time is it?" he asks.

I tell him it's 7:15.

"Then no," he says. "I'll sleep it off and wake up tomorrow morning sick, but I know I got more, so I'll get high. Then I'll start the wild goose chase. I'll do whatever I gotta do to get money. Commit some crimes."

When I ask him if he wants to get clean, he sits up earnestly.

"Yeah, I do wanna get clean so bad, so bad, real bad, I wanna get clean," he says. "But it's just so hard. When you're full-fledged kicking, it is unbearable, un-fucking-bearable."

He lists the symptoms for me: Your stomach hurts. You can't go to the bathroom because you have a buildup of shit. You can't get it out because there's too much, so you have to take a laxative. You get the chills; you're always cold. Your bones hurt. You're excruciatingly uncomfortable in your own bones. You get cramps, aches. You start burning, so you take a cold shower, you take four showers because that's the only time you feel a little normal. But as soon as you get out, the feeling comes back.

But, he tells me, the physical withdrawal is nothing compared to what happens inside of your head.

"The dope sickness, that is nothing, that is 10 percent of the problem," he says. "I mean it fucking hurts and it's horrible, but the feelings that you feel, man, that's what gets you. That is what fucking takes you down. The guilt, the shame. The guilt will fucking kill you, man."

Pat felt guilty too. I know this, not because he told me, but because when I was picking through the boxes of his belongings, I had unearthed his rehab papers. "One thing that is very important to me is my family," he had written. "I have my family motto tattooed across my arms, and yet I lied and deceived them all. I was in jail on Christmas and everyone in my family knew about my problem. This saddens me very much because I can't stand hurting those I love."

The diamond studs in Luke's earlobes catch the light of the dusk. His hair is fine and straddles the border between brown and blond, like my brother's. I ask him whether he thinks he's a good person. He thinks for a minute before answering.

"I don't know, man. Because I don't really have a chance to show that side. I do think I'm a good person, I'm just . . ." He trails off and starts nodding.

His hand seems to have forgotten its cigarette, which smolders sadly, nearing its end. I think of Pat, smoking on the balcony of my apartment, breathing luminescent wisps into the black sky as I watched the slump of his shoulders. I remember the sickening gnaw of being out of control, and hating myself for not knowing what to say to him.

"I think you're a good person for doing this," I say to Luke, meaning sharing his story, but he doesn't respond.

He comes back to life suddenly, his head snapping upward from his chest, remembering that Anna will be here soon. He envies people like her, who are in relationships, who have someone to care about them.

"Sometimes you look at your life and if someone cares about how you're doing, it just feels good to know that," he says. "For someone to wonder what you're doing during the day and hope that you're okay. That's all I'm chasing is companionship."

Right now, he says, he has very few friends left. He has nothing. He thinks maybe getting a girlfriend would help him out.

"I can't take care of myself," he says wistfully, before heading back inside for one more hit before Anna arrives.

3 | TWO SATURDAYS

I. 1988

First comes the dew. It melts on blades of grass outside my window, smelling like seawater. When the sun rises, it filters through the hanging prism, spreading tiny rainbows across the warm brown rug. An owl calls from the tall pine tree that grows down the block, saying goodbye to the night.

I have just turned ten: old enough to boss around Caitlin, who is nearly six, and Brian, almost four, but still young enough to want to spend most of my free time playing with them. So far they don't seem to mind my rule over our little world.

Saturdays are our favorite day of the week: we get to spend it all with our father. Every Saturday morning, my sister and brother and I jump out of bed and gather under an afghan quilt in front of the television— the one day of the week we can watch cartoons. Dad makes breakfast: waffles with butter, syrup, and powdered sugar for us, bacon and eggs for himself and our mother. Then he takes us on a bike ride to Burton Park or nearby Foster City, where we ride in a staggering line on the bike path that winds along the bay to the San Mateo Bridge, the smell of seagulls and salt flats in our noses.

Every Saturday night, Kathy, our parents' longtime friend who is like a second mother to us, comes over for dinner. Dad grills hamburgers or makes tacos, and after we go to bed, our parents and Kathy watch movies rented from Rod's Video downtown. My sister and I, who have the two upstairs bedrooms, sneak onto the stairwell in our pajamas and eavesdrop on grown-up conversations.

On this Saturday morning, our parents call us into the family room for a special surprise. It's a Hallmark envelope addressed to the three of us. The card inside has a picture of a baby splashing in a bathtub with one lock of hair sticking up in a curlicue.

Dear Erin, Caitlin, and Brian,

Three is terrific, but four is fantastic! I am your new baby brother or sister and I can't wait to meet all of you in July. We are going to have so much fun playing together.

Love,
Daly Baby #4

Caitlin and Brian look up in confusion, but I instantly understand. As Mom explains to the younger kids that soon there will be a new baby in the family, I run to the phone and call all my friends to tell them the news. No one else my age has a sibling a decade younger. We can't wait for July.

PAT IS BORN early in the morning on July 15, the hottest day of the year. Our grandmother, who is staying with us, relays the news from our parents at the hospital.

We jump up and down cheering. We cut a long strip of butcher paper and make a WELCOME HOME sign in big block letters using scented markers that leave smudges on the tips of our noses. When we hear our parents' car in the driveway, we stampede out the front door. Mom's stomach is fleshy and buoyant when she hugs us. Dad is carrying a tiny bassinet, and inside is Pat. He is wrinkled and reddish, like a dried-up pinto bean.

We all sit on the weathered couch in the family room and take turns holding him. He doesn't do much—just scrunches his little fists up by his face—but we adore him instantly. My parents play classical music on the stereo and videotape us, asking us what we think about Pat. We all say we love him. There is softness in the air, the feeling of being bundled in blankets.

✖

PAT QUICKLY BECOMES our new favorite plaything. We treat him like a doll, talking for him in made-up voices that take on different personalities: Superman, opera singer, circus ringmaster. He giggles uncomprehendingly at our antics. When he learns to crawl, we cajole him around the house like a puppy, enticing him with "dog treats"—Cheerios—and making him fetch Ping-Pong balls. We pretend to be his adoring, maniacal fans when he pulls himself up on his toes to reach the piano keys above his head. On his first birthday, he sits in his high chair and smears chocolate frosting all over his face, banging his head backward in delight against the fraying yellow vinyl.

Pat becomes even more fun as he grows older. By age two, he is a natural court jester and has a knack for goofy faces that send all of us into fits of laughter. He never walks; he only runs. His energy is boundless. It's clear he's wired differently than the rest of us kids: while we're all athletic, we're not physically adept the way he is. It's like his body is specifically engineered to scale countertops, doorways, trees, even the rooftop of our two-story house. There is no walking, only bouncing, somersaulting, cartwheeling. He runs around the back patio in Brian's hand-me-down T-shirts, which hang down to his knees, and black hightops. He learns to do handstands and can backflip on demand, which we make him do constantly and from a variety of challenging locations: the retaining wall of our front steps, the top of the backyard play structure, the midpoint of the cottonwood tree.

At school, Pat makes friends easily and displays a particular kindness toward those who are different. His best friend in kindergarten is a classmate with Down syndrome. They run through the tall grass framing the bog at the edge of the playground, pretending to be wild horses.

II. 1993

My father speaks in hushed tones as he holds my mother's hands across the kitchen table. He brings her hands to his lips and kisses them. There are half-chewed bits of waffles and pools of syrup on the table, mostly left behind by Pat, who's now immersed in *Pee-wee's Playhouse*. Cait and Bri are playing with the Speak & Spell, trying to make it say words like *pencil neck* and *stupid head*. Everything about the day is too bright, too blue, too warm, too sweet.

"Are you ready to tell them?" my father asks. My mother slowly nods and they rise from the table.

Years later, I learned that the cancer had been festering inside my father for years. A routine blood test at Dad's annual physical turned it up, just one month before Pat was born. In the maternity ward at the hospital, Dad had held Pat in his arms and told Mom this was his reason to fight to live. But how do you explain cancer to three children under the age of ten?

Is it any easier to explain it five years later when your children are fifteen, eleven, nine, and five?

There are tears, and questions, and assurances that feel like promises. Dad holds Pat on his lap and locks eyes with Mom. He tells us of what's to come: doctors, hospitals, chemotherapy, a bone marrow transplant.

The sun through the sliding glass door suddenly seems invasive, the little ants on the patio its warriors.

That afternoon, I go to a movie with my friends, crying silently as we sit in the blackened theater. The world has shifted slightly on its axis. In those first few hours, the change is nearly imperceptible. But over the next few months, a transformation unfolds. Saturdays now mean transfusions, treatments, procedures, surgeries. Our parents try to maintain a sense of normalcy, but the house, once bursting with life and anticipation, settles into a hollow silence. We have lots of help from Kathy, who moves in with us, and from our parents' many other friends, who shuttle the kids to after-school activities and bring us foil-wrapped Pyrex dishes full of lasagna and chili con carne. And of course Pat is eager to pitch in, concocting delicacies like "grilled cheese sandwich salad," a bowl full of toasted bread and ripped-up American cheese slices tossed with mayonnaise and ketchup. But at night, the house no longer feels warm.

When it is Pat's bedtime, I tuck him in the upper level of his bunk bed, sandwiched between legions of stuffed animals, and stroke the back of his neck at his hairline. It seems to help him fall asleep. I have nicknamed him Bunny, a silly endearment he now insists I use at all times, though he is nearly six years old. In return, he has inexplicably omitted the *i* from my name.

"Goodnight, Bunny," I say, stroking his neck.

"More, Ern, more," he whispers as he drifts away.

4 | REMEMBERING

"AS SOON AS the high hits, you understand that this is the feeling you've been looking for," Anna tells me on the way to Luke's house. If you take the pills, you won't feel. If you take the pills, you won't be in pain.

Anna's father had cancer too. She was fourteen when things really started to go downhill, when his face became sunken and yellowed and the house began to smell like stale sheets. In the afternoons, she sat with him in his bedroom, picking at the plaid creases of her Catholic school uniform. She didn't tell him about the boy in math class who poked her fat rolls and called her a whale. Instead she sang: mostly jazz tunes, sometimes opera, while her father drifted in and out of sleep.

Her dad would ask her where his pills were, and Anna would bring them to him.

Soon he was staying in the hospital for weeks at a time, leaving the medicine behind. It beckoned to her. One night she and a friend went into her parents' bathroom and opened the cabinet. Her friend wanted to know what the big deal was; after all, Anna's dad seemed really happy whenever he took the pills. Anna agreed. It seemed like he didn't even care that he was dying. When she swallowed her first pill, she was washed in numbness. Everything bad was erased: she did not have a care in the world, and she loved it.

Anna began sneaking a few pills when no one was looking: morphine, Dilaudid, OxyContin, fentanyl. They made her feel glazed, protected by an unseen shell. At school, the insults about her weight didn't sting as much, and as a singer, the pills made her bolder. She joined three different choirs and started writing pop and blues songs. On weekends, she and a friend performed at local restaurants and street fairs.

Her access to painkillers improved when she had gastric bypass surgery at age fifteen. The doctors prescribed big bottles of liquid hydrocodone, which she'd chug like a cocktail late at night alone in her bedroom. Long after the scars had started to fade, she pretended to be in pain, and the prescriptions kept coming.

When her father died four days after her sixteenth birthday, the pills were the only way to quiet the hollow nagging feeling that bit at her from below, fanning upward from her gut like bile.

Anna tells me about the first time she shot heroin. She had moved hundreds of miles away from her family in Dana Point, California, away from the house that held her father's ghost. By then she was taking pills by the handful—ten, twenty, sometimes thirty a day—but the numbness she craved had worn off. She was sitting with her friend on the front porch, and he offered to shoot her up. He promised he'd just give her a little bit, and told her not to freak out. All she needed to do was breathe.

Anna was scared when she saw the blood come up through the syringe, but as soon as it hit her, it was the best feeling she'd ever had.

"And that is when it started," she says now. "That is when heroin took my life over."

Shadows lurk like phantoms in Anna's brown eyes. They conceal the things she's seen, even though she is just twenty-two. Living in a drug den, with writing on the mildewed bathroom walls and a dead cat in a box on the kitchen table. Letting men touch her in order to get her fix. Watching her friend flatline from an overdose before the paramedics brought her back to life. Overdosing herself, waking up in the emergency room, and overdosing again within an hour of her release. Today she marks nearly eighty days clean, but the darkness sneaks in at the corners.

"It's hard, because it's more than making your mind up about it," she says of staying sober. "The body creates needs."

One problem is Luke. She became close to him while he was dating her cousin and they were all using. Sober, she still cares about him and wants to help him, but she doesn't like to hang around him anymore because he's always high. Anna is desperate not to fall down the rabbit hole again; she feels her addiction pulling at her whenever she sees Luke. She wants to be part of the minority of addicts who make it out alive, and are able to stay clean.

"I want to remember my life," she says, knocking on Luke's door.

✖

INSIDE THE SOBER living house, the air is stale and laced with smoke. Luke's roommate leads Anna to the bedroom, where Luke is perched on the corner of his bed, leaning over a folded paper towel on the floor. His eyes are pinned and paranoid as he ushers her into the room and locks the door behind her. He is in the middle of cooking up a shot, and Anna knows it.

She flops down on his roommate's bed and folds her arms with purpose. Anna has walked away from situations like this many times since she got sober, but right now she wants to stay. She misses her friend.

But Luke is oblivious to her presence, obsessed with the task at hand. Every movement is precise and calculated, facilitating the flow of the liquid from spoon to syringe to bloodstream. His head drops to his chin, and the room is silent. Anna looks only at her phone, not at Luke, not at the drugs.

When he comes back to life, he is animated and intense. He bounces around Anna like a windup toy and pulls her outside for a smoke. She follows him reluctantly, dragging her feet. She sits at the patio table and lights up. When she returns her attention to her phone, he stands behind her and leans his face downward in front of hers, inches from her lips, as if to kiss her. Then he jumps onto the table and does push-ups, babbling incoherently. She rolls her eyes as if to dismiss his antics, but many emotions cross her face: Frustration. Love. Sadness. Resolve. Fear.

Earlier, she had said, "It's sad that we have to watch all of the people around us die for us to realize maybe we shouldn't be doing this anymore."

Finally, Anna has had enough. Luke knows she must go, knows why she is leaving, but still he follows her out onto the street. Before she gets into her car, he pulls her close and hugs her for a long, long time. He deflates into her, resting his head on her shoulder, facing inward toward her heart. It seems like he's crying. But when he finally raises his face, there are no tears.

As Anna drives home, she thinks of all she has lost. Her father, her friends who overdosed. She wonders if she will lose Luke too.

✖

FROM THE CORNERS of the darkness, the voices come from hidden faces. One by one, they share their stories of pain. On a table in the center of the room, three candles cast a glow just bright enough to illuminate a stack of recovery pamphlets, but not the faces surrounding them, not Anna.

"I was high and threatened to kill myself in front of my mom," one voice says. "She said, 'Son, go kill yourself, you are already halfway dead.'"

Another voice says, "Every bad thing I never thought would happen to me in my whole life has happened because of drugs."

There is comfort in the darkness. It cloaks the voices, shrouding them in a veil of anonymity, offering solace and protection. There is no fear in this room, only raw, untempered honesty. The truth: their truths.

In the end, it was Anna who ended up getting lost. She broke up with the father of her baby girl, and he ran off to Florida, taking their daughter with him. In the battle to reclaim her daughter, she began to lose focus and stopped going to meetings. A deep depression and hopelessness set in. The fear of permanently losing one of her two children was paralyzing, taking precedence over all other emotions. She finally thought, "Fuck it. What's the point? Why am I even sober?" And just like that, she became lost again.

Everything was a blur, and then she woke up to the paramedics pumping on her chest. A few more minutes and she would have died, they told her—but she still didn't care. She went into a detox program, followed by a sober living house, but that feeling was still there inside of her: *Fuck it*. And it began all over again.

Another month, and she woke up in the passenger seat of her mother's car. Her mom said to her, "I can't be around you anymore." Anna floated up into the air, outside of her body, above the car. She looked down on the girl below, so sad, so broken. She realized she didn't have one more relapse in her, and she decided that she could either die or try to get clean one more time.

In the latest rehab, she was completely out of her element. Everyone else was young like her, but many of them had lots of sober time, and they seemed so confident and stable. Anna felt like she stuck out like a sore thumb. But she was desperate to get better, so she stood up in a group session and said, "I want what you guys have. Tell me how to get it." She started taking their advice. She woke up at 6:00 AM, walked the trails, did yoga, got coffee, went to meetings, kept busy, listened, surrendered. She learned to take things step by step, abandoning the mind-set of *How many days do I have sober?* in favor of *Am I sober today, this minute?*

Anna began to feel at home, safe, peaceful. She realized that at the core, she wasn't happy with who she was and that she used drugs to be

someone she wasn't. She also admitted that she used to suppress uncomfortable feelings, including the fact that she was mad at her dad for dying
and leaving her. And this made her understand that if she were to die,
her kids would have to grow up without a mom, just like she had to
grow up without a dad. It would mean more to them if she were able to
stay sober than if she died, she thought. Maybe she was worth something
after all.

Bit by bit, the life force inside her began to surpass the death wish of
drugs. It was as if she had been trying to hang herself or throw herself
off a cliff, over and over, wanting to die, but at the same time not quite
wanting it all the way. Anna didn't know what would happen in the next
minute, the next hour, the next day, but the important thing was that
right now, she was sober, and the life force was winning out.

Tonight she listens as the faceless voices tumble forth, and she tries
to learn from them. They tell her that life will knock her down, but
she can make the choice to be strong in the face of hardship. That the
healthier she gets in sobriety, the more she'll see how sick she was while
using. That if she stays humble, she'll gain strength.

The words float from the faces into the flames of the candles and
wrap around fidgeting hands that emit the smell of just-smoked cigarettes. Anna touches her arm in the darkness, in the spot where her latest sobriety date is tattooed: 11-11-12. In a week she'll be leaving for
Florida to try and reclaim custody of her daughter, and she needs all the
strength she can get.

She thinks of her father, remembering the words he wrote once to
her on a card: "My darling, sweet, loving Annalisa, I am so very proud
of you."

She hopes that one day, her daughter will be proud of her too.

5 | THE FALL

MY FATHER'S EYES are blue like opals.

They shine with fever and chemicals. His face puffs up, giving him the look of a Buddha statue, slack and stoned. He lies in bed with his leather briefcase open beside him, trying to work. But the hallucinations get in the way.

And the vomiting. He tries to do it quietly, but we can hear him.

He wears wool hats and socks to quiet the chills. In the garage, he parks his wheelchair next to his windsurfing board, which hangs neglected in the corner.

I find him standing in the hallway, his toothpick legs protruding from the folds of his striped bathrobe. I hold him close to me and cry. His thin arms circle me like fraying twine as he says, "Shhhhhh."

I pull away and Pat is in the doorway. He looks down at the floor. He is only nine, but I know he understands. I know he *knows*.

Is this when we begin to lose Pat?

Or is it a few months later, when the lights of the ambulance slice through the moonshadows in the kitchen, where we huddle in our pajamas as the paramedics wheel the stretcher out the front door?

Is it the morning we return from the hospital a family of five instead of six?

Or is it later still, sitting in the front pew before the coffin draped in roses?

6 | RUN LIKE HELL

THE AIR IN the car is heavy with steam and sweat, my exhaled breath forming a ghostly footprint on the tinted glass of the window. Summer mornings in South Florida are characterized by an omnipresent humidity, with the skies not so much promising as threatening to quench the thirst of the sticky streets. But I make no move to crack the window.

The cop in the driver's seat beside me tugs at the edges of his Kevlar vest and toggles between his walkie-talkie and his cell phone. The police department here in Pinellas County has agreed to let me ride along with the narcotics team as part of my research on the painkiller addiction epidemic. I sink back against the headrest, trying to be as still as possible while he and his team pinpoint the location of their suspect. I think of Anna, who has come here to find her daughter, and wonder whether she has succeeded in her mission.

We've been hanging out in this unmarked car across the street from Park Drugs Pharmacy in Pinellas Park for nearly an hour, and the horizon around us is darkening, even though it's barely 10:00 AM. The cop is mostly silent, focused on his mission. His team includes two other undercover officers in a second unmarked car, two additional two-man patrol vehicles hiding in the parking lot, and a cop conducting surveillance from inside the pharmacy itself, and they are lying in wait for their latest target in the ongoing battle against the illegal market for pills.

Up until recently, Florida was the epicenter of the nation's painkiller addiction epidemic, home to ninety of the nation's top one hundred oxycodone-purchasing doctors and fifty-three of its top one hundred oxycodone-purchasing pharmacies.[51] Billboards cropped up along the highways heading into Florida, telling people exactly how to get to specific pain clinics—so-called pill mills that sold painkillers for cash up front—to get their fixes. At one point in one of the worst-hit counties, there were more pill mills than McDonald's restaurants.[52] Out-of-state licenses were a common sight, the cops say, with groups of people piling into buses or vans and driving from neighboring states like Alabama and Georgia to visit multiple clinics for cheap pills. The police were routinely called to motels to pick up the bodies of "pill tourists" who had overdosed and died. Sometimes people didn't even wait to get back to their motels, overdosing right there in the lobbies of pain clinics after filling their prescriptions.

These days, thanks to a recent crackdown by state officials, the number of pain clinics is dwindling and the cops are picking up fewer dead bodies. But for regional law enforcement teams like this one in Pinellas County, it's clear the problem is nowhere near solved. Their working lives have been consumed by "Pharmageddon," and they are plagued by the sense that no matter how hard they work, their progress is constantly being subverted. As the narcotics officer tells me, it's like fighting against an ocean wave that keeps growing in force and size; they have taken to calling it "the Blob."

"It doesn't matter how smart you are, how much money you have, what your social status is—if you do painkillers you will get addicted, and you will become a part of the Blob," he says. "It's beyond the resources of law enforcement, the medical profession, educators, the rehab community. And we're going to end up losing a generation because of it."

For the past few years, Pinellas County has had one of the highest prescription drug addiction rates in the nation, and there is a seemingly limitless bounty of players for the cops to go after: dirty doctors, unscrupulous pharmacies, pill pushers, and of course addicts. But because prescription drugs are legal until they're diverted for an illegal use, it can be tricky to pinpoint the exact behavior that warrants an arrest. Raids on pill mills are regularly conducted, but privacy laws often get in the way of introducing patient records in court. Intervening in a street sale is an option, but if the buyer produces a pill bottle with his or her name on it, he or she can't be arrested. And dealers often insulate themselves from being caught by positioning themselves at the top of a vast network—a pyramid scheme of sorts—made up of "recruiters," who in turn hire tens and sometimes hundreds of "patients" to visit doctors and obtain fraudulent prescriptions. Many times illegal immigrants are involved, with recruiters showing up at fields and offering farmworkers as much as $150 a day to pose as patients.

The Pinellas County cops have several different methods of attacking the Blob. In some cases they go after clinic owners or seek out small-time dealers, conducting "buy-bust" operations in which officers solicit pills in local bars and strip clubs in the hopes of making arrests. Or they'll ask around to see who can direct them to a fake MRI manufacturer; some clinics claim to require an MRI to prove the existence of a physical problem, though it's often just for show. However, these sorts of fishing expeditions don't always yield catches, so the cops increasingly rely on confidential informants, or CIs, to point them toward more specific targets. Sometimes the bottom feeders agree to rat out the big fish once they get arrested and find themselves facing the possibility of jail time, like this morning when one young man came in to sign up as a CI in exchange for the police putting in a good word with the county prosecutor pursuing his case. As he filled out a form stating his willingness to wear an audio tap, he told detectives about his main source for pills: a guy he met while working at an auto repair shop who was running off fake scripts and prescription labels on his computer. He gave the man's home address, where he promised cops they would find entire garbage bags full of pill bottles.

Other CIs are more nefarious. This morning's stakeout was launched when the chief pharmacist at Park Drugs called the police after a customer submitted a prescription for OxyContin that was written by a doctor who was born in 1921 and had been retired for twenty-five years. Just last week, the customer, a young woman with a criminal record, tried to fill the same prescription at a different pharmacy, which put her name on a warning list distributed to local businesses. Now the pharmacist has offered her up for bait.

But it turns out the pharmacist is no angel: the cops have been eyeing him since they shut down the medical clinic across the way last year. When that clinic was taken down, the pharmacist lost about $1 million a year in revenue, leading the police to suspect that patients were being directed to his pharmacy to reap the benefits of his loose hand in filling prescriptions. They already know he regularly fills prescriptions using counterfeit pills, selling half of the real supply out the back door and using the other half to satiate his own Oxy addiction. By feeding the cops occasional information to help them make arrests, he thinks they'll let him operate under the radar. He doesn't know that while they're using his tip-offs, they're simultaneously building their case against him. And lucky for the cops, he's usually too doped up to hide the evidence when they come around.

Today the pharmacist blinks suspiciously through the glass at the tall counter, but as soon as the plain-clothes officers flash their badges, he unlocks a side door and eagerly welcomes them into a back room. The cops set up a surveillance camera near one of the back windows near a pile of shoes and an old mattress. The pharmacist bounces with excitement as he shows the officers the fake script submitted by the target, the young woman with the OxyContin prescription. He doesn't even notice one of the cops standing near the counter, pilfering through a stack of stolen driver's licenses and Medicaid cards.

But right now, the focus is on the young woman, who is set to show up any minute in a white Lexus registered to the mother of her boyfriend. The cops' suspicion is that her boyfriend—a young man with a hefty Oxy habit himself—is using her as a pawn, having her fill prescriptions under her name and selling the pills at a markup.

The somber sky finally ruptures, spilling forth an angry gush of rain that blankets the oiled streets. A car pulls up, driven by the boyfriend, and parks under the flailing leaves of a palm tree. The young woman jumps out of the backseat, unaware that her every move is being monitored by eight police officers ready to pounce. Once she's inside the pharmacy, the surveillance officer calls out her actions on the radio, giving the team the opportunity to move in on the vehicle without alerting her boyfriend to their presence.

Pills in hand, she exits the pharmacy and walks back toward the car. But just as she reaches it, a cacophony of sirens and lights goes off. Panicked, she tries to open the door. In a grand gesture of self-preservation, her boyfriend has hit the locks. It's too late for both of them, however, and with officers shouting for the pair to put their hands up, the two have no choice but to surrender.

As they are handcuffed and body-searched, a crowd gathers at the Wendy's across the way. The flashes of red and blue are amplified by their reflections in the warm puddles of rainwater. People stare and whisper, awed by the presence of so many grim-faced cops in bulletproof vests.

"It's like a never-ending story," an officer sighs, slamming the patrol car door.

✖

THE YOUNG WOMAN rubs her left wrist where it's being pinched by the handcuffs binding her to a chair, staring fearfully at her interrogator as I again try to blend in. She has been sitting in a room with cement walls and no windows since her arrest, periodically wiping away tears with her one free hand. Her face is crumpled between the eyebrows, giving her the look of a lost child. It makes me sad, even though I know she's in the wrong; I wonder if my brother had the same disoriented look in his eyes as he sat waiting in the holding cell, high, after one of his several arrests.

"I swore to myself I'd never be in handcuffs," she says softly, to no one in particular.

Although the room is sealed, muffled sounds make their way through the metal door. This is a special compound at a secret location where members of the narcotics task force conduct training, interview informants, and question suspects. It houses a team of drug-sniffing dogs, and sometimes they get riled up and start barking. Right now there is also the woman's boyfriend, who is hollering at the officers in the holding room across the hall. His cursing and the dogs' barking, together with the cold cinderblock walls and drafty rooms, amplify the compound's aura of isolation and terror.

"I don't want to see behind the bars of a jail cell," the woman cries. "Are they going to put me in ankle chains?"

The interrogating officer doesn't answer. Instead, from inside her wallet, he pulls a stack of business cards for various pharmacies and doctors. Then he holds up a baggie with the confiscated pills: two bottles of 30-milligram OxyContin with 180 pills apiece, a bottle of ninety Xanax bars, and thirty potassium chloride pills. (In addition to painkillers, fraudulent scripts often include innocuous medications to make them appear more legitimate.) The woman had paid $800 in cash for the lot, and if she'd had the chance to turn around and sell the pills on the street, she could have made more than $10,000.

The woman says the blame lies with her boyfriend, whose bellowing can be heard from the adjacent room. He is high on OxyContin. His addiction has been getting worse, she says: he's started doing so much Oxy that he regularly walks into walls or slurs and nods off. She says she feels bad for him, so she helps him out with things like filling his painkiller prescription, which he has because of a neck injury in a car accident a few years back.

"I'll do anything," she cries. "I'll go to church and pray and do good by God and my kids, and if he doesn't too, I'll leave him."

The cop puts her personal belongings back in her purse but sets the pills and the business cards aside.

"You need to start thinking about your kids," he says. "If your boyfriend gets high on Oxy and drives the kids to the grocery store and gets in an accident, you'll be responsible for not taking them out of harm's way."

The woman nods and fingers her handcuffed wrist as if to remind herself that this is really happening.

Her boyfriend, for his part, has suddenly gone quiet. The painkiller's euphoric high has faded into a deep, anesthetized sleep that not even the barking of the dogs can penetrate.

✖

AFTER THE TWO suspects are sent to central booking, the cops head back to the main office to file their reports. The head narcotics officer is especially relieved; this is his last shift before a two-week vacation. But first, he'll have to wade through all the emails and phone messages: tips from CIs, requests from school officials to speak to kids about the dangers of prescription drugs, updates from the coroner's office regarding investigations into overdose deaths—mostly due to pills, but now increasingly heroin too.

The other day, he received a phone call from a sheriff in Georgia, where many of the pill pushers have moved in light of Florida's crackdown. The sheriff wanted the cop's opinion on a fake MRI case that had come across his desk. He'd never seen anything like it before.

The cop had only one piece of advice for the sheriff.

"I told him to run like hell," he says, his lips folding into a thin line.

7 | CHOOSING TO BELIEVE

MY MOTHER'S BREATH on the other end of the line comes in spurts, like carbonation escaping from a bottle. It is winter in New York City, where I have moved for graduate school, and the wind assaults me as I climb the subway stairs. She is trying to tell me something about Pat, but her spurts and the din of the city make it difficult to understand.

Pat is fifteen, and things at home have been tense. He has been sullen and distant, Mom tells me, and she recently transferred him to a private school in San Francisco after he earned poor grades at the public school near our house. She fears that he's falling in with the wrong crowd too: he has come home smelling of alcohol and cigarettes more than once.

Whenever I talk to Pat on the phone, though, he seems to be the same old Pat: cheerful and full of life. He wants to hear all about New York: the snowstorms, the subways, the warm pretzels, the crazy people. He talks animatedly about school—mostly to tell me how much he hates algebra or how mean his history teacher is—but still, he is passionate about being on the pole-vaulting and diving teams, and he loves skateboarding and snowboarding with his friends on the weekends.

I also know that he is under a lot of pressure from Mom—not intentionally, but because life for her since our father's death has been a struggle emotionally. I feel protective of her, because I know how much she is hurting. But I also feel protective of Pat, because he has borne the brunt of her despair. With the rest of us out of the house —Cait is working as a teacher at a special education school, and Bri is just finishing up college—his every move is subject to scrutiny. And he is not an easy child for her: he doesn't conform to her standards, doesn't follow her orders, doesn't pick his battles. We have all urged him not to push her to her breaking point just because he can. They are like two bulls butting heads, and neither will back down.

He explains it to me: "I get in trouble because I always feel the need to fight back. I don't know why."

"Well, just stop being a punk," I tell him.

"I *will*, Ern!" he replies, giggling a little to show he isn't taking me seriously. And then he adds, "I love you soooooo much! When are you coming home? I can't wait to see you!" The little boy grabs my hand again, making me forget my unease.

As for the drinking and smoking, I blow it off. Barely an adult myself, I identify more with the teenage desire to experiment than with the parental urge to protect. Besides, it's nothing I didn't do in high school, so it can't be of too much alarm. I also decide it would be hypocritical to come down on Pat for drinking and smoking when I am sometimes guilty of those vices myself, albeit legally.

I'm further calmed by the memory of Pat's promise to me earlier that year, when I had come home during a break from school. He had taken me out to lunch at a local deli using money he'd earned at his summer job at Blockbuster, which had long since replaced the Rod's Video of our childhood. He ordered our sandwiches proudly, the kid brother taking care of his older sister for a change. We sat at a rickety wire table on the sidewalk as he filled me in on his life. The big news that summer was that his friend Victor had gone to rehab for cocaine. Victor hadn't been in our family's good graces since Pat came home from kindergarten one day with a smudged footprint on his white T-shirt. When we asked Pat about it, he had said, "Victor stepped on me." I found it unsurprising that Victor had become a troubled teen, but I was keen to know what Pat thought of drugs.

"The insides of his nose are all eaten away," Pat told me in a disgusted tone. "It's gross."

I had been relieved. Pat had always been a risk-taker when it came to physical challenges, and I worried that his adventurous spirit and eagerness to please could put him on a dangerous path in terms of mind-altering substances. Perhaps to seem more "cool older sister" than finger-wagging parent, I instructed him that alcohol and marijuana weren't really that big of a deal but to stay away from the bad stuff. I didn't define "bad stuff." He slurped soda through his straw and laughed at my authoritarian tone, but when I pushed him, he made the promise: "I swear to God, Ern! I will never, ever do drugs. Geez!"

I think back to this promise now, as Mom begins to tell me, between gasps, what she has found in Pat's backpack: Cigarettes. Lighters. Rolling papers. Weed. A glass pipe. Foil.

Needles.

Hot steam blasts from the steel grate below my feet, shrieking into the bitter night.

No, I scream in my head. *No, no, no.*

"Breathe," I say out loud to Mom. "Calm down. Breathe." I breathe with her, slowly and loudly: in two, three, four; out two, three, four. There has to be some explanation for this; she needs to confront him. She needs to remain composed.

We hang up, and the city is a blur of light and sound. I refuse to believe there were needles. I refuse to believe this is something that can't be fixed.

✖

PAT INITIALLY CLAIMS that they aren't his needles. He was carrying them for a friend, and it was a stupid mistake. Then he admits they were his—but says he was only using them to grow magic mushrooms. When Mom relays his proffered explanation, I launch a frantic online investigation. I learn that, indeed, one method of cultivating psychedelic mushrooms involves mixing spores grown on a piece of aluminum foil with water and drawing them up with a syringe. I grab hold of this information and use it to appease myself and Mom. Yes, it's terrible and something needs to be done. Pat needs to be punished, grounded; he needs to learn his lesson. He already seems contrite: when I berate him on the phone later that night, there is no resistance, only meekness.

"I'm sorry, Ern," he says. "I won't do it ever again."

I choose to believe him.

✖

12-6-04
Dear Ern,

Wassssss UP??? Guess what? Right now your B-sides CD is recording. I can't wait for you to get it. It is 9:33 right now and I have a lot of homework. UGG. I hate homework! JUST KIDDING!! I LOVE HOMEWORK. JUST KIDDING I HATE HOMEWORK!!! I wish I didn't have to do it. So, I got your letter a few days ago and I love it. This weekend I went snowboarding with my friends Brandon and Ross. It was fun. We woke up at 4:00 a.m. and drove up to Dodge Ridge. I didn't like Dodge Ridge that much. The snow sucked. It was all icy. Before we went snowboarding Ross, Brandon and I (did you notice my good grammar?!) were playing on a snow skate (like a skateboard for the snow w/ no wheels) and I fell onto the cement and hurt my hand, my ankle and my lower back/butt. I didn't notice that I had hurt my lower back/butt until I got home. I was taking a shower and I noticed that I had a HUGE scab on my back. It's pretty gross. But I had a good time. GUESS WHAT!! Do you remember me telling you about Jasper's mom? Well guess what she got me. She got me a PlayStation 2! She is so nice. I haven't told Mom and I can't set it up because she took mine and Brian's TV away! She is so stupid. I might just set it up downstairs. Oh well! I'll get our TV back one way or another. Man, it's taken me a long time to write this note it is now 11:34. JUST JOKING

I was only kidding. But just sos (I wrote "sos" on purpose because that is what my math teacher says. "Just sos you know alls you got to do is...") That is how he talks. Anyway just sos you know I would spend an infinite amount of time on your letters because you are the coolest, nicest, prettiest, most beautiful person EVER and I LOVE U SOOOOOOO x infinity much. But I have to go. Write me back soon!! I LOVE YOU.

LOVE,
Pat

P.S. I love your signature! I am going to practice mine.

Letters from Pat arrive throughout my years in New York. They are effervescent and spastic, jumping from one thing to the next with the unbridled energy of a child and only briefly touching on what I know is the reality of life on Cedar Street these days, permeated by the tension between Pat and our mother. From afar, I analyze my brother, piecing him together based on his letters and our phone calls, and the earful I'm getting from Mom. But whenever I try to dig deeper with him, he finds a way to throw me off track. His fallbacks are humor and charm, and his anecdotes and adulations easily sway me away from my worries. I have always been a sucker for Pat.

But as his adolescence progresses, the rest of us are increasingly unable to ignore the constant bickering between him and our mother. They are both wrong and both right. Pat is bitterly unhappy at the private high school in the city, complaining about the ninety-minute commute on the bus from the suburbs and the difficulty of the classes. While he is smart, he has to work hard at academics, and he'd prefer to be out on the field or in the water. Our mother doesn't understand this; her first three children were model students who *wanted* to learn. Pat is different, we tell her—not bad different, just different. She counters that he has to apply himself academically if he's ever going to get into college, which in our family is more of an expectation than an option. We are among the lucky ones whose parents saved all their working lives for our college educations, and in Mom's view, Pat is throwing this opportunity away.

There is also the matter of the DUI. Pat and two of his friends are arrested on the barren state highway near our family's cabin three hours north. Pat, at the wheel, has a blood alcohol level of 0.08, and California has a zero-tolerance policy for minors. Pat is booked into the county jail and charged with a DUI. Again, there are excuses: he had only two beers. His friends were too drunk to drive. He was trying to be responsible. He didn't *feel* drunk. Mom is livid, not only because of the risk Pat took with his life and the lives of others but because the incident makes it glaringly obvious that Pat is on a troubled path.

We all breathe a sigh of relief when Pat graduates from high school and moves down to southern California to enroll in San Diego State University. But the fights continue. As always, it is difficult to take sides in these scuffles, because they are dispatches from a distant battleground spun by opposing rhetoric. One Christmas Eve, Ben and I are in Utah with his family when I get a phone call from Cait: Pat has come home from college with tattoos on both arms. He has put a definitive end to one of his ongoing battles with Mom: she had explicitly told him that she'd yank his college funding if he got tattoos. Perhaps less angered by the tattoos themselves than by his blatant disrespect, she has stormed out of the house and driven to the cabin to be alone. Christmas is ruined.

I laugh bitterly when I learn what Pat's tattoos are. Split between his inner arms they read, "Deo Fidelis et Regi." The armorial motto of the O'Dalaigh clan of Ireland, from which our family is descended: "Faithful to God and King" or "Faithful to My Family."

But then I realize where Pat got the idea: from the Gaelic crest hung above the old brown armchair in our den, where our father used to sit and play the guitar.

8 | BUYING TIME

OUTSIDE THE HOSPITAL, the pavement glitters, millions of tiny diamonds framed by neat rows of flowerbeds. The outside world feels too bright, too happy. Something about it makes Ethan want to plunge back into darkness. Something about it makes him want to die.

He dreams of death, longs for it. He doesn't know why, only that he wishes he had died back there inside the hospital. Death had been so close, opening its arms and beckoning. Ethan had wanted so much to fall down that shadowy hole. But the doctors had pulled him back up into the mess of tubes and fluorescent white lights. The mess that is his life.

The coma had given him eight days of respite from the chase, the incessant cycle: shoot up, get high, come down, get sick, get more drugs, repeat. Ethan has brought himself to the brink many times, but something always pulls him back, unwilling. This time it was his dog. After he'd filled his veins with a cocktail of heroin, Opana, Xanax, and Soma, he'd sat down on the stairs near his bedroom. It was cool there, and he was so tired. The fight was dragging him down. He dove into the sweet stupor, hoping he'd never wake up. But the dog kept licking his face, tethering him to the world, refusing to let him go.

The doctor who signed off on Ethan's release papers said that if it hadn't been for his dog, Ethan would be dead. He said this as if Ethan should be happy about it.

That was forty-five minutes ago. Ethan pulls his cell phone from the plastic bag of his belongings and turns it on. He needs to get a hold of his dealer.

It's the only way to get back to the darkness.

✖

THE PROBATION OFFICER at the jail in Santa Ana holds Ethan's head in his lap. As Ethan fades in and out of consciousness, he imagines what the officer is thinking: *This kid just can't get it right. This kid is going to die.*

Ethan lets himself pass out, oblivious to the swarm of people awaiting sentencing outside the courtroom. The last thought in his head before he falls asleep is that it would be a blessing if he died. He is so sick of the way he is living; sick of hurting the people who love him the most; sick of being loaded.

Ethan is facing sixteen months in prison for a hit-and-run; he wasn't high when he mowed over the pedestrian, but he had drugs in his car and was on his way to get more, so he panicked and fled. He has already spent six months in the county jail for the incident, but sobriety was one of the terms of his probation, and he failed his latest drug test.

He knows the officer is considering his criminal history, which is typical of most young opiate addicts. Age fourteen: arrest for possession of marijuana and drunk-and-disorderly behavior. Age fifteen: arrest for possession of prescription drugs without a prescription and driving under the influence. Age sixteen: arrest for possession and intent to sell prescription drugs. Age seventeen: arrest for possession of heroin. Multiple overdoses, including one three months ago that resulted in a five-day coma from which Ethan was not expected to emerge, but did. The odds of his survival are dwindling: without help, it is clear that Ethan is going to die, whether he wants to or not.

The officer rouses Ethan and offers him a final choice to present to the judge: serve the prison term in full, starting today, or enroll in an inpatient drug treatment program—and promise to complete it. Ethan knows the odds are stacked against him. If he chooses jail, he'll have a chance to get clean, but there are still ways to obtain drugs while incarcerated, so it isn't a sure bet. Even if he refrains from using while behind bars, without a treatment program his mind-set will remain unchanged. He will likely bide his time until his release, when he'll begin the vicious cycle of addiction all over again. And if he doesn't get help, he'll likely end up back here. The majority of inmates imprisoned under California's infamous "three strikes" law, which allows sentences of twenty-five years to life for anyone previously convicted of two serious felonies, are addicts like Ethan: nearly 70 percent of convicts with a third strike show a high need for substance abuse treatment, compared with 48 percent of all inmates in the state.[53]

The officer had urged him to get into a program once before, when Ethan was being released from his six-month jail stint. He had told Ethan that he needed help or was going to die.

"Catch me if you can," Ethan had said dismissively. He wasn't ready.

Today, though, Ethan is vulnerable and tired. His friends have been dropping like flies: arrested, disappeared, dead from overdoses. He is twenty-three and has his whole life ahead of him. So he figures he'll give it a shot. He has nothing left to lose.

✖

THE OCEAN IN southern California is cool and warm at the same time. Cool enough to refresh and cleanse, to wash away your sins. Warm enough to swaddle you, hold you close, make you feel safe. When Ethan is clean, the ocean is the only place in the world he wants to be.

He came here high too, of course. The drugs muted everything: the screams of the gulls, the pull of the clockwork waves, the gritty scent of seaweed and sand. But on days like today, he can dive into the waters and feel acutely alive. He tastes the bittersweet salt on his lips and he feels closer to God as the ocean pulses around him, illuminated by the rays of the dawn.

There is a brightness that shines in Ethan with six months free of opiates, a cautious energy in his eyes. When he surfs he feels himself growing stronger. He has always loved the ocean most when the waves are huge, but he's starting to realize that for himself and many of his surfer buddies, it is the same when they get high: everything must be done to the extreme.

When he first started buying the pills that were being passed around his high school, mostly Xanax and Soma, it didn't seem like a big deal. The pills made surfing feel surreal, like a dream over which he had control. And there were more pills at home: his grandfather, who was dying of cancer, had tubs of them lying around. Ethan didn't know what they were, so he started experimenting. He found that he liked opiates the best: OxyContin, Norco, Vicodin, morphine. As a child, he used to put his towels in the dryer before he took a shower so that when he got out, he could surround himself in fluffy heat, and that's how these pills made him feel. Once he knew the names of the medications, he started heading down to Mexico and picking up pills for cheap. But it was also easy to get the pills from local doctors, who required no medical history or physical examination—just a copayment in exchange for a prescription.

Then came the withdrawals, the kicking legs and sour stomach and waves of nausea. Many of his friends were going through the same thing, until someone figured out that a gram of heroin could stave off those symptoms for three or four days, as opposed to a couple of hours for a pill. Ethan and his friends started snorting heroin, then smoking it, then mixing it with water and heating it in a spoon before slamming it into their arms with a needle. He cringes now when he thinks of some of the worst of these experiences: the chances they took with their young lives. But at the time, it was all just part of their attitude. Live life to the fullest, as his friend Joey used to say.

Ethan burrows his toes into the sand as he waits for his wetsuit to dry. Joey was one of his best friends from childhood. They'd grown up playing T-ball, surfing, and later doing drugs. Joey was sober now too. Ethan had been seeing him at recovery meetings over the past couple of weeks, but the two friends hadn't had a chance to really hang out, just them—sober—in a long time. Yesterday morning, Ethan had caught sight of Joey down by the courthouse, where he was heading to check in with his probation officer. He hadn't had time to tell Joey about his new idea: getting together a group of sober surfers and skaters who would speak to teens and young adults about the dangers of drugs. They could call it Hope Division, and their motto could be "Surf, Skate, Hope." The two friends had made plans to get together this afternoon at the beach to surf, and Ethan was hoping to talk the idea over with Joey then.

Ethan realizes that even though he's been on the beach for nearly three hours already, he is still glad to be coming back later on with his friend. When he returns to his parked car, he changes out of his wetsuit and packs up his surfboard. On the dashboard his cell phone blinks with a missed call from Joey's mom.

9 | SAYING NOTHING

MY BROTHER PADDLES before me in the still, calm waters of the inlet. His shoulders are crisp and strong in the tropical heat, moving rhythmically with the pull of the kayak's oars. He calls back to me, "Slowpoke!" I'm ten years older and slower than Pat, plus my kayak is leaking. He rows backward to find out what the problem is, but even after he graciously switches boats with me, I still can't keep up with him. He laughs and darts deeper into the watery maze of mangroves, their spidery vines brushing the tops of his sun-bleached hair.

"Ern, come on!" he shouts. "There's a crocodile over here!"

It is the summer of 2008, just after I've finished graduate school and Ben and I have moved back to San Francisco. We are on a family vacation in Costa Rica. Mom has taken a sabbatical of sorts and is living with a local family and teaching English in a small village in the southern part of the country. We had all been surprised when she announced the trip, since she had always been more of a homebody. Secretly, I suspected it had something to do with Pat. Although she sometimes comes off as dictatorial, she loves him fiercely. Unfortunately, the more she tries to make him conform, the more he pushes her away.

This vacation was supposed to be fun: a family reunion in a tropical paradise. There have certainly been good moments, like our adventure kayaking through the mangroves, or a few days ago when we went ziplining through the rain forest. But there has been a distinct undertone of strain. Pat and Mom are at it again, and nothing seems to ease the tension of their hushed conversations, the spats they constantly tumble into while the rest of us try to pretend away the bitterness.

Money has been a constant issue between the two of them. Pat has been kicked out of the dorm rooms, apparently due to noise violations and graffiti. He claims it wasn't his fault that people always flocked to his room and partied—how could he be expected to control the actions of others? When Mom called the school to find out what had happened, the counselor wouldn't release any more information because Pat was eighteen. He was a good kid, the counselor said, but the dorms weren't right for him.

Pat has moved into an off-campus house with a group of friends and has all but dropped out of classes. His latest idea was to switch to community college, where he'd have a more flexible schedule and therefore more time to work at his day job at a pizzeria, as well as to skateboard and surf. Or he might just drop out of school altogether and become a surf instructor. Mom finally told him in exasperation to do whatever he wanted. But she reminded him that the money in his college fund was for classes and books, so if he dropped out of school, he'd be on his own financially. While she had hoped this would serve as a threat, Pat has taken it as a challenge, telling Mom he just doesn't think college is for him, and he's not going to waste her money on something he isn't sure about. He wants to start filing his taxes independently and forge his own path. He is leaving her behind.

We are in a seaside town on the Oso Peninsula, a day's journey from the village where Mom is staying, when Pat goes to an ATM to withdraw cash and comes back empty-handed. Mom is baffled, and furious: just six months ago, she had deposited funds for the spring semester into that account—$10,000. Naturally, Pat has a million excuses. He loaned a friend some money. He sprained his ankle and went to the emergency room, but he forgot his insurance card so he had to pay up front. His books were really expensive this year. His former roommate owes him three months' rent.

As these excuses spill forth, Pat is meek and apologetic. Mom does not raise her voice, but it's clear she is frantic. Since Dad died, she has taken great care with our family's finances; she's the type of person who religiously pays her bills on time and still practices what we kids see as the antiquated ritual of balancing her checkbook. I leave them together to hash it out, but when I come back an hour later, things seem to have settled into an uneasy peace. As angry as Mom is, her instinct is to help, and she wants Pat to have a clean slate. They've worked out a short-term financial plan to get Pat back on track, with the goal that he'll eventually repay her. Pat hadn't wanted Mom's help, telling her that he would find a way to fix his mistakes. But Mom wants to handle this problem as a team, as our family has tackled every challenge in the past.

"We will get through this together," she says.

That night, my sister and I go to the local grocery store and buy a small cake and a box of matches. We bring the cake back to the hotel room, stick a lit match in the middle of it, and call Pat into the room. It is his twentieth birthday. He grins and hugs us, and blows out the match. His sunburned shoulders, slick with aloe, reflect the whirring light of the ceiling fan. He seems happy and lost at the same time.

As we eat the cake, I'm distracted by Pat's left leg, which he's tapping on the ground like a jackhammer. I swat at him playfully and he grins. When he finishes the cake, he bolts out the door, saying he's going to take a walk. I wonder why he seems so antsy. I decide he's probably still embarrassed about the missing money.

The rain, warm like blood, flows in rivulets through the gutters outside, sounding like tears.

✖

THE NEXT DAY we all decide to rent bikes and ride them to a nearby beach, where Bri and Pat can go surfing and Mom, Cait, and I can spend a lazy afternoon sunbathing and reading. While Bri and Cait are renting the bikes, Pat and I stop off at an Internet café to check our email. It's been awhile since I traveled out of the country for so long, and I'm relieved to discover that everything is fine on the home front: no work- or apartment-related emergencies. And since Pat is here with us, there's no fear of getting any upsetting news about another one of his mishaps.

Beside me, Pat snorts good-naturedly and slaps the wobbly wooden table with his fist; the Spanish keyboard makes punctuating a challenge. I tell him I'm about ready to go. He agrees but keeps on typing while I stand up and dig into my bag for cash to pay the café owner.

In the cramped space, I have a full view of Pat's screen as I wait for the manager to give me my change; he is still attempting to type. I don't mean to spy on him exactly— I know he's probably emailing the girl he's allegedly been dating, a relationship that has been the source of great embarrassment for Pat at the hands of his teasing siblings. But in that way of being unable not to rubberneck at the scene of a freeway car crash, I cannot look away.

I read the words as they meld together, weaving a story I don't understand: "you know that im just as deep if not deeper than you. you have to tell me how rehab was cuz if i cant clean up or get a little better when i get back ill be right there with you . . . that shit sucks ass to come off of. you saw me."

Suddenly the manager is talking to me, handing me the bill, and I look away from the screen. And then, abruptly, the story disappears into the ether as Pat sends the email and stands up, grabbing his backpack. He turns around toward me and grins his trademark smile, bouncing toward the door.

"Let's get outta here!" he says, and I am confused. I grab my change from the manager and follow my brother blindly into the light. I don't know what just happened. I cannot comprehend what I just read; it's as if the words weren't English at all, or any other human language, but were instead imparted from some alien world, some world other than mine. I am literally speechless, without words to describe or address the situation I have witnessed. So I say nothing.

I feel my brother grab my arm. He's pointing to a pile of coconuts, sitting inexplicably in the gutter-like trenches that line the streets. He sifts through the pile until he finds one that is perfectly oblong, with hundreds of delicate tawny threads matted along its exterior. The guide on one of our rain forest hikes had explained how to crack open a coconut, and Pat has been eager to try out the technique. He stuffs the fruit into his backpack and we walk on.

The unnerved feeling inside of me deepens. What did he mean by "im just as deep if not deeper than you"? Pat seems just fine. Maybe a little wayward in terms of his finances and future goals, but mostly he's happy and light, like always. He'd said, "that shit sucks ass to come off of. you saw me." What was the "shit," and what had there been to see? Why did he say, "you have to tell me how rehab was cuz if i cant clean up or get a little better when i get back ill be right there with you"? Get clean—from what? Rehab—for what? Already, my memory is slippery, and I'm not sure if I'd read his words correctly. They have been muddied by my uncertainty, my fears, my disbelief. I do not understand what I saw, or think I saw. Did I even see it? My head feels swollen in the humidity, my throat cinched closed as if tightened with a drawstring. Still, I say nothing.

Outside the bike rental shop, we meet up with everyone else. We spend a few minutes getting used to the bikes, wobbling around in circles. We head off toward the ocean in a spaced-out procession down a

dusty road lined with brilliant green fields. Once again, Pat takes off
ahead of me, his Hawaiian-patterned board shorts quickly fading into
the emerald horizon, out of my eyesight, out of my reach.

When we arrive at the beach an hour later, Pat isn't there. Bri takes
off down one of the small roads that feed into the main one, thinking Pat
may have accidentally taken a wrong turn; he can't have gone too far.
Mom, Cait, and I wheel our bikes up the thick dunes and descend on the
other side toward the cerulean sea, which fans outward and all around
us under a matching sky. It is magnificent, and I am crumbling inside,
and again I say nothing.

It is another hour before Bri returns with Pat, who he'd found back
on the main road. Pat says he just got lost, but I don't know what to
believe as he throws down his backpack and extracts the coconut. I
watch as he smacks the fruit along its equator against a large piece of
driftwood and twists it into two halves, his veins bulging with the effort.
I wonder suddenly what has gone into those veins, and the panic in my
stomach shoots down to my feet, paralyzing me.

I am a journalist; I am trained to ask questions, to seek answers, to
be objective rather than emotional, to find the truth. But my brother
looks up at me triumphantly, and the pearly meat of the opened coconut
glistens in his hands like freshly fallen snow, unbroken yet by footprints,
and though I do not know why, I say nothing.

10 | COME BACK

ALICE KNOWS JOEY is gone as soon as she enters his bedroom. He is sitting on the edge of his bed, facing the door, his head thrown back, his mouth open. His nail beds and lips are a deep shade of purple, and his eyes are unmoving. On the floor at his feet is a needle half-filled with an amber-colored liquid. Though Alice knows it's pointless, she bends over next to him and begs her youngest son, her little Joe Bug, not to leave this world.

"Get back in your body, now!" she shouts at him. "Just get back!"

Joey doesn't move.

"Ted, I think Joey finally did it," she yells.

Her husband runs into the room.

Ted lifts Joey into his arms like the child he once was. He lays his tall, handsome twenty-three-year-old son down on the floor. Joey's body is like Play-Doh; his legs fold upward like a rag doll, almost behind his head, and Alice unbends them out of this unnatural position. As Ted performs CPR, Alice calls 911. Ted sobs as he pumps Joey's chest, but Alice has yet to cry.

She thinks back to the night before, when Joey had come home after dinner to plop down on the couch next to Alice, who was watching TV. He seemed exhausted: he said he'd been surfing all day and had applied for a job too. Alice wanted to believe him, but these days with Joey, who knew? His niece's birthday party was the next day, and Alice didn't want Joey to forget—she could tell he'd been having a hard time lately and had recently lost his phone.

"I'm not going to have any problem with you tomorrow, am I?" she asked.

"No, Mom," he said, and he went off to bed, which Alice thought was strange. Usually, it was Alice who went to bed earlier.

Now Alice turns away as Ted leans over Joey, away from the terrible scene of a father's tears falling onto his fallen son. When the paramedics arrive, she and Ted huddle in the living room and grasp hands, praying.

"God, you are the Almighty and all-powerful," they say. "If it is your will, please put Joey back in his body. Please just put him back."

When the paramedics come out and say they're sorry, Alice still does not cry. She tells me later that she and her husband always knew this day would come. Alice and Ted weren't like some of the other parents, the ones who preferred to keep up the facade of a perfect life, the ones who refused to admit that their children were addicts, even though everyone secretly knew the truth. No, she and Ted had openly accepted the fact that Joey was an addict, once they'd found out how bad things had really gotten for him. Addiction ran in the family, and Alice had always made it clear to her three kids that because of their genetic history, they had to be careful when it came to alcohol and drugs. Scientists estimate that genetic predisposition accounts for between 40 and 60 percent of a person's vulnerability to addiction, Alice informed them.[54] If they flipped that switch in their brains, they would forever have to deal with the consequences, and life would be a whole lot harder. But Joey had needed to find that out for himself.

Recently, he'd told her that he wished he'd listened to her all along. His mom had been right.

Unlike many other parents, Alice and Ted believed that Joey's addiction wasn't a moral failing on his part. They believed that addiction was a disease, and they had done everything they could to help their son: mental health services, outpatient treatment programs, seven inpatient rehabs, psychiatric hospitalizations. Joey would get better for a few weeks or even months, but he always slipped back. Once, when he woke up in the hospital after an overdose of OxyContin, Xanax, and cocaine, he said sleepily to Alice, "I shouldn't be alive, Mom. I should be dead for everything I put in me."

"I just love drugs," he'd added. "I just love them so much, and I don't know why."

Alice had told him he'd better find out.

As for herself, Alice never harbored any illusions that Joey was immune from tragedy, but she always allowed herself to feel hope for him. She refused to enable him, calling the cops on him and throwing him out whenever it was necessary. But her constant mission was to stay strong for Joey, to remind him that he had a disease that required treatment, to help him believe he was a good person who deserved to make it. He had been knocked down so many times, but he kept getting back up, she pointed out to him when she could tell he was struggling. Sometimes, when he was clean, she could catch glimpses of his inherent innocence, the little boy he once was, digging for sand crabs by the ocean. Before the pills, before the heroin, when his life stretched ahead of him like an endless highway, winding toward an unseen end.

Now the little boy is gone. The kid with so much talent and potential, who had so much to add to the world, has disappeared. There is only a ravaged body in his place, the body of a man, his tattooed arms framing his face like a kaleidoscopic halo.

Finally, Alice lets the tears break through, recalling the words Joey wrote for a school assignment when he was sixteen: "In my future, I can see many things happening. In 15 years, I will be 31 years old. By the time I'm that old, I hope to have already started a family. I wish that I will have a beautiful wife and two kids. I want my family to be as loving and caring as possible. I really want to make my dreams come true."

✖

THE CHURCH AT the top of the hill bakes in the arid sun as it fills slowly with
mourners. Alice and Ted sit side by side before an altar awash in lilies,
their heads leaning inward to form a heart. It looks like defeat and tri-
umph at the same time: sadness, love, and everything in between. Alice
tells herself she can look at the situation one of two ways: that Joey's
death is a tragedy, or that she was blessed with his life for twenty-three
years. She recalls an old Armenian adage: "Everything is written on your
forehead. God knows it all: the day you're going to be born, and the day
you're going to die."

A few rows behind Alice and Ted, Ethan holds his head in his hands.
Ever since Alice called him last week with the news of Joey's death,
he has felt as if he is on the edge of a colossal precipice, a wide chasm
threatening to swallow him whole. The funerals are starting to melt
together in his mind: twelve, thirteen, fourteen friends gone in just two
years; so many that he can barely remember them. All of them under
age twenty-five, and all of them dead because of pills and heroin. And
now Joey.

Ethan does not cry. He is filled with numbness, a sense that nothing
matters. Joey had looked great that day by the courthouse; he had seemed
fine. But Ethan knows outward appearances can lie. What was it that
brought Joey back to the darkness, sucking him back into the vortex?
He was so young, so full of life. Ethan feels two opposing sides battling
within him: the voice of his addiction, and the voice of his soul—*him*,
Ethan, the essence of his personhood, all the good and flawed things
that make him a human being worthy of living. He knows exactly how
Joey felt: the shame and the guilt, paired with the unbearable urge to be
numb. And while it hurts that Joey is dead, Ethan isn't naive enough to
believe that this is the last friend he'll lose to an overdose. *It's happened*

so often lately that it's expected, and it's going to happen to someone else, and it's going to be soon, he thinks to himself.

During the service, many of the older mourners weep at the improbability of the absence of the young man in the pictures on the poster boards at the front of the church, hugging his parents, surfing unimaginably high waves, riding roller coasters with his niece. At the podium, Joey's sister remembers listening to his heartbeat when he was still in Alice's womb.

"I have loved my baby brother ever since that moment," she says.

Still, Ethan does not cry.

As Joey's godparents sing an Armenian folksong, Ethan glances at those around him. Only the older people are crying. The younger ones, the ones around his age, sit in silence. They are beaten down, deadened. One young man in a flannel shirt folds his arms over his chest, his blond hair catching the glimmer of the overhead lights as his chin drops downward, nodding uncontrollably. His eyes are glazed, but not with tears. Ethan remembers the feeling so vividly that he can nearly taste it: he has attended plenty of memorials high, either because he would be obviously sick if he didn't fix before the service, or because it was easier to deal with death that way. Sometimes he and his friends would even get high to celebrate the life of a friend who had passed away of an overdose, telling themselves, *We party hard. We all hang out, we all get loaded together, and this is what our friend would have wanted us to do.* Now Ethan sees how messed up that is, but it doesn't stop him from feeling the familiar twinge, the desire to fill the hollowness.

A slideshow is being projected onto two huge screens mounted on the church's walls, the timeline of a short life from beginning to end. In the photographs, Joey is grinning, free. He is unafraid, at peace, and Ethan envies him.

After the service, Ethan waits in line to sign his name on a blown-up picture of Joey, enveloped by translucent sea spray, riding the waves into the horizon. Behind him, a kid Ethan doesn't know whispers to his companion, "I've got to go see my guy in Santa Ana." Ethan envies this kid too.

Ethan signs Joey's picture with their joking catchphrase: "Dude, bro, dude, bro!" He adds, "I'm going to miss you and your stoked attitude. Love and miss you bud. See you later." Then he walks back to the parking lot, the palm trees rustling nervously. He gets into his car and heads toward Santa Ana.

✖

NOW THAT HE'S locked up, Ethan dreams of wide-open spaces. The hills surrounding San Juan Capistrano, the Appalachian Trail, and the ocean, always the ocean. All around him, the walls are papered with the things his cell mates dream of: girls mostly, and trucks and motorcycles. But his space is covered with pictures of waves. He misses the ocean so much that it physically hurts.

Inside the jail, his once-tanned skin has grown pasty, emphasizing the tattoo on his finger. He has picked up a work shift doing errands for the guards, mopping the floor or running paperwork from office to office. It's not the job he minds so much as the hours: 4:00 PM to midnight, which means that he's usually sleeping during outside exercise time.

"Is it sunny out there today?" he asks wistfully when I come to visit him. His voice is muffled and distant through the prison telephone, his orange prison scrubs blurry through the grimy Plexiglas.

Because of his work schedule, in the ten months Ethan's been incarcerated he's seen the sun only a handful of times—in the past three months only once. The last time he saw it was when the guards conducted a random raid on the cells, looking for contraband. When the inmates were shuttled outside, he took off his shirt and lay down on the ground, trying to soak the delicious warmth into his bones.

The drugs—Xanax mostly, and heroin—crept back in after Joey's memorial. The relapse was brief but brutal: he got into another car accident while high, this time hitting another vehicle, breaking the passenger's leg. When he got to the holding cell, he was shocked by the graffiti scrawled on the wall. "Dude, bro, dude, bro," just like he and Joey used to say.

Ethan took it as a sign and made a pact with himself to stay clean. It's been a constant struggle, because drugs are everywhere in jail, but the time he's spent locked up marks the longest stint of sobriety he's had since he started using: ten months. This past New Year's Eve, he even convinced one of his fellow inmates to commit to sobriety too—after all, you just need two people to hold a meeting. The kid has ended up being his best friend in here, but he's bailing out in a few weeks, and Ethan will be on his own again.

Every day he feels bad about what he's done in his life. He tries to stay positive, like his mom raised him to be. Good comes from everything, he tells himself, and there must be a reason he's here, a purpose to the turn his life has taken. He tries to help some of the young kids who get thrown in jail and are kicking heroin, without being annoying and preachy.

"This is not the lifestyle you want for yourself," he tells them.

Someday, when he gets out, he wants to keep helping kids like him. Maybe he'll finally launch the Hope Division, or move abroad and open up a sober surfing operation.

He knows something saved him, but he doesn't know what it was.

11 | LOSING FAITH

FROM FAR AWAY, the lump in the parking lot near the university campus doesn't look like a body. More like a sack: a laundry bag, perhaps, or a large backpack filled with books. But when the cops get closer, they realize the lump is indeed a body—a young kid, barely breathing, facedown on the concrete. When they rouse him, he is disoriented and belligerent. They handcuff him and find bottles of pills in his pockets. He is booked into the San Diego County Jail a few minutes after midnight: inmate number 8196065. Pat.

My sister has been staying at the Cedar Street house during Mom's absence, so she's the one to receive his collect call. The voice on the other end of the line is faded and fuzzy.

"I'm in jail," he says softly. "I don't know when I'm going to get out."

The catch in his voice is agonizing, but Cait is furious. It's a week before Christmas, and Mom is flying home from Costa Rica in three days. We haven't seen her since our trip to visit her over the summer, and we've been planning a huge homecoming party.

"What did you do now?" she asks tersely. "What do you want me to do?"

Pat doesn't give a lot of details, but says he was arrested for public intoxication. He doesn't know when his court date will be, but he's definitely going to miss his flight home tomorrow, and he asks Cait to try to change it.

"Please, don't tell anyone," he begs her, as if no one will notice his absence.

When Cait tells us the news, I am livid. Once again, Pat has managed to ruin what should have been a joyous time for our family. Knowing Mom will be devastated, we decide to give her at least a few hours of happiness before the dark cloud descends again. When we meet her at the airport, we'll be vague about Pat's whereabouts. Then we'll take her home, have a nice dinner with her, and tell her the truth after she's settled in.

At the airport, it takes one look at her face to know this plan isn't going to work.

"Where is Pat?" she asks immediately, panic and fear in her jet-lagged eyes.

An hour later, the car is packed to drive down to San Diego in the morning.

✖

ON CHRISTMAS DAY, we all meet for dinner at our grandmother's house. Mom will be here soon, along with Pat, and we are pretending that everything is normal. This incenses me; I have been enraged ever since Pat returned yesterday with Mom. Of course he hadn't told us the whole story: he had been arrested for public intoxication but also for possession of OxyContin without a prescription. It turns out that the house where he'd been living had been under police surveillance for months and was finally raided, resulting in Pat and three of his roommates being arrested. At his court date in January, he'll be facing up to a year in jail and $2,000 in fines. Yet he is still full of excuses: The pills weren't his. He wasn't intoxicated; he was just passed out. It's his roommate, a known drug dealer, who the police were after—he had just gotten caught in the middle.

When Pat walks in the door and kisses our grandmother on the cheek, something inside me cracks. Little seems out of place: he is, as always, blond and tan and young and beautiful. Soon he is gallantly showing off the napkin-folding skills he has acquired at his latest job waiting tables. I pull him into our grandmother's bedroom and scream at him until I am hoarse.

"Just stop doing drugs!" I yell. I am sobbing, clutching at him, wringing my hands. I do not understand why it has to be this way.

The little boy stares back at me. For the first time since this saga began, I ask him point-blank for the truth.

"What have you done? Have you snorted shit? Have you shot up?" I demand, without asking him to define *shit*.

He looks ashamed as he answers in a voice so quiet I can barely hear him.

"I've done pretty much everything," he says.

I lose it completely, begging him now. I tell him I love him and don't want to lose him; I implore him again to just stop doing drugs. He doesn't fight back: he seems deflated somehow, and sad. He hugs me, his hair damp against the desperate crush of my tears, and makes another promise.

"I will, Ern. I will," he says. "I'm sorry."

Did I ruin us that night? Did I alienate him, make him feel so outcast, so far away from the rest of us that he just has to go and do more of whatever he was doing?

Or is it the next night that I cause the break, yelling at him after he has hurt Mom yet again, threatening to leave the next day for southern California, telling her he doesn't need her, saying "Fuck this shit" as she starts crying, then breathing heavily, then hyperventilating, then screaming as she feels him slipping further away?

I yell at him more, and his response is as placating as always.

"I'm sorry, Ern," he says. "I love you. I'm going to get better, I promise."
I choose to believe him.

✖

THE NEXT DAY, Mom and Cait drive Pat down to San Diego for his court
date. That night, he overdoses while lying in bed next to Mom. The
paramedics arrive just in time, and in the ambulance on the way to the
hospital, Mom squeezes Pat's fingers, which grow limper as the chemicals overwhelm his system.

Pat wakes up in the still hours of dawn, just in time to face the judge.
Cait is fuming and tells him he could have died if Mom hadn't called for
help when she did. Pat says this is ridiculous. Everyone is overreacting.
He would have slept it off. But he whispers faintly as he turns away, "I
found the pills, and I couldn't resist."

They barely make it to the courthouse. The judge orders Pat to enroll
in a thirty-day outpatient rehab program as a condition of avoiding jail
time. He must live with Mom and abide by her house rules.

"Good luck, Mr. Daly," the judge says, and Pat hangs his head.

✖

BRIAN CALLS TO ask if I can pick up Pat and Mom from the airport that
night. He is already on his way back to the Bay Area from his apartment
in Santa Cruz, but he won't be able to get to the airport in time. Cait
isn't answering phone calls; she is too angry. She is driving the car back
up to San Francisco and will meet us at the Cedar Street house later on.
My sister, the one with infinite patience, the one who always finds the
good in bad situations, has finally broken. I say yes and hang up. I have
no idea how this has spun so far out of control.

As Ben and I drive to the airport, waves of nausea rise up from my stomach. I want to see Pat and make sure he is alive, but I don't know how to fix him. I feel guilty: for not being a better sister, for being unable to stop his pain. I am shell-shocked with incompetence, floundering in my inability to control what lies ahead.

He looks stale and ragged as he walks toward me. I force myself to be steady, thinking this is what he needs: for me not to collapse. In the car, Ben drives, and Mom sits in the front seat, steering the conversation toward the weather. I sit with Pat in the back, holding him in my arms.

He cries all the way back to Cedar Street. I hold him like a baby and run my fingers through his gossamer hair, listening to his sobs. He does it shamefully, hanging his head in my lap and covering his face with his arms.

"I'm done with it," he cries. "I want to get my life back on track." It sounds real when he says it.

"I love you," I tell him. "You're a good person. There is so much good stuff ahead of you. You're going to make it."

I pull him upward and look into his eyes—glassy—and realize he is high.

✖

PAT'S REHAB PROGRAM is at a local hospital, where Mom drops him off every morning and picks him up every night. During the car rides, he has little to say, but he seems complacent. Then one night after dinner, he walks into the bathroom as Mom is brushing her teeth. He stands above the toilet and pulls out a ziplock baggie full of small white pills.

"I'm finished," he tells Mom, flushing them away.

We are all enchanted by this story, taking it to mean that Pat has finally turned a corner. Still, there are setbacks. Mom begins attending Nar-Anon meetings, angering Pat, who claims he isn't an addict; he's just been partying too much. After one meeting, Mom tapes a handout on drug addiction on the closet door in her bedroom. When Pat discovers it, he rips it down. The next day, Cait walks into the kitchen to find him crying in Mom's arms.

"I'm sorry I've hurt you guys," he sobs, with a distinct slur in his voice.

"I love you," Mom says. "Please, Pat. I will do anything to help you get better. I won't let you go easily. You have the power to write your own story, make your own new beginning."

Cait pulls Mom aside and whispers accusingly that Pat is high. Mom just cries.

"I know," she finally says. "But just for once, it's so nice to hear him say he's sorry."

Pat shows me a different side. In our frequent phone calls, he sounds tired but mostly upbeat, which I interpret as a sign that he's at least trying. But strangely, he has started to complain about a host of odd physical symptoms that make little sense to me: He can't sleep. His mind is racing uncontrollably. He keeps passing out and feels nauseous all the time. His body feels tingly and itchy. He has been prescribed an antidepressant, a mild sedative, and naltrexone, an opioid antagonist used to curb cravings for opiates, and I assume these symptoms are side effects of the medications. I tell him to talk to his doctor about all of this and mention that I myself have used antidepressants and sedatives periodically over the years. At this information, he perks up, asking me which drugs I was prescribed, and the dosages. He is particularly interested in my experience with Klonopin, which I have used to treat panic attacks, and with Ambien for sleep. I think of how Pat has always seen himself as the black sheep of the family and wonder whether knowing that his big sister isn't perfect might help him feel less alone in his turmoil. But another part of me distrusts his motive: is he angling to figure out which legitimate symptoms he can fake to persuade doctors to issue more prescriptions?

The pressure between Mom and Pat is building again, so I invite him and my siblings to spend the night at my apartment. We drive to the beach at Fort Funston, where the dog can run off-leash. In the car, Pat is in charge of the iPod, and we joke about our ten-year generational gap: he refers to Nirvana, one of his favorite bands, as "vintage," while I remember exactly where I was at age sixteen when Kurt Cobain's suicide was announced. On the shore, he walks with Bri ahead of Cait and I, and I stare at his baggy jeans, his rumpled flannel shirt, his ratty sneakers. There are so many secrets hidden inside of him, and I don't know how to break through his shell and discover them.

Later, back at the apartment, he asks if he can borrow my cell phone to call a friend. He makes the call from the back balcony, quietly, out of my earshot. He goes into the bathroom, and when he comes out, I am sure his pupils are pinned. I confer hurriedly with the others as Pat settles in front of the TV. We have assumed that he is clean because the rehab program is drug testing him, and while he's not acting all crazy and out of control, we worry that if he's high, he might overdose in his sleep. Cait describes the sound of Pat's snoring when he overdosed in San Diego: clogged, sporadic, heavy. We decide not to confront him and risk making him feel attacked; it's the first time in months that we've all been able to hang out, drama-free. We spend a tortured night together, listening through the shadows for "the snore."

It never comes.

✖

IT IS AFTER midnight when I get the call. I've acquired the habit of sleeping with my phone under my pillow, in case it is Pat, or someone calling about him. This time it's a missed call from "Bunny."

Pat is in Los Angeles, living with his girlfriend after having completed his rehab program. When I call him back, he says he just wanted to check in. He tells me he's getting stronger—he has started working out again and skateboarding—and has been going to recovery meetings. Rather than return to school, he has decided to become an electrical lineman. I think it's a great idea: why shouldn't he be high in the sky, at the edge of the horizon, where his taste for risk is appeased in a healthy way? We discuss how he needs to practice walking me down the aisle at my upcoming wedding, a role he has assumed with guileless enthusiasm.

"It's so cool that you're getting married!" he says, and I feel momentarily like we are children again: the little boy, my baby brother, comes running into my open arms, eyes shining.

I catch a note of forlornness when Pat says goodbye, something despondent in the downward deflection of his voice. It's so miniscule that I barely pick up on it, and yet it nags me as I replace the phone under my pillow and settle back in under the sheets. I argue with myself: *Call him back. It's one in the morning. Find out what's wrong. Don't be paranoid. Tell him you love him one more time. You already did; he already knows.*

Exhaustion wins out. He has promised me he is okay.

I choose to believe him.

✖

I WONDER SOMETIMES about that last conversation with Pat.

I wonder if he wanted to die.

PART II
ANGER

THE CITY BLINKS ITS LIGHT, POLICE
SIRENS SOUND, FAINT MUSIC FROM
ANOTHER APARTMENT COMES AND GOES
WITH THE BREEZE. AND THEN, JUST
AS IT HAD THAT AFTERNOON, THE OLD
CRAVING RETURNS . . . LIKE SKIN THAT
FEELS PERFECTLY FINE ONE MORNING
AND THEN IS ABLAZE WITH AN ITCH THE NEXT.
IT LOOKS THE SAME: SKIN–HARMLESS,
UNFETTERED SKIN. BUT ALL AT ONCE
IT'S SCREAMING TO BE RAVAGED WITH
FINGERNAILS AND RUBBED RAW.

—BILL CLEGG, *NINETY DAYS*

12 | UNTRUE

IN THE CRUMPLED early hours, I lunge awake. It can't be true. The phone call, the tears, Mom's screams.

The dawn filters into the room. It is real. Pat is dead.

The house is full of swollen eyes. Mom in her bed with Kathy beside her. Caitlin in a sleeping bag on the floor, surrounded by pillows cobbled together from hallway closets. Brian, cradled by Elise. Ben, beside me, finally sleeping, turned toward the window. The dog on the brown carpet below. Me, awake. And Pat, in a metal slot in a wall in a morgue five hundred miles away.

I throw off the heavy covers, under which Pat slept and hid bags of pills. I fumble with the doorknob, which he used to key open with scissors when we fought. I hurl past the staircase and run to the bathroom, where he had once nodded off and fallen, cracking his skull against the toilet bowl (true), telling Mom afterward that he had been tired and had fallen asleep while peeing (not true). I vomit in the toilet, where Pat also vomited while he was detoxing. I want more to come out; it won't. I sob.

✖

THINGS BEGIN TO happen quickly, and we all seem to spin off into separate orbits, solitary planets revolving around the same sun. Soon there are all the usual things that follow in tragedy's footsteps. The house becomes filled with everything that comes in the wake of death: voices, casseroles, phone calls, flowers, hugs, cards, ringing doorbells, sweets. The things people do when there is nothing else to be done. People from the past materialize out of nowhere. At any given time Mom is surrounded by at least three people. Caitlin goes shopping for clothes in which to bury Pat. Brian visits each of our relatives to tell them the news, accompanied by our family friend Tom for support. Tom, who is a lawyer, also deals with the necessary documents and records associated with death. Ben makes funeral home appointments and organizes a motorcade for the procession. Elise starts putting together a program for the service. I compose Pat's obituary. Everyone else, without asking, cooks, cleans, irons, and launders.

I sit at the desk in the bedroom as I write, looking down at the rope swing in the backyard, hating Pat for all the things he didn't tell me. Hating him for not giving me a better chance to save him. Hating him for leaving us all behind.

My sister comes into the room, crying, and the sight of her brokenness fills me with fury.

"Why was the door locked?" she sobs as I hug her uselessly. "Why did the paramedics have to break down the door?"

I have no answer for her.

✖

THE MORNING WE drive to the funeral home is overcast and quiet, and we travel slowly. By now, the shock has sunken into a dull sick feeling, almost like the bone aches and stomach butterflies of the flu. We are all here, our little family that keeps getting littler. Ben is here too; he has agreed to do the talking. He used to help a mortician friend collect dead bodies and bring them to the morgue for embalming and has an easy familiarity with death that always seemed a little unorthodox. Now it comes as a relief.

The funeral director is a young woman with dark hair and glasses who meets us at the door and offers the appropriate condolences. We thank her because we have to. Mom holds it together until we are seated around a glass table in the director's office.

I don't blame her when she begins to cry. A little more than a decade ago, she and Dad sat in this room and had the same conversation with a different funeral director about him. Dad knew he was going to die, and he wanted everything to be set so that there would be no decisions to be made when he did. And it was indeed seamless, passing in a smooth, sad wave of black clothes and Irish hymns and funeral limousines, a line of cars stretching backward on the highway as far as I could see.

And now it is today, and everything is uncertain. We don't even know where Pat's body is. The funeral director says it is probably still in Burbank, where the autopsy is being performed. A lengthy conversation ensues: how to contact the coroner's office, whether to contract a refrigerated truck to transport the body five hundred miles up to the Bay Area, when to expect the toxicology report, how much to pay the priest, which newspaper to post the obituary in, when to have a private viewing and whom to invite, what clothes to dress Pat in, which flowers to order and how many, whether to cremate Pat or bury him, and, if he is buried, where and in what type of coffin.

While all this is going on, I become fixated on a brochure propped among the rosaries and urns. "LifeGem® Diamonds . . . because love lives on," it reads. "The LifeGem® is a certified, high-quality diamond created from the carbon of your loved one as a memorial to their unique life."

It takes a minute before I comprehend that this brochure is trying to sell me on the idea of wearing my dead brother around my neck in the form of a diamond.

"I'll take one of these," I announce, startling our mother. She looks up from her enormous binder with all of Pat's documents with eyes so puffy that it seems as though she's been stung by a million tiny bees. She appears lost.

The funeral director nods and says we can talk about that possibility if we decide to go with cremation. I had forgotten—we haven't yet decided on what the director is calling a "mode of disposition." Mom wants Pat to be buried in the same plot as our father. The space was intended for her; in fact, the headstone already has her name on it. The director says we can get a new headstone with all three names, as long as all three bodies will fit in the plot. Whether or not that can happen depends on the cemetery's particular restrictions on length, width, and depth. *How many coffins can you fit in one plot?* It runs through my head in a singsong.

Mom is, by now, frantic. We have to rush over to the cemetery to see whether she can be squeezed into the same plot as her husband and son. If not, she says, she wants Pat to have the plot and she will be cremated.

"I want him to be with his father," she cries in the car. "I don't want him to be alone. I don't care about me."

Ben drives, silently. Bri rubs Mom's back and looks out the window. Cait says we will do whatever Mom wants. I sit and say nothing; I am still thinking about the Pat diamond.

They know us at the cemetery. I always ask to use the bathroom in their administrative offices because the cemetery is so far away from wherever I usually am. Also, I rarely come here, and so I always get lost when I try to find Dad's grave. One time I ended up wandering up and down the perfect green rows for hours, hysterical because I was such a horrible daughter that I couldn't even find my own father's final resting place. Ben, who was with me, had to ask the gardeners for help. They patched into the office, which sent the magic plot number back via walkie-talkie. It was right there; I don't know how I'd missed it. I could just see the prim ladies in the office rolling their eyes. The same thing had happened to Bri though, which made us both feel better.

The cemetery ladies, while prim, are very nice to us today, and after they tap on their computers and make a few phone calls, suddenly everything falls into place: the three bodies can be accommodated. The appropriate staff members are available for a Tuesday funeral. The current headstone can be removed and replaced. The new one will have three names. We all say how great this is.

Mom looks off into the distance at the vast manicured lawn, checkered with white stones and statues of angels and beyond them the rolling hills. I wonder if she is thinking, *How did it come to this?* She clutches her binder and nods. It is done.

As we pile back into the car, I remember the Pat diamond. I can't have one now that he is being buried. My Bunny is really gone.

13 | STRANGER THAN FICTION

BLASTS OF BOILING heat fill the cement room, assaulting the pores and choking the throat. Even after the furnace shuts down, the heat lingers. A small pile of ashes in the shape of a human body lies behind the oven's thick steel door, marked by the spidery line of a spine and a rounded swell where the skull once was. Full disintegration can take less than an hour, depending on the size of the corpse.

Many of the corpses that come through this mortuary in Laguna Hills, California these days are of young people who have died of drug overdoses, mostly pills and heroin. In Orange County, where the mortuary is based, more than two hundred young people have died from drug overdoses since 2007, and deaths from heroin overdoses have nearly doubled.[55] As we walk through the carpeted and silent halls, one of the mortuary employees tells me the parents of these corpses are usually in a haze. The hardest moment, he says, often comes when they are led into the room containing the "memorial products": hardwood and bronze caskets, biodegradable urns, sterling silver keepsake jewelry, prayer cards, flag cases, crucifixes.

"They can't escape the truth of death once they cross this threshold," he says. "The surreal becomes reality."

The mortuary's director always hopes that in such situations, the death of one young person may change another one's life for the better. But many times he sees the same faces, tear-stained and horror-stricken, returning through the doors of the visitation parlor. Again and again, they regard the lifeless forms of their friends, the invincibility of youth blurring their vision. Some even continue to glorify the drugs that killed their peers: one time, at a young man's funeral, several of his friends approached the open casket and tucked a baggie of heroin in his shirt pocket. A mortuary employee swiftly removed it, hoping the family hadn't seen what had happened.

"It's hard to know what runs through their minds and hearts when they're viewing a friend like this," the director says. "The truth is stranger than fiction."

For some reason, the truth doesn't sink in.

✖

JOEY SAYS TO Alice, "It was all a mistake, Mom. I tried to get back in my body, but I couldn't."

This is what Joey says, at least according to the psychic Alice recently visited at the urging of a friend. Alice is skeptical; she isn't sure whether she believes the psychic as she trims her treasured rosebush in the scalding heat of the noonday sun. The rosebush is a dramatic splash of apricot and coral, a hybrid bloom known as "Just Joey" that she has nestled next to what used to be rows of broccoli plants. Last year, Joey had spent days loosening the soil and setting out the seedlings for those plants, which sprouted hardy green stalks that clenched into the earth with their roots. Alice had hated to see them go when it was finally time to rip them up, after all that work Joey had done—especially now that he was gone. But now she has her Joey rosebush, bright and sweet, just like her Joe Bug.

Though Alice isn't sure about the psychic, she does believe that Joey came to her in the weeks after he passed away, because she felt him with her own body. On that first wrenching night, Alice noticed a presence on Ted's side of the bed as she was trying to fall asleep. It wasn't exactly a figure, but it moved like one, coming closer, settling down on the sheet behind her. She felt love pouring out of the presence, washing her in a feeling of warmth and comfort.

"Joe Bug," she said sleepily, without thinking. "I love you."

In the weeks that followed, Alice would wake up and sense the presence at the foot of the bed or hovering near her left side. It was invisible but real and seeking forgiveness, wanting to make sure she was okay. Alice began talking to it soundlessly, saying the words in her head: *I love you, Joe Bug. It's okay. There's nothing to explain, nothing to forgive. I know you love me. Go on your way.*

Sometimes she wanted to rouse Ted and tell him about the presence, but she didn't. He was having a hard time and didn't like to talk about Joey's death much. Often, during the day, she'd walk into the garage to do the laundry and find her husband standing there staring into space.

"I was just thinking of Joe," he'd say.

In June the presence stopped appearing in Alice's bedroom. She willed it to return, but nothing happened. She sat on Joey's bed, looking down at the floor. A contractor had been called to the house the day after Joey died to replace the carpet, which had become saturated with his blood after the paramedics came to try and save him. They'd rearranged the furniture, so everything looked different, but all of Joey's clothes sat in two big black trash bags stuffed inside the closet. Sometimes when she misses Joey, she hauls the bags out and pilfers through the piles of T-shirts, sweatpants, jeans, swim trunks, and ski jackets, holding each item up to her nose, inhaling deeply.

His scent is beginning to disappear too.

✖

ALICE HAS ALWAYS been a big reader, especially when it comes to addiction. She'd taken the approach of an open dialogue with her kids, hoping that educating them about the fact that addiction is a brain disorder with a genetic component would help them make smart choices when it came to substances. Though this approach hadn't worked with Joey, Alice hasn't stopped reading about addiction after his death, and the more she reads, the angrier she becomes.

It's the way society treats addicts that angers Alice the most, despite the overwhelming scientific evidence explaining why they do the things they do. She learns that the prefrontal cortex, the part of the brain involved in critical decision making, isn't fully developed in adolescence, when drug use often starts.[56] If a teen uses drugs, this further impedes the development of the prefrontal cortex, slowly ingraining the habit in the brain's wiring. It isn't surprising that those like Joey, who start using drugs at a young age and try desperately over the course of their adolescence to stop, fail over and over again—their brains literally become predestined to relapse.[57]

Alice also reads that addiction isn't a moral failing, that drug use isn't about a person's lack of willpower or character, something to be punished rather than treated—a conviction she's had all along. In David Sheff's *Clean*, she reads that addiction alters the flow of neurotransmitters, creating physical, measurable, long-lasting changes in the brain. Someone who is truly addicted is driven by a physical impulse to use drugs, which leads to destructive and immoral behavior if those drugs are out of reach: lying, stealing, committing crimes, hurting those they love, she reads. "It's true that addicts ingested, smoked, or injected illicit drugs into their bodies," Sheff writes. "However, this action didn't cause the addiction. If it did, all people who took drugs would become addicted, but most don't."[58]

Another passage stands out to Alice: "When people are addicted, their consciences are muted but not completely silenced. They feel guilt and shame. Their loved ones can't understand what's happened to them, and neither can the addicts. They're horrified. Retreating from an over-whelming psychological burden, they're even more likely to succumb to craving. Meanwhile, they keep using to prevent withdrawal. And they keep using so they can avoid facing the devastation—the harm to rela-tionships, career, finances, and so on—their drug use has caused."[59]

Alice wonders why, if science so clearly shows that addiction is a disease, society doesn't care for addicts as if they have an illness that deserves to be treated in a hospital. She thinks, How is it any different than people who make poor choices when it comes to diet and exercise and end up with heart disease or diabetes? These types of patients are able to go to the doctor and get treatment for their conditions; why not addicts? The American Medical Association has even officially recog-nized obesity as a disease, spurring more insurers to pay for treatments; why hasn't this been the case for addiction? Alice wonders.

She remembers the day, not long after Joey's death, when she received a call from Sky High Sports, a trampoline house in nearby Costa Mesa. Joey had been there recently with a group of sober friends. Apparently, while flipping into a foam pit, he'd lost his cell phone. The manager had finally retrieved it.

On the phone was a missed call, and a message. Joey, knowing he was in trouble, had been calling around, trying to check himself into a rehab facility, but no one had an available bed. The message was from a rehab where a space had finally opened up, and they'd take Joey.

To Alice, it seems Joey had always been cheating death—even from birth. She'd needed to have an emergency delivery due to a prolapsed umbilical cord, and Joey had almost died. A series of childhood illnesses, including spinal meningitis and a bout with the chicken pox that had landed him in the hospital with a staph infection, gangrene, and celluli-tis, had plagued him the first three years of his life. Then there were all the accidents: the falls off his bike, the snowboarding injuries, the crazy risks he'd take surfing waves at the Wedge, one of the most coveted and dangerous surf spots in the world.

And of course, the drugs. Going through boxes of paperwork, Alice unearthed a notebook containing Joey's story of drug addiction in his own words—hundreds of pages he'd written while locked up in jail after one of his several arrests.

"It's a miracle this kid lived as long as he did," she says.

But the missed phone call makes her feel so sad for him. Joey knew he needed help, and he was actively seeking it—the resources just weren't there for him.

✖

"EVERYONE DESERVES A second chance," reads the handout Alice is holding. "Many people who experience a loss in their lives often say that they are suffering from guilt, when in reality, they are suffering from something much, much more painful: SHAME. We need to work towards removing any sense of shame we feel. We have to come to a point where we no longer feel that we are bad, and realize that the world is a broken place and every once in a while we all contribute to that brokenness."

Alice wishes Ted had agreed to come with her tonight. There are only four men in a room otherwise crowded with women and coffee and sugar cookies, but she wonders if he might have been able to bond with them, to finally be able to talk about his son's death. This is her first time at SOLACE—"Surviving Our Loss With Awareness, Compassion and Empathy"—a weekly support group for people who have lost a loved one to drug overdose or are close to someone currently suffering with addiction, and Alice already feels at ease. The group's founders and coordinators, Elaine, Margie, and Patty, are three moms who each lost a son to an overdose, and they know how intimidating it can be to share the intimate details of addiction and loss. Because of the stigma surrounding drug abuse, many have kept silent about the turmoil in their lives. So the trio works hard to create a supportive environment where new people like Alice can feel comfortable and accepted. Here, there is no judgment, no shame. Most of the attendees are moms who have lost children to pills or heroin or both; some are parents whose children are in jail or rehab or out on the streets; there are a few siblings and significant others with brothers and sisters and partners who are gone or currently addicted. But everyone here has the same weathered look, and they are encouraged to speak freely about their emotions.

"I keep begging God to die," says one woman who lost her son. "He was my whole world. What do I do now?"

Elaine, who is leading the group with Margie tonight, agrees that moving on isn't easy. But, she says, you have to push yourself and make a conscious choice to go forward.

"Our kids wouldn't want us in misery," she says. "They wouldn't want us to kill ourselves. We all deserve to live significant lives, not just survive."

Another mom chimes in that she has been feeling hopeless lately too. But on the way to tonight's meeting, she decided that instead of lying down and dying—which is what she wanted to do—she was going to live to be old and gray.

"Every year from now on, I'm going to live for my son, because he can't," she says.

"Sometimes I wonder if they died because their suffering would have been too great if they had lived," a third mom adds. "They were all so sensitive, too sensitive to the hurt in the world. Maybe we are somehow better able to handle the struggle, and we just don't know it."

One of the few men, a father, shares that he was late to the meeting because he found his son overdosing on the kitchen floor, wracked by seizures.

"When he came to, I asked him, 'Is this it? Is this how you're going to die? What do I need to do to help you?'" the man says.

But the young man had refused to say which drugs he'd been using, and the father came to the meeting feeling helpless. He knew his son had overdosed on benzodiazepines in the past, but lately he'd been hanging out along the Bristol Street corridor, a known place to pick up heroin. The other parents in the room exchange furtive glances and tell him to hope for the best but expect the worst. They know from experience that sugarcoating the situation will hurt, not help.

When it is Alice's turn, she says she feels blessed to have had her son in her life and that she believes he was supposed to die when he did.

"I learned a lot through my Joey dying," she says. "I learned what a wonderful person he was. I just keep wondering, Why do we treat these kids as dirty junkies?"

She bangs her fist on the table for emphasis and looks earnestly at the other parents.

"Why don't we treat them as if they have a brain disease?" she asks. "Why doesn't health care pay for them to get the help they need, get them into detox, get them into rehab, just like any other sick person?"

The room is silent.

14 | WAX

THEY LINGER UNDER the yawning mouth of the church's wooden doors, eyeing the open casket. Pat is visible, even from where they stand, unsure of what to do. They are so young, his friends, and yet they know more about the dark parts of my brother than I do. I see their hands shake as they begin to walk toward us. I wonder if they are high.

We stand next to the casket, my family and I, with Pat lying inside. His stillness is unreal and eerie. It makes me feel like I am being watched. I want to rewind time—not just to make Pat alive again but to understand how he died. I want to unearth his secrets.

I want to see his eyes, his pupils as they dilate under eyebrows that had become bushier as he became a man. They glaze over slowly, like water over glass. His skin, brown from the sun, as the blood stops flowing and it turns gray. His lips, his feet, his hands as they turn purple. His mouth as it falls open and goes slack with spit and foam. His bladder as it releases and his bowels as he shits in his pants. His lungs as they collapse, his heart as it goes still. His brain as it halts its frenzied rush: slower, slower, slower, stop. His face smashed up against the door where he has fallen in a drugged haze.

Moonlight blankets the room where he lies, silent and unmoving. When the sun rises, there is pounding on the door, there are vibrations against his head that he cannot feel. There are screams he cannot hear, lights he cannot see, a stretcher with black plastic wrap that conceals the brightness. Then there are cold steel tables, saws, tubes that pump him full of chemicals. Stitches that bind him back together. I want to see it all.

Now, as I stare down at him, his face looks like it is melting. But when my warm lips meet his forehead, he feels like ice, caked in layers of pancake makeup that try to conceal the bruises from his fall against the door. He feels like wax, like something that should be bitten into. His fingernails have powder underneath them. His expression is ghoulish and masklike. Only his hair is still soft. I stroke it and whisper in his ear, "You will always be my Bunny." I wonder if he would want forgiveness, so I add, "I'm not angry."

Whispered prayers fall like echoing voices heard from the other side of a long tunnel. Hands pinch rosary beads. Hymns rise to the ceiling of the church and swim in the glitter of the small round lights, then slip away easily into the sky. I sit in my slim skirt and clawing shoes, my eyes fixed on the polished mahogany draped in a shower of roses before me. I want my brother to wake up again.

But he is leaving, spiraling downward through the floor and earth, and as he leaves a rupture splits my heart.

After the funeral, there is a gathering at Tom and Betty's house. People dressed in black fill the rooms and spill out into the garden. There is Pat's childhood friend with Down syndrome. There is his third-grade teacher. His soccer coach. Our next-door neighbors who moved away. There are so many people that I become dizzy with the condolences and hugs, the awkward conversations about what happened, telling the story in a way appropriate for fleeting conversation. Everyone who is here loved Pat, and loves our family, and unlike strangers, they're asking because they truly care. But for some reason the love in the room makes it harder for me to come up with a way to explain Pat's death—especially since I don't fully understand it myself. "Pat got really fucked up" is what I want to say, but mostly I end up just shaking my head and shrugging.

I leave the house and go for a walk. Tom and Betty live in the hills, and the dusk is just beginning to unravel over the rooftops below. I replay my last words to Pat before they closed the coffin forever, and I realize that I lied to him.

I *am* angry at Pat. I envy him because he gets to be numb. I want that numbness too, because then I would be able to go bravely back into the hurricane of sniffles and Saran-wrapped trays. I want to stop the tears. I want to just exist, floating on some hazy plane, complete neutrality. I want to lessen this new realization that I am angry, bit by bit, as if handfuls of sand are being thrown onto a smoldering campfire, one after the other, finally concealing a festering rage.

On the way back to the house, I pass by a group of Pat's friends sitting on the curb, smoking. I nod at them without speaking. I am angry at them too, I realize, for not helping Pat, for partying with him, for failing to let his family know how bad everything had become.

They look back at me, silent, keeping their distance.

✖

THE NEXT DAYS and weeks unfold haphazardly: minutes and hours implode inward and somehow also linger endlessly. My sister and I stay with Mom, fearful of leaving her alone in the immense, unfilled house.

I always find myself awake in those dark predawn hours, floating—placid and still—as if I am a small piece of bark that has been set adrift in a stream. I feel nothing—no headache, no fear, not even a sense of my physical body. There cannot possibly be a God.

This realization only makes things worse. I stare at the ceiling, willing myself not to look at the closet door, where four names were etched, long ago, into the white paint with a paper clip: Erin. Caitlin. Brian. Pat. The impossibility of God runs through my head like a record negligently put on repeat. Pat didn't die because God took him: he died because he stuck a needle in his arm. Dad didn't die because God no longer wanted him to suffer: he died because he was sick. Other people die because they're old, or they get hit by a bus, or they put a gun to their head, or someone murders them. There is nothing further to elaborate, no analysis or contemplation. It's simple, logical, factual. Horrible but true.

There are those who mitigate their grief with the promise of eternal comfort. Well-meaning visitors, dear friends, cherished neighbors. They hug Mom on the couch as she cries and say that it's tragic, but Pat is no longer suffering. What they mean is that his battle with addiction is over, leaving him at peace; that he met his end painlessly, riding a wave of morphine. He simply fell asleep and didn't wake up. These are the things people say because they want to believe them.

I believe that Pat isn't anywhere.

He is gone. He was a precious and fucked-up mass of bones and skin and personality and soul—a mass of matter that was felled by a chemical. He was not a part of some higher being's master plan; he was a product of science, and his death makes absolute sense. We say it is senseless, but we mean that it is nonsensical on a larger scale: nonsensical, without sense, that he picked up a needle, filled it with heroin, and injected it into his veins, stopping his respiratory system. But the mere fact of his death is totally logical.

✖

AFTER ABOUT A month, Mom wants to be alone again. We are uncomfortable with the thought of her rattling around in the big house by herself, but she insists. I am sick with worry about her, but I also know—and I know that she knows—that at some point we have to cross that chasm between us and the world that exists outside our grief, so I reluctantly return to San Francisco.

I climb the musty carpeted stairs of our old Victorian in the city, thinking back to that morning one month ago, to the adrenaline and the ache that wouldn't come out. I dread running into my neighbors, kind as they are, who don't know what to say to me. I fear the pile of unopened mail, with its Hallmark envelopes from friends, relatives, colleagues, people from childhood long forgotten. I haven't been home since Pat died.

Later that night, racked by insomnia, I stand at the window, looking out onto the empty city street roiled by fog. The pale thin skin of my arm stares up at me in a challenging manner. It's very odd how the ordinary tasks of life can bring up this image of Pat's death: my little brother, with a needle in his arm. Holding a pen, sweeping the floor, stacking the dishes, sitting on the toilet, folding the socks. Those in our family have always been thin. I wonder, as I look down at the translucent skin shielding my blood from the lamplight, if this makes us weaker.

Weaker or stronger?

Weaker, because the vein is that much more exposed.

Stronger, because pain brought to the surface and dealt with results in resiliency.

Weaker, because if my brother felt anything like I do, no wonder he pumped numbness into his veins.

Stronger, because I choose to live and not to kill myself.

How easy it would be, how seamless. How lovely to be free of all restraint, disposed of all sadness, relieved of all guilt. I envy Pat in these moments when the veins beckon. I've never done hard-core drugs and never intend to. But my veins pop and clamor. They want to know why I don't ease this horrible realization of life and death.

There is one vein in particular that stares up at me, the one in the middle of my right arm. It asks me why I don't know the answers to my questions. It pulses at me: *How did you let this happen?*

My hands tap, my breath falls, my veins bulge in the dusk of the early spring night. None of it seems real, as none of the past seems alive. I am breaking with a reality that makes no sense. No matter what it takes, no matter how much it hurts, I want to understand.

To leave my brother behind, to say goodbye to him there in the dirt, that would liberate me. But I can't. He holds me back, pulls me down, tugs me aside.

Look at me, he says. *I am here. I need you to hear me.*

I listen.

15 | SIGNS

"I WASN'T ALWAYS like this."

Elaine reads her son Josh's words, written in the days when he was hopelessly hooked on pills but before he'd descended into heroin. Before her knock on the unlocked bathroom door was met with a tomb-like silence and she called for her husband, having promised him she wouldn't open it again after Josh's near-fatal overdose four days prior. Before Josh was found slumped over the toilet seat, track marks slicing the flesh of his wrists. Before the paramedics had dragged him out by his feet and worked on him for forty-five minutes while a policeman held Elaine as she cried. Before the ambulance transported Josh to the hospital, where the nurse was the same one who'd been on duty during his first overdose, the one who said when he was pronounced dead that he was the nicest young man she had ever met.

Time had stopped then, as it stops now, six years later, when Josh's words, in death, tell her the truth he couldn't bear to admit to in life.

"I wasn't always like this," Josh had written.

Well, that is not exactly true. I think that for most of my life I have had this problem trapped inside of me. Usually I wake up gasping for breath as if my dreams are deep water that I always just barely escape. I pull the sheets off me and get up. The air is cold and it burns my skin. I know what I need; I am walking toward the bathroom. With every step, pain shoots through my body. I am almost there.

I close the bathroom door and turn the fan and bath water on. I take the last difficult step and stand on the toilet to get what I need.

The top of the cupboard is covered with prescription bottles. I open the cupboard. Another 30 or 40 bottles lie here, stacked precariously. I am not sure why I do not just throw them out. After all, these bottles are supposed to be a secret, my secret, and nobody is supposed to know about them.

I probably sound like someone who you would keep your kids away from, and avoid looking at on the street. But I'm not. I look just like everybody. Becoming a junkie can happen to pretty much any human being, given the right circumstances. If anyone asked my parents, my girl, or my friends, they would laugh if you said that I am a junkie. That is what makes me feel even worse. This secret, my secret.

I think back to when I discovered how I felt about these pills. It was a beautiful, warm night, it had rained earlier and smelled wonderful. I was driving around in my small convertible, letting the wind whip around me. I took just two of these pills right before I left, and I was overpowered by positive emotion. I felt better than I ever had; nothing could have harmed me that night. The stupidest part of this whole thing is that on this night, I had everything in the world I could ask for. I had the girl I loved, the car I wanted, a great job, a family.

The pills are starting to take effect, and I can feel myself starting to go back to normal. Not high, just normal. These pills are nothing compared to what I want and expect them to be. I can take 20 at a time, and they still will not accommodate me. According to many, I should be dead of liver failure by now.

Come to think of it, I really wouldn't mind being dead. It would be better than this half-existence that I am currently living.

By now, Elaine knows these words practically by heart. But knowing them doesn't make them sting less. Though she tries not to fight the pain anymore, the way she did in the beginning, she still finds it hard to accept Josh's death, that his life was cut short at age twenty-seven, when most people's lives are just beginning. He'd always had a strange fascination with the so-called Twenty-Seven Club, a group of famous musicians—Jimi Hendrix, Janis Joplin, Jim Morrison, Kurt Cobain—who had all died at age twenty-seven of drugs and alcohol. Josh's death at the same age now seems like a cruelly fulfilled prophecy to her. She wishes he had not become a member of that club.

While she knows it's impossible, she would do anything to have Josh back: her kind, sensitive son, whose lifelong terror of vomiting made his heroin abuse all the more incomprehensible. Besides vomiting, Josh's worst fear growing up was that something bad would happen to his mother, and even during the darkest moments of his downward spiral, Elaine knew how much he loved her.

She feels the same way about her son as his description of his addiction to drugs: "Sure, it might take me a whole day to obtain some, but wouldn't you put in just a meager eight hours to spend the night with your true love?"

Josh had wanted to become an adolescent psychiatrist and work with addicted teens, and over time Elaine has learned to view his death as a bittersweet gift from him: his passing means that she must carry on his torch, helping those whose lives have been shattered by addiction and loss. Although she knows that the statistics surrounding recovery and long-term success are grim, she believes most addicts—especially the young kids—want to stop using, and she wants to help them. There are many opportunities for intervention: in 2010, for every painkiller overdose death among eighteen- to twenty-five-year-olds, there were seventeen treatment admissions and sixty-six emergency room visits.[80] She wants to show these kids love and acceptance, make them believe they are beautiful people inside, make them want to want life instead of death.

She wants for them what Josh could never have.

Many of the parents she has met through her addiction resources organization, Project JOSH, and those in SOLACE, the support group she runs in Orange County, like to talk about signs. Signs from their children who have gone away; signs from God. They hunger for these signs as if starving; they rely upon them as proof that their sons and daughters still exist somewhere, watching over them. To them, these signs are not coincidences but evidence. Elaine comes from a clinical background, but she is okay with this, because she too believes in signs.

Just the other day, she received an email out of the blue from one of the girls Josh had dated when he was in his early twenties. The girl—now a married woman with children—had lost touch with Josh years before and was excited when Facebook offered Josh's brother Zach as a person she might know. She began to explore, thrilled at the thought of reconnecting with her old friend Josh, the sweet boy who took her miniature golfing on their first date, called her every morning at 1:00 AM like clockwork, and always drove with one hand so that he could hold her hand with the other.

"I can't really describe the feeling in my chest when I saw that Josh had died," she told Elaine. "It was like a kick and then a thousand bricks laying on me. How could the boy I knew die that way? I'm sad he never found his peace in this world. I'm sad he never got to do all the things he wanted. Long ago, he wanted to help children. He often talked of going back to school. I'm sad that he never got past his demons."

Elaine is taking it as a sign that she must continue to fight Josh's demons, the ones that live on in so many others.

16 | DIGGING FOR BONES

PAT'S AUTOPSY ARRIVES in a flat and brown envelope. Ordinary. I've both wished for and dreaded this moment: the unveiling. The truth. I hold it in my hands, turning it over, acid searing my stomach.

My brother's autopsy states that

> the body of Daly, Patrick Daniel, a 20-year-old male, was discovered at approximately 1013 hours on 02/04/09 on a carpeted bedroom floor. He was last known alive at approximately 0330 hours. His left arm was flexed upward, with his closed hand resting near his face; his right hand came to rest underneath his right side torso. His lower body partially rested upon stacked blankets, which appeared to be his sleeping area. An uncapped syringe was found underneath his chest, over which he was slumped, with the cap found behind his left leg. The tip of his tongue slightly protruded, clenched between his teeth. Rigor mortis was extreme to the jaw region, appearing severe throughout the rest of the body. He was dressed in green underwear and black shorts, and was wearing a rubber band and a bracelet on each wrist.

Those bracelets: the shredded scraps of black shoelaces he'd salvaged from an old pair of Converse sneakers that he'd worn in elementary school, doodling on the white rubber in class.

The body weighs 150 pounds and measures 66 inches. EKG pads are present in the posterior shoulder blade and buttock areas. The head is normocephalic and covered by blond hair. A recent puncture mark is present in the right antecubital fossa. Tattoos are present and identified as "Deo Fidelis" in the right medial arm and "et Regi" in the left medial arm.

"Deo Fidelis et Regi." The marks that had caused the Christmas Eve blowout two years ago, when everything was just beginning to fall apart. The marks that branded him a man, and supposedly indicated his love for his family, when he was still a little boy hurting us over and over again.

The subcutaneous fat of the abdominal wall measures 0.5 inches. The stomach contains 100cc of brown/tan coarse soft fluid. The brain weighs 1,680 grams. The tongue shows a metal bar approximately 0.3 inches from the tip. Decedent died of heroin/ morphine intoxication. Mode: accident.

Heroin. Not pills. He died of a heroin overdose. I had known this, but seeing it spelled out is different. Pat really did it. He fucking shot heroin and died like a junkie.

I smooth the crease of the folded paper back around the staple and slide the packet back into its manila envelope, collapsing the arms of the metal brads to lie flat. I shove the autopsy into the crevices of my closet, behind a bin of winter scarves and old bathing suits. I leave the house and run, the golden crescents of the afternoon sunlight swallowing me like a slick, warm dream.

My feet slam against gravel, and with every step Pat invades me. He is lying in the upper bunk, surrounded by stuffed animals, as I sing him "All the Pretty Little Horses" to make him giggle. (I have a terrible singing voice.) He is pouring sugar on his Frosted Flakes and chewing with his mouth wide open. (He knows it annoys me.) He is answering my phone calls with a loud "HI ERN!" He is folding a piece of origami paper into ten thousand incarnations and writing little notes to me on the hidden flaps: "You are a goddess to me. I love you soooooooooo-times-infinity much!!! I will be your Bunny forever, even when I am 90 and you are 100. Anyone can tell that you are the most beautiful girl in the world."

It cannot be. The light of the dying sun taunts me, filling me with a pervasive sickness, the understanding that I am alive and he is dead. I knew, rationally, that Pat was addicted to drugs. I understood, for months and perhaps even years, that he was teetering on the edge of a great precipice that one day would surely consume him. But in my heart, I hadn't accepted this reality. I paid the county of Los Angeles $88 to learn the truth about losing my brother, as if seeing the words typed out in an official report would clarify the disconnect: Where is Pat? Why isn't he answering his phone? Now that the truth is so neatly laid out before me, it is shockingly real. It is undeniable and unfathomable at the same time.

The balloons of heroin found under his body, one full, the other empty; the burnt spoon in a balled sock; the fact that his right lung weighed 830 grams while his left lung weighed 680 grams; the presence of ventral lividity. All fade backward and congeal into a singular fixation: He had a tongue ring?

✖

A FEW DAYS after reading Pat's autopsy report, I fall victim to a sickness. Not something treatable, like a cold or the flu or even depression, but a nagging ache somewhere deep inside. Most often this sickness comes on quickly and unannounced. It is the sickness of losing Pat, and of knowing how he met his end.

It comes while walking the dog under the too-blue morning sky.

It comes while driving, thinking of Pat in the backseat on our way to the beach, where he wandered ahead of me as I stared at his falling-apart jeans, wondering about all the things I didn't know about him but knowing that he was high, hating him for it, and hating myself for saying nothing to him.

It comes while washing the dishes, for no reason at all. The words of his autopsy swim in the suds like tiny worms: He is no longer Pat. He is "the decedent."

Losing him feels like being homesick. You are somewhere you shouldn't be, and all you crave is the familiar. There's nothing out-wardly wrong; perhaps you're even happy. But in your gut, there is a tiny nag. A small space that feels empty and yet alive because it aches. A dull realization that there is an unfilled hole left by something that once was there.

When I think of the autopsy, still lodged deep in my closet, I am assaulted by images of my brother. At night the fog spreads its fingers across the windows like a veil, making me wish I could dive into it head-first, making me wish for blindness. Pat lies on the bedroom floor, indigo lines fanning outward from the puncture mark in his arm. The inky poison permeates his body again and again, creeping through his veins like a slow-moving spider, and I am helpless to stop it from reaching his heart. The autopsy has brought these images to me, and now I cannot forget them.

Worse, I cannot change them, because they are the truth.

Why did I deny this truth when it was happening right before my eyes? Why does the image of my brother shooting heroin sicken me with shock? I should be well accustomed to this fact; after all, I'd asked him point-blank that last Christmas about which drugs he'd done, and whether he'd shot them up. His answer to me had been both nonspecific and all-inclusive: "I've done pretty much everything."

So why does the truth, now, pack such a punch to my gut?

Pat died with a needle in his arm.

✖

A FRIEND OF the family—a longtime alcoholic—dies. His struggle had been long, but his downward spiral took a turn for the worse when his wife died of cancer, leaving him and their two kids behind. At his funeral, our family gathers in a pew several rows back from where his children sit. Though they're in their twenties, I still think of them as kids, all of us sucking on Charleston Chews while playing pinball during the hot summers at our cabin. I stare at the back of their necks, remembering what it feels like to be the ones everyone feels sorry for, the way I feel sorry for them now.

I am surprised when one of the eulogizers tackles the elephant in the room head-on. "When she died, he found life nearly impossible," he says. "We all wish we could have done more. Pray for him, pray for his kids, and pray for yourselves, because you are all like him. We are all human."

It isn't until later that night that I am able to cry. The tears come while I chop onions, which sear my eyes and force the sadness out. I hate addiction.

There is no reason why some fall and not others, and it is terrifying.

And perhaps even more terrifying: when they fall, we go on. There is the pain of their addiction, the terribleness of their downward descent, the horror of their deaths. And then there is the moving forward.

The marching on.

17 | OVERTAKEN

THE PANEL MEMBERS sit on an elevated podium above Jodi, a semicircle of strangers to whom she is about to bare her soul. Jodi has been racked with waves of nerves since she arrived in the California State Capitol early this morning. She must remember to stay brave, to walk the fine line between passion and reason. If she thinks in real terms of her son Jarrod, she'll become overwhelmed by emotion. Better to separate herself from the words on the notepad before her, the story of her son's death.

Jodi searches the faces of state legislators considering claims that the California Medical Board failed to hold some physicians accountable for overprescribing powerful narcotics, contributing to California's prescription drug addiction epidemic. Some of them shuffle papers; others stare at their watches or into the crowd behind her. None of them looks directly at Jodi. Above their heads is a panoramic mural depicting early western settlers, a pioneer couple regarding the rolling hills flush with redwoods and the immense stretch of sky, melting into the Pacific Ocean in a seamless haze of blue.

Blue like her son's eyes.

A line from a movie emerges from the recesses of her memory: *I hope the Pacific is as blue as it has been in my dreams.*

These days, her dreams are mostly nightmares. If the ocean does appear, it isn't a blue one but a mass of murk and filth, dark slimy things swimming in its core. Jarrod is there too. He is drowning, and she can't save him. The dream makes no sense; Jarrod loved the water. Her first-born had kicked his way out of the amniotic sac five and a half weeks before his due date with feet that were flat like flippers—one of them crooked—and a shock of jet black hair. A decade later, when his little brother, Blake, was six, Jarrod taught him how to dive into the sea off the rocky cliffs overlooking the Kauai bay where the family vacationed every year. In the sun, his hair became so blond that it was almost white, and his skin turned dark and slick, the droplets rolling from his arms and legs as if magnetically repelled. Jodi and her husband, Bill, used to joke that Jarrod had been reincarnated from a seal.

Jodi had asked the pediatrician if Jarrod's crooked foot would straighten out.

"What do you want, a perfect child?" he had responded jokingly, to which she had thought, *Well, yes.*

Jarrod's blue eyes confront the panel now from his high school graduation picture, which Jodi has placed on the table before her. The men and women facing her glance at it quickly, then look away, and something deep inside her begins to burn. Although the paper in her hands quivers slightly, she forces her voice to hold steady and calm. She will not relent.

"This is my son, Jarrod," she says to the room, the words bouncing from the domed ceilings above and disappearing into the painted ocean beyond.

✖

LATELY, JODI SPENDS a lot of time in her garden. She has worked as a florist for many years, and it feels comforting to be surrounded by flowers in their various stages of life: hopeful buds, proud blooms, withering petals. And bees—always the bees. They bring her back to Jarrod.

Jodi was in the garden on the day Jarrod died. It was January 2010, and there was a light dusting of frost on the grass that morning, the only sign that winter was under way in Mission Viejo, a suburban community in southern California's Saddleback Valley. Jarrod's nineteen-year-old friend had just died after a seven-year battle with cancer, and Jodi was handling the floral arrangements for the service. Bouquets of lilies, a memoriam wreath, sprays of roses. As she worked, Jodi thought about Jarrod. Long before his friend passed away, Jarrod hadn't been acting like himself, and Jodi and Bill were worried.

Though he'd always suffered from anxiety and low self-esteem, Jarrod was also friendly, thoughtful, and compassionate. His teachers and neighbors often commented on how smart and considerate he was, and he always had plenty of friends, many of them girls who trusted him enough to cry on his shoulder about their immature boyfriends. He also loved to make people laugh. Just two weeks prior, on a ski vacation to Big Bear, they had all been hysterical over his imitation of Jeff Daniels in the movie *Dumb and Dumber* getting his tongue stuck to an icy ski lift chair.

But Jarrod had started coming home acting strangely: extra quiet, extra happy, and sometimes extra irritable. Jodi discovered that he was smoking pot to ease his anxiety and to fit in with his friends. He got pulled over for driving under the influence and was charged with a DUI a few weeks before his high school graduation.

"I do not plan on doing anything that will put me, my family, or loved ones in harm's way," he had written in an assignment for his traffic school class. "I know that I have to think before I do something. I want to be a good role model for my younger brother. I don't want him to make the same mistakes I made."

Then, during an argument with Jodi, Jarrod had threatened to jump out of the moving car. Jodi and Bill decided to take him to see a doctor who was known at the time as one of the best in Orange County. Jodi went into every visit with Jarrod and closely monitored his prescriptions of the antianxiety drug Klonopin and Cymbalta, an antidepressant. As a mom whose home medicine cabinet contained nothing more potent than cough syrup, she thought she was on top of the situation.

What Jodi and Bill didn't know was that Jarrod had been doing more than just weed. A couple of his close friends had been visiting a doctor in nearby Rowland Heights who accepted cash payments in exchange for prescriptions for various pills: Vicodin, Xanax, OxyContin, and even Opana, a painkiller more potent than morphine. Jarrod's friends shared the pills among themselves to get high and had grown to depend on them. A couple of times, when the pills ran out, they'd even tried shooting heroin.

Jarrod's parents also didn't know that three days before, he'd told his doctor that he was having trouble sleeping because he was so devastated over his friend's death. The doctor handed him a couple of sample boxes of Seroquel, an antipsychotic medication, along with a script that said to take three to four pills at bedtime. Jodi, who had informed the doctor of her concerns that Jarrod was exhibiting addictive behavior, was usually present during her son's appointments. But this time, for reasons she didn't yet understand, Jarrod had asked his mom to stay in the waiting room.

Around eleven that night, Jodi and Bill said goodnight to Jarrod, who was sitting on the couch in the living room watching a movie with some of his friends. A few hours later, they woke up to find the hall light still on. They went downstairs to find Jarrod sitting where they had last seen him, unconscious and barely breathing. While Jodi called 911, Bill gave Jarrod mouth-to-mouth resuscitation and pumped his chest.

It was too late. Jarrod died at 3:47 AM, in the same hospital where he had been born nineteen years earlier. The official cause of death: Opana, which Jarrod had snorted, in combination with the Klonopin and Seroquel he had been prescribed.

The morning after Jarrod's death, Blake made a poster board for people to sign and sat on the corner at the end of their street, holding a vigil. A bee came and landed on Blake's poster, and all day long it refused to leave. Blake said the bee was Jarrod, and Jodi agreed.

Today Jodi sits in the garden with a stack of Hallmark cards, watching for bees. The cards tell the story of her family's life together, the milestones that marked their journey, the joys they shared over the years.

"Dear Jarrod," reads one card. "There are so many reasons you make us proud. We love you more than all the rain drops in the world (and it's raining really hard right now!) Love, Mom and Dad."

"Dear Dad," reads another. "Happy Father's Day! I love and appreciate everything you do for me. I cannot wait until I have a kid, so I can try to be just like you. I love you more than all the baseballs in the world! Xoxo, Jarrod."

"Dear Jarrod, Happy birthday! You're the best brother in the world except when you tease me. Thank you for sticking up for me. You are always there for me and I love that. I love you so much. Love, Blake."

The light turns mellow and golden as the sun begins its descent behind the hills, and the buzzing of the bees between the flowers seems to slow. Jodi touches the mole on her neck, just above her left collarbone. Jarrod had an identical mole in the exact same spot. The summer is fast approaching, and in August Jarrod would have turned twenty-three. She wonders whether his life would have continued on as an unbroken nightmare; whether he would have gone down on some other terrible night or whether he would have conquered his demons. She isn't sure, but she does know one thing: she would give anything in the world to be able to kiss him goodnight.

She swats at the tears sliding down her cheeks and presses her fingertips below her eyes, as if to glue them down, erasing the evidence of her sorrow. Time marches on: Blake's senior prom is this weekend, and he'll be home from school in a few minutes to pick up a check to buy his date's corsage. The young girl will be wearing pink, soft and warm like the rose petals emitting a scent so sweet that Jodi thinks her heart might break in two.

✖

ONCE AGAIN, JODI steels herself to face the crowd. At least this morning the audience is a bit less intimidating than at the Capitol a few weeks ago, though not by much: five hundred high school seniors, the graduating class of 2013 at Fountain Valley High School, Jodi's alma mater. It's nearing June, and the mood in the gym is restless and buoyant. But an eerie hush falls over the kids, jam-packed into the rising rows of bleachers, as Jodi takes the stage. Behind her, a screen displays a still shot of the opening scene of her documentary, *Overtaken,* a short film in which several young adults tell their stories of pill and heroin addiction.

"This is my son, Jarrod," she begins.

The crowd watches, unmoving, as the film plays. Afterward, Jodi leads a woman in a flowing turquoise shirt and silver earrings to the stage. The woman says that her son started taking Vicodin and other pills to get high as a freshman. Soon after, her jewelry began disappearing, as well as all the spoons in the kitchen, and she began finding foils with burn marks hidden around the house. Her six-foot-two, two-hundred-pound boy had progressed to heroin, and he became emaciated and drawn. He tried to get clean and even enlisted in the navy after he graduated, but a few days after Christmas 2011, she and her husband received a phone call that her son was on life support after an overdose. He'd relapsed again, and his body was unable to tolerate the same amount of heroin after a period of sobriety. They waited to disconnect him from the machines until the doctors could find recipients for his usable organs, the woman says, her voice choking.

The kids look on silently as Jodi introduces a hesitant young man in a green baseball cap who says he has been clean from heroin and pills for two and a half months. The crowd claps.

"The last day I used was going to be my last day living," he says. "I took twenty-five Xanax bars and a gram of heroin. I was trying to die. It didn't work, I guess."

Finally Jodi introduces Connor, a former painkiller and heroin addict who is now twenty-three and clean. He strikes a conversational tone with the audience, telling them he had always felt different from the other kids in school.

"I was the weird guy in bio class, puking into my sleeve after drinking and smoking too many doobies," he says. "It was fun, but the fun didn't last that long."

OxyContin became his drug of choice, he adds, and asks whether anyone knows what that is. A short boy with a smattering of acne raises his hand and shouts, "Is it the pill form of heroin?" Connor slaps his hands together in approval.

"Yes, my man, thank you!" he says. "Because of OxyContin, I started doing heroin, and that led me to actually run over my mom in my car because she was interrupting my fix, and my most important thing in that moment was, 'Damn it, I'm not going to spill my spoon.'"

Connor opens it up to questions and is immediately bombarded. The kids want to know how long it took him to go from pills to heroin (a few months, Connor says); what to say to a friend who says he's taking Xanax as a prescription but seems to be addicted (Connor's advice: say you're scared for him); whether going to rehab shows on your record (it doesn't, according to Connor).

The bell rings, signaling the end of the assembly. The kids cheer and pour out of the auditorium in a raucous stampede, but a few linger behind and approach Connor. One of them asks for a copy of *Overtaken* to show to her addicted stepsister; another wants to talk about a friend who died of a heroin overdose. Jodi looks on as the room filters and empties, an abandoned backpack under the front bleacher finally the only remains.

On the drive home, she stops at Ruby's Shake Shack, a burger joint perched on the cliffs overlooking the Pacific Ocean. She sits on an outdoor bench facing the waves, throwing french fries to the portly squirrels that live under the wooden deck of the café. They eat the treats gingerly, as if picking at fine caviar, and Jodi laughs. She looks into the expanse of shimmering blue spread out before her.

Tomorrow she will drive back up the coast again, this time to check in on her friend Ellie's son Dale, who is on his sixteenth day free of opiates in a sober living home in Norco, about an hour's drive from Mission Viejo. She will tell him all about Jarrod, hoping his young mind will be able to absorb the finality of loss, the hole in the world that is left when someone whose life was only just beginning is taken away forever.

18 | WHERE ARE YOU?

Date: Tue, 27 Jan 2009 07:10:37 -0800
From: bunny <bobbyandjorge1@yahoo.com>
To: emdaly@hotmail.com
Subject: Re: Where are you?

heyyyy ern!
im soooooooooooo sorry i was going to call you and tell you that yes i am in
burbank but wasn't able to because j and her mom and kathy all came over for
dinner on saturday and then i left on sunday . . . and then i was thinking on the
car ride down here that i'd call you when i got my cell phone activated as soon
as i got down here but the cell phone didn't work haha . . . but anyways i am
sooooo sorry i forgot to call you . . . i'm going to call you tonite so we'll talk
soon . . . but i have to go to kaiser down here and have my intake appt to start
up a program down here . . . but i love you sooooo much ern and thanks for all
your support . . . luvs ya

love pat

IT IS PAT'S last written communication to me. He did call me that night,
which was the last time we spoke—was he high?

The answer doesn't matter, although I know the answer is yes.
Coming across this email only makes me want to sleuth more. If I can't
ask Pat for the truth, I certainly have the right to find out for myself. And
what rights does a dead person have anyway— especially one like Pat,
who chose death?

I justify my snooping with these ideas and hack into his Facebook and MySpace pages, and his email account, which I read in its entirety. The task takes days, but finally I unearth the email I have been looking for: the one I'd seen Pat writing in the Internet café in Costa Rica as I peeked over his shoulder.

I remember the snippets I'd seen, but the whole story slaps me in the face:

> wow im so proud of you. your a stronger person than i am. even if you fuck up you know i wont judge you. and you know that im just as deep if not deeper than you. you have to tell me how rehab was cuz if i cant clean up or get a little better when i get back ill be right there with you. wut are you going for? jus everything? i hope its not oxy cuz that shit sucks ass to come off of. you saw me. but even if it is, i know you can do it. your the strongest girl and person i know so dont worry. i always got your back. i gotta go, my sister is here with me. im always thinking about you. i love you so god damn much i cant even describe it. good luck, be strong. youll get thru it . . . LUVVVSSSSS YAAAA . . .
>
> love love love
>
> Pat

I shouldn't have seen the snippets then, just as I shouldn't be seeing the whole story now. But I can't un-see my brother's words. Nor can I deny the fact that I had done nothing, when at least part of the story had been laid out right before my eyes. Why had I stopped dead in my tracks when I discovered something I did not want to know—something that clearly warranted action, something so obviously suspicious that it demanded the very opposite of inaction? So I hadn't known about the Oxy, but even if I had, wasn't it enough of a red flag to read the words *rehab* and *being in deep* and *getting clean*?

I recall myself, standing in the tiny café, the ceiling fans casting tornadoes of air downward to disturb the flies, the smell of coffee and burning trash. I remember looking down at my brother and thinking, *What do I do?* And I did nothing. I remember walking with him down the sidewalk and thinking, *What do I say?* And I said nothing. I think of the look in his eyes when Mom asked him where all the money had gone, the incessant, nervous tapping of his foot on the floor, his absence when we all showed up at the beach. I did not ask more questions, I did not search his backpack when he was in the shower, I did not confront him about the things I shouldn't have seen but did.

As much as I don't understand my brother, I also don't understand myself. A slow, small burn starts festering inside of me, a mixture of self-hatred and guilt. How could I have this information spelled out so clearly in front of me and done nothing about it? I'm like those despicable human beings in what psychologists describe as the bystander effect, one of a crowd of people standing by, idle, while a victim desperately cries out for help. I had always thought that if I were part of such a crowd, I'd be the one to step forward—I'd have to. Otherwise I would essentially be just as evil as the perpetrator of the crime.

I had not stepped forward.

✖

EIGHT BOXES CONTAINING the remnants of Pat's life sit in a pile in Mom's garage. His girlfriend's mother had shipped them up to us after he died, and they have sat there alone in the dark, unopened. Mom finally asks me if I'll go through them because she can't bring herself to do it. I agree, secretly pleased to have an excuse to continue my probe into my brother's downfall, which has begun to feel like hurting myself in a way that feels good. The more I learn, the more it hurts, and the more I investigate. It is desperate and obsessive, and sometimes I feel him looking down on me, screaming at me to stop.

His screams make me want to do it more.

One morning when I know Mom is at work, I drive to the house and back my car into the driveway. I take a deep breath before descending into the garage, where I confront the pile of boxes. I have no idea what they contain.

The tight air is dusty and mildewed as I begin to slash through the packing tape, and I wonder how it's possible for decay to set in after just two months.

First are just the ordinary things: an unopened pack of disposable razors, a Mighty Mouse CD case with no CD in it, an unopened tub of Stridex pads, a ziplock baggie with a bunch of skateboard bearings, a Zippo lighter. Piles and piles of dirty laundry, mostly flannel boxers and socks. I find two of his most worn T-shirts—one that bears the name of his favorite band, Kalifornia Redemption, and another that simply says "STUD"—and set them aside, along with his Chuck Taylors and the leopard-print slippers he'd stolen from Cait so many years ago.

I thumb through the pages of his school notebooks, which are mostly empty. I find a folder that contains his court papers from last December, after he was arrested for possession of OxyContin without a prescription, smashed between the pages. "The defendant appears to have a significant substance abuse issue that has gone unnoticed by his family," the pretrial services report states.

I am confused: I remember this report very clearly; I'd read these very words before. Mom had pulled me into her bedroom and shown me everything when they returned from San Diego after Pat's overdose and court date. I had read these words and gone out to Pat, who was sitting at the kitchen table eating cereal from a plastic bowl with Tony the Tiger on it, one we'd sent away for as kids after cutting the UPC panel from the back of a Frosted Flakes box. I had looked at him and simply stared, not being able to merge the two Pats in my head: the sweet-toothed brother of our youth, and the drug-addicted brother of now. But had I said anything to him? What did I do with the knowledge that he had "a significant substance abuse issue that has gone unnoticed by his family?"

Holding the report now in my hands, I am baffled that I had gone on with my life having that knowledge. That we had all gone on with our lives. What had been wrong with me, with us? Had I simply walked away from him, that day in the kitchen, leaving him to his Frosted Flakes and apparently unnoticed drug addiction?

How had I failed Pat so completely? What further evidence did I need that my brother was going to die, and why didn't I stop him? How had I not thrown him out of his chair onto the green tiled floor, bolted him down, smothered him in my tears and love until he was safe from his demons?

I think back to that day in Costa Rica, reading Pat's email over his shoulder, the universe spelling it out for me: *Your brother is in trouble.* How had I not grabbed him by the arm, looked him in his eyes, and said, "You need help, and here's how I'm going to help you"?

Another folder falls out. Inside it are all the documents from Pat's rehab program: intake forms, privacy policies, daily schedules, phone numbers. There are two versions of a list, one in Pat's scratchy handwriting and one that is typed: a first draft and a final copy, I suppose. The list is of all the drugs he ever did, when he did them, how often he did them, and how much. It begins with alcohol and pot, at age fourteen, and quickly expands to include every drug I've ever heard of—and some that I haven't. Special K, acid, 'shrooms, tweak, crack, cocaine, ecstasy, salvia, DXM, GHB: the ones he did once or only occasionally. Then, the ones he did often, in high amounts, for years: Vicodin, Valium, Perc, Xanax, Norco, Oxy, and, finally, heroin. The list is unimaginably long; the typed version takes up nearly two full pages, single-spaced. It feels impossible, the way Pat's absence feels impossible. How was there time to do so many drugs? His life was short; how did he fit it all in? Was he high literally all the time?

And: how had I fallen so stupidly for his lies?

I feel a surge of resentment toward Pat for minimizing the extent of his problem, followed by despair. I guess this is what he meant when I asked him at Christmas which drugs he'd done: "I've tried pretty much everything," he'd said.

Oh Bunny, I think, *if only you'd told me the whole truth about how deep you were in. Why didn't you just tell me?*

The last document is a five-page questionnaire about the consequences and effects of one's drug use. Each page is filled to the margins with Pat's writing, his final confessions, spelled out in the faded scratch of a dulled pencil tip.

> As my addiction got worse over time, I became much more on edge and little things began to anger me. I started doing things I never would have done had it not been for my addiction. For example, stealing from stores, using needles, and drinking at odd times in order to curb my withdrawals. When I was high I often acted much meaner and sarcastic than I usually do. I said things to people I care about that I wish I could take back, but I can't. I lied to everyone I cared about: my family, my friends, and my girlfriend. EVERYONE. And even once my addiction became apparent to my friends and girlfriend (not my family yet) I continued to lie to the ones closest to me. And once my addiction became apparent to my family, I continued to lie, which ultimately led me to overdose.

Asked to give an example of how his addiction had caused him to violate his own morals, he had written:

> "I totally hurt my family and broke their trust through my addiction. They had no idea I was using and everything came down at once on them. I overdosed and scared them all and I don't know if I can ever fix the hurt and problems I caused them."

I am filled with something beyond anger, beyond fury, beyond rage: it is a white-hot heat, and it burns so hard that it blinds me. The midday sunlight whispers through the small window above, the silence cut only by my breath. I reach for a nearby glass of water and throw it onto the cement floor with all my strength. The glass seems to shatter in slow motion, making a piercing snap as a hundred oddly shaped bits spread themselves in a diamond constellation. I pick up one shard and press it against the back of my hand in a long, deliberate line. I am hoping the snakelike scratch will fill with blood as red as my pain.

It isn't enough to numb the sickening thud: Pat wasn't just partying, being a dumb kid, making bad choices. He was truly an addict. He had been lingering at death's door for years, right under our noses, and up until now I had refused to believe it.

I had failed him. He had lied, yes. He had hidden himself from me, from all of us. But even so, I had failed him.

19 | SIXTEEN DAYS

DALE TELLS HIS girlfriend Alyson to give him the needle so he can clean it.

Alyson doesn't respond, even when Dale's buddy Noah nudges her on the shoulder. She is slumped against the wall of the gas station bathroom, where the three of them are crouching around a cluster of small amber rocks bubbling in the cradle of a spoon. The grubby ceramic tiles on the floor are starting to swim in Dale's vision, a kaleidoscope of squares upon squares. The first shot of heroin he cooked up and shot— along with the Xanax bars he ate awhile ago—is kicking his ass, jumbling the words that are in his head but are having trouble coming out of his mouth.

"Give me the needle," he says again slowly, to the silence.

Dale feels the blackout start to wash down around him and thinks to himself, *Gotta get help*. He gropes around in the mess of Alyson's purse until he finds the bag of unused dope. He hides it in the waistband of his pants. He fumbles with the steel lock and finds himself inside the gas station, where he tells the attendant in what he hopes is a calm voice, "I think someone's overdosing in your bathroom." Suddenly the cops show up—but why? He was trying to get the paramedics there, not the police, who are now questioning him, and he feels the little plastic baggie start to slip out from underneath him, slithering down his leg and landing on the ground in front of everyone, and he is cuffed and in a cruiser and then on the floor of the holding cell, which is colder than ice, colder than the gas station bathroom, colder than anything he's ever felt in his whole life, and holy fuck he's high.

✖

DALE IS IN another bathroom, this time at his friend Mike's house. The cops released him after three days of kicking it in a jail cell—his first time behind bars but one of the many times he's had to white-knuckle an opiate detox, usually because he's run out of drugs. The whole cold turkey thing is getting old. Dale is pretty sick of having to go through the withdrawals: throwing up everywhere, picking at his face, being unable to sleep, the twitches, the restless legs, losing his mind. And the only way to avoid the withdrawals is to do more drugs. He doesn't even remember what it's like to not need opiates coursing through his veins just to feel well, just to be at baseline.

As he cooks up a gigantic shot, he thinks back to the first time he used heroin, just before he turned seventeen. Dale was no stranger to drugs. He'd gotten started on Adderall and weed in middle school and quickly found that he liked most narcotics: 'shrooms, LSD, ecstasy, speed, coke. But it was the downers he loved most—painkillers like Vicodin, Norco, Oxy. When he smoked heroin for the first time, it felt like being grabbed by an invisible hand that wouldn't let go.

Those were the days when he was still swearing he'd never use needles. But one night he met up with his friend Brady, who was hooking him up with some dope. Dale asked for some foil to smoke it off of, but Brady didn't have any—he used to stick to smoking, but ever since meeting a girl in rehab who was an IV heroin addict, he only slammed. Dale sat thinking over the situation for twenty minutes. He was hesitant to use the needle but desperate for his fix. He knew that once he went to the needle, he'd never be able to turn back. It wasn't even like Brady was pressuring him to do it. Brady was a good kid, and he felt bad because it was Dale's first time slamming. Though he finally agreed to cook up the shot, he refused to put the needle in Dale's arm. And then, there it was, the moment of no return. That was the most euphoric high Dale had felt in his whole life. Ever since then, he's been chasing its memory. He chases it with every shot, hoping—though he knows it is hopeless—that it will bring him back to that moment, when the world was beautiful and everything felt possible.

He chases it with this shot, which hits him to his core. But he knows instantly it's not the same. He is chasing a ghost.

✖

ONE MONTH LATER, another huge shot, this time in the back of Mike's car. After Dale shoots it, everything goes silent and black. When consciousness returns, he heaves himself up from behind the front seat and catches his face in the rearview mirror. He has been out for a long time, not breathing. His face is still blue.

The last time he overdosed—the time in Mike's bathroom—he'd staggered into the living room, where his friends were sitting around watching TV, knocking over a trash can on the way in. He'd put on a pair of sunglasses and collapsed on the couch. That was the last thing Dale remembered. The next thing he knew, he was strapped down naked on a hospital bed, with burn marks on his chest from the defibrillators. His friends had called 911 when green foam started leaking from his mouth. In the ambulance on the way to the hospital, he'd been injected with naloxone—a drug that reverses an opiate overdose—four times, but he was so high that his heart had stopped beating for two whole minutes before the paramedics were able to bring him back to life.

He looks at his blue face in the mirror and thinks of some of his friends who have died of heroin overdoses—including Brady, the guy who had fought so hard to keep Dale from moving to the needle. Brady was a really cool person, and he didn't deserve to die. Dale wonders if he deserves to die. For some reason, whenever he's about to slam, he's not worried about his own death. But now he thinks of his dead friends and how much their families and friends have suffered.

This is for real, he thinks. *I could really die from this drug.*

✖

A LOT CAN change in sixteen days. With the drugs washed from his system, Dale feels calmer and more focused than he has in a long time. He also feels relieved that he has a place to sleep, even if it's just a bunk bed in this residential treatment facility in the middle of nowhere. It was getting lame, crashing in friends' cars, deserted parks, abandoned shooting galleries.

Dale feels disgusted when he thinks about heroin now. And perplexed: he can't explain why he keeps going back to it, time after time, overdose after overdose. He hates how just one taste of it turns him into a complete junkie, how his personality totally changes and all his morals go out the window. His hygiene too.

"That drug just really calls to me," he tells Jodi, a friend of his mom's who is visiting him here. "As soon as I do it, heroin becomes my lifestyle. I literally become heroin."

Jodi nods quietly. She wants to know whether this time he's really committed to sobriety. It's his fifth time in rehab, and his mom has agreed to pay for the first thirty days, but after that he's on his own. She has Dale's half-brother and half-sister to worry about, and there just isn't enough money to keep paying for endless treatment of a problem that never seems to end.

Dale says he doesn't know what's keeping him here—at nineteen he's legally free to walk out the door anytime he chooses.

"I just feel done," he says, picking at the friendship bracelet tied around his ankle. "I just want to try out the whole normal thing. Get a job, get a car. Stay here for a few months."

"Well, you have to believe that God wants you here," Jodi says. "There's a reason you survived. And you have to know that your mom loves you."

Dale smiles out of politeness, but he wiggles his foot nervously. Since coming to this rehab, his relationship with his mom has been more open than ever before. They are finally talking to each other like human beings instead of fighting, and he tries to call and tell her that he loves her. But he knows how much she is hurting—voices can't lie.

When it is time for Jodi to leave, Dale lights a cigarette and walks her to her car. He thanks her for coming and puts the cigarette down in a crease in the pavement so that he can give her a hug. After her car pulls away, he picks up the cigarette and shuffles across the deserted parking lot to his bunk room, where he sits on the stoop to finish smoking. He thinks of what he'd say to a younger version of himself, a kid on the verge of tasting that first insurmountable shot.

It's just not worth it, he'd say to the kid. *You'll lose everything. Nothing will make you as evil as heroin.*

It's the worst thing that's ever happened to me.

20 | *TRANQUILIDAD*

IN THE DREAM we are at a party, the cacophony of drunken voices ebbing around us like water sloshing against the sides of a glass. Pat sits in the corner, slumped against the wall, giggling senselessly. I know he's not drinking the beer he's barely holding onto; I know he's high. I can't stand it anymore. I walk around the party searching for Ben, and when I find him I insist that we leave. "He's fucked up," Ben agrees. "But you should at least tell him goodbye."

When we find Pat again, he's sitting at the kitchen table eating a pizza, his hands shiny with grease. He looks up at me with eyes clouded and glazed.

"Pat, I'm going to go now," I say gently, and he tries to stand up to give me a hug, but he's so high that he falls back into the chair. I kneel beside him and look straight into his eyes, stroking his arms.

"You are my precious, beautiful Bunny," I say. "I love you."

I look down and see that he has wet his pants, a dark stain creeping down the inner folds of his shorts. He starts to cry. He looks straight back at me, and everything passes between us: his addiction, his self-hatred, his helplessness—my helplessness.

Then suddenly he shoots up from the chair and in one swift move grabs my neck with both his hands. He chokes me, cinching his fingers closed around my throat, and in the moment I lose consciousness, I wake up.

"Are you mad at me?" I whisper into the night. I wonder if Pat wishes I would stop poking around in the ashes of his life.

I want to apologize to him. I have realized that most of my reactions to addicted Pat came out as anger, and I wonder how this felt. All the yelling, all the berating.

"I love you I love you I love you," I say, wanting so much to fall back asleep and get back to him.

✖

MY MOTHER CALLS me with a pinched sound in her voice. I ache to lift this heavy weight from her, to ease the sadness off her. She no longer feels like my mother but like a child, a small, sensitive thing that needs nurturing, protection, and encouragement, and I am desperate to please her, to make everything okay again, even though I cannot.

She is calling because she has developed a roll of film, and on it is the last picture I ever took with Pat. The dam breaks, that pinched sound giving way to throaty sobs.

"I don't know if you want to see it or not," she cries. "I can send it to you."

"Of course I want to see it," I tell her, even though its finality falls like a brick. If there is a last picture of me with Pat, it means that's where I'll have to hold him forever—whatever the look on our faces, whatever we're doing, will be the last documentation of us together.

When the envelope arrives, I open it reluctantly. The picture is of me in my wedding dress, standing with Pat at the top of the stairs in the Cedar Street house. We are practicing walking down the aisle. His T-shirt has holes in it, and he's pulled his dirty white socks as far up as they'll go. His hoodie is pulled over his head, barely shielding his pallid eyes. But he holds his arm nobly for me and grins broadly.

The picture is quintessentially Pat, and I frame it and set it on my desk, where I sit and try to write about losing him. But the words refuse to come, clogged somewhere between my heart and my throat, stymied by a rage I can't name. I am angry at Pat, for leaving us, for lying to us. I am angry at myself and the rest of my family for being too afraid to face his addiction.

These are the immediate things that anger me, but as the weeks go on and as my last picture with Pat stares back at me, I realize that my anger is spreading outward, becoming less targeted and more complete. I become angry at everything: I am angry about losing Pat, of course, angry at the brutality of death, the unfairness of life. Eventually, I become angry at things as seemingly innocuous as the changing of the seasons. Time marches on; the world persists in its eternal orbit. All the pleasures and duties of life continue. But something is missing. With Pat gone, there is no more drama. I no longer sleep with the phone by my head; the desperate searches for rehab programs are over; we don't attend Nar-Anon meetings in stuffy hospital rooms. There are no more court dates or ambulance rides to the emergency room. There is no more wondering about how to save Pat. This should come as a relief; instead it only emphasizes the choking emptiness inside me.

The family my mother lived with in Costa Rica calls the Cedar Street house. The news of Pat's death had devastated them, particularly the young girls, the ones who'd giggled with starry eyes as he, the blond young American, gripped their hands as they danced one night when we visited their village during our family vacation.

"Tranquilidad," the grandmother of the family says to Mom, over and over. Tranquility.

"Oremos a Dios por la tranquilidad," she says. "La vida es dura."

Pray to God for tranquility. Life is hard.

"I am too mad at God to pray to him," Mom finally tells her. "But please pray to him for me."

She hangs up the phone unsteadily.

My wedding day comes, a day I have dreamed of since I was a little girl, and even *this* angers me. The invitations had been addressed and ready to mail the week before Pat died and had lingered unsent in a bag by the front door, until our family friend Betty had pulled me aside. Everything she had said made sense: Pat would have wanted me to move forward with the wedding; our family needed a positive event to bring us together; this would give Mom something joyful to focus on and help her through her grief. I hadn't wanted to go through with it; I would have preferred to just go down to city hall and get the marriage license. It seemed garish to focus on trivial things like cake flavors and flower arrangements when Pat was dead. But when Betty said she'd handle all the details, I numbly said yes.

Today I stand at the top of the stairs and think of Pat in his hoodie, holding my arm. I look skyward as if for a sign or some resolution. Again, I am left with nothing, only the feeling that I am filled with a tarry black liquid, boiling furiously, endlessly. I am happy, so happy, to be marrying Ben. But that happiness feels faraway, as if it's been locked inside a box to be opened at a later date.

"Tranquilidad," I tell myself, taking a deep breath before I descend.

✖

I WAKE UP in Mexico, the rhythmic pounding of the ocean outside the door. Everything has passed by in a blur, both beautiful and sad. There were flowers, orange and pink, and faces that smiled. Champagne toasts and dancing. Ben looking down at me as I looked up at him, his hands on my back, holding me up.

It is just after sunrise, and the space where he was sleeping next to me is wrinkled and still warm. Out the window, I can see his footsteps in the sand. He goes out in the mornings for coffee and brings it back to me. I walk out into the sand too, close to the tide. The early sun is already hot, but the waves are cool, complacent.

Last night I dreamed that I was floating in these waters. There were people sliding across the liquid lines, figures that moved across the horizon in sprays of seawater that distorted their faces, their surfboards zigzagging toward the beach. I looked for Pat but could not find him.

The iridescent waters lap at my ankles, and the sand gives way to my feet, welcoming them, surrounding them, making them disappear. There are no surfers or beachcombers; there is no one around. I could walk into the sea and try to find my brother. A smooth slipping, a calm descent into the depths. This is how I would like to go.

"What is death but a negligible accident?" I remember reading somewhere, and I see my brother slipping away, the ocean swallowing him up, quietly and easily, as if he is weightless.

I turn around and walk back to shore.

✖

ONE NIGHT A few weeks later, after the bittersweet chaos of the wedding and honeymoon have begun to fade, it comes to me. First softly, like a tap on the shoulder; then more sharply, the azure pinpoint of a growing flame.

Understanding.

As if possessed, I pick up a pen, and finally I begin to write:

I understand you. Of course you wanted to get away, to stop the pain. So do I. From you. From everyone. I want to go to sleep and forget everything that's ever happened. But I want to wake up because I can't imagine not feeling that sun, that glorious sun, so warm on my skin that it feels unconscionable that you are dead and I am here.

At least when you went away, you just went to sleep, swirling sweetly downward, succumbing to the rush of numbness that gave way to an

eternal dark. An easy death. Tranquilidad. Your physical body didn't suffer; your heart didn't know about the approaching stillness. My sweetheart, I want to do it too. But why, why didn't you want to wake up?

Was it pull of your addiction? Or just the stupidity of your youth?
Did you want to die? Or did you think you could just shoot up and come
back? How were you so far removed from life that you could take that
chance? How could you laugh with me and take me by the hand, as if
you cared, as if you weren't going to die, FUCK YOU for what you have
done to my life and yet I miss you more than anything, your picture hurts
me, your face hurts me, everything about you hurts me. You have broken me you fucking little bastard how do you expect me to go on when
your autopsy is in a box in my closet and I am in purgatory, forced to go
on living while you are allowed to die, to be done with it all, you had no
problem leaving us destroyed in your wake, you had no problem breaking our hearts so that you could get high one more time. Don't fuck with
me I know exactly how you died. Slumped over a needle, you fucking
liar. You lied to me you sack of shit. You had no intention of getting clean,
you weren't going to meetings or looking for jobs, you died with two balloons of heroin and a burnt spoon in your balled-up sock you piece of
shit. FUCK. YOU.

I throw the pen against the wall. I hate Pat. I hate him for what he
did to us, to Mom. He took a broken woman and broke her even more.
How could he be so selfish, so astoundingly cruel? How could he not see
how much she loved him, how she ached for him to love her back? How
could he not see that her heart was such a precious and fragile thing?

I think of him, sitting in our father's armchair after his overdose,
playing the guitar. I had rocked back and forth as he sang, thinking how
distant he was, stunned by the knowledge that he had almost died the
night before. I didn't know my own brother anymore. He was like a cari-
cature of himself, but I'd hugged him anyway before going off to bed. I
called him Bunny, even though he was—yet again—high, and therefore
not my Bunny. I had kissed his hot forehead and silky hair, not knowing
that in less than a month, I would kiss those same spots as he lay in his

coffin. Dead because he was an idiot, dead because he was weak, dead because he was my brother, and why did I ever think I would be lucky enough to have him always by my side?

I have a million reasons to be furious with him, and it all amounts to nothing. Because more than anything, more than my anger, more than my disgust, more than my resentment, I just want Pat back.

PART III

BARGAINING

WHAT WOULD I GIVE TO **BE ABLE** TO **SAY ONE SMALL THING** THAT **MADE HIM HAPPY? WHAT WOULD** THAT **ONE SMALL THING BE? IF I HAD SAID IT IN TIME** WOULD **IT HAVE WORKED?**

–JOAN DIDION, *THE YEAR OF MAGICAL THINKING*

21 | THE TALISMAN

I LEAVE SAN Francisco early in the morning, the spidery fingers of frost just beginning to mist away in the cautious sunlight. I am embarking on a gruesome road trip, trailing my brother's ghost down the California coast. There are secrets hidden in his old haunts, things I need to learn beyond the sterile proclamation of the toxicology report.

It is often said that an addict's loved ones can develop their own addiction to the addict, becoming preoccupied with the addict's well-being even at the expense of other relationships and obligations. In much the same way, I have become addicted to my brother's death, and I will be stuck here in this limbo, inert and fixated, until I find the answers I seek. Until I find a way to explain to myself the hole Pat has left in our lives.

The urban skyline soon gives way to the wide stretch of the Pacific Ocean, shimmering and infinite. It's the kind of sheer and unabated beauty that makes you think of God. I remember driving along this stretch of the coast years ago, after my father had died. The way the faraway clouds gathered at the edge of the sea, illuminated from behind and above, made me wonder if that's where Dad was: protected, eternal, floating somewhere in a universe I couldn't comprehend. Then—perhaps because I was young and idealistic—it was possible to force myself to imagine him there, in his striped bathrobe and worn brown moccasins. To say hello and imagine he heard me. But the scene today only feels like an absence.

✖

WHEN I REACH the house in Burbank, it is yellow and pleasant. Sitting calmly under a cloudless sky, its stone walkway bordered by emerald grass, the house gives no indication of trauma or darkness. It is unobtrusively, sickeningly normal. The ground-floor bedroom has a big, bright window framed by navy shutters, and if I peer inside, I will see where my brother died.

When Pat's girlfriend's mother answers the door, she pulls me into a hug and into the house. I wonder what went through her mind when I called her a few weeks ago and told her what I wanted to do. I don't know much about this woman, only that she struggled to get help for her daughter and was kind to Pat, providing him with a place to stay while he got back on his feet. She was home on the night he died; he and his girlfriend had smoked heroin on the living room couch while she was upstairs in bed, and her husband had broken down Pat's locked door the next morning. I remember, vaguely, that she called the Cedar Street house in the hours after we told Mom that Pat was dead. Though her sobs had made the call incoherent, she had managed to tell Mom she was sorry. I had felt only bitterness at the time, but standing before her now, I realize that I had simply needed someone—anyone—to blame. It wasn't her fault. She is just like any other mother who's lived through addiction: Tired. Helpless. Hopeful. Sad. Wordlessly, she hands me a packet of Kleenex and points me in the direction of the bedroom.

As I walk down the hallway, I wonder how she and my mother can both go on living in these houses. I suppose we all must move on; of course she shouldn't be expected to pick up and leave her home just because my brother died here. I just wonder how she doesn't remember it, his body and the roar of the sirens, every time she passes the bedroom door—but then again, maybe she does.

The bedroom is tiny, with walls painted blue and a treadmill in the corner. The last time Pat called me, he'd explained that he was out of breath because he was walking on the treadmill. He was trying to burn off some of the excess energy and boredom, the feelings that sometimes made him want to use. I'd been so pleased at this healthy way of dealing with his addiction, not knowing he was also scoring heroin and stashing needles in his backpack.

The autopsy floods back to me: "His left arm was flexed upward, with his closed hand resting near his face; his right hand came to rest underneath his right side torso. His lower body partially rested upon stacked blankets, which appeared to be his sleeping area." I calculate the measurements in my mind: there is a twin bed now that seems to be too large for this tiny room; it must have replaced the stack of blankets, because if Pat had rested upon them but also fallen against the door, bruising his face, that means that the exact spot where he died would be approximately here, right where I stand now.

A numbing rush, like the surge brought on by of a shot of heavy liquor, comes over me. The sensation brings me to my knees, and I sink to the floor. I touch the door, painted a flawless, porcelain white. Did his face make a whacking sound, a slap, as it fell? Or was it more of a thud, something that could easily be passed off in the dead of night as the groan of the house or the cat alighting from couch to chair? I run my fingers through the carpet and, as if I am out of my body, watch them clutch at the nubby fibers, as if through doing so, I will be able to mine some molecule of my brother's essence. Did they clean this carpet after he died? And with what—bleach? That powder the paramedics pour on the pavement after a car crash to absorb the blood? But I don't think there was any blood—maybe piss or vomit or shit?

There are three mirrors on the wall next to the door. They are long and narrow and curvy, like a trio of glass snakes falling from the sky. My reflection is dissected across them, like a child in a funhouse. The room is too small to contain my brother, and yet I continue to search the rug, the door, the treadmill, the disappeared pile of blankets, willing these objects he once touched to conjure him back.

Here is the spot where Pat died; it holds his absence, the reality that *this* is where he left us. I can hear a television faintly a few rooms away; the kitchen faucet turns on and off.

The sun is nearly set, and he is nowhere to be found.

✖

IT IS HAPPY hour when I reach the motel in San Diego. Swarms of giddy tourists clog the sidewalk, staggering from bar to beach. It's nothing special, sandwiched between a Thai restaurant and a liquor store. I enter warily. Another place where my brother almost died.

Room 217 sits at the end of a long hallway framed by peeling panels of wood laminate and exposed pipes. It is claustrophobically small, with barely two feet separating the twin beds and a smudged window sliced by an iron grate. I sink onto one of the beds and think of Pat calling me from Cait's cell phone all those months ago. They were headed to this motel, but first Mom had wanted to go to the house where Pat had been crashing with friends so that he could pack up his belongings. Despite the nature of the trip, Pat seemed to be in good spirits. I had told him to call me after the court hearing the next morning and that I loved him.

"I love you too, Ern!" he'd said cheerfully before hanging up.

A few minutes later, Cait had called me from a rest stop. She said that one minute Pat seemed overly happy, and the next minute he was falling asleep to the point where he was snoring. It was odd behavior, and in our ignorance, we'd wondered if he was on something or if maybe he was just tired. Anyway, if he was on something, what were we supposed to do? Should they drive directly to a hospital? Turn him in to the cops? She had to hang up before we could decide.

When they arrived at Pat's house, Mom and Cait were shocked: it was filthy. Mold grew on the walls, and there were piles of dirty clothes everywhere. The police had dumped everything on the floor in the raid a few weeks before, and nothing had been cleaned up. Pat disappeared into the bathroom while Mom and Cait picked through some of his sweatshirts, looking for anything salvageable. After awhile, Cait grew suspicious and knocked on the bathroom door. Pat answered that his stomach was upset and emerged a few minutes later, stumbling to the car. A fight began when Mom mentioned the state of the house.

"Don't worry," Pat slurred. "I'm going to run away to Mexico. You'll never have to see me again."

On the way to the motel, they passed a small house near the university, and Pat suddenly lurched forward from the backseat. He begged Mom to stop for just a second and jumped out of the car, running toward a dark-haired kid who was standing on the lawn. The two whispered and hugged, and as quickly as he'd left, Pat was back. As they drove away, he tapped his fingers against the glass and closed his eyes.

By the time they arrived in the motel lobby, Pat was embarrassingly high. He could barely stand up, and his arms were dangling loosely at his sides.

"Great place you got here," he said sarcastically to the clerk, draping himself over the front desk.

Cait pulled him aside as Mom got the keys and demanded to know what he was on, saying she needed to take him to the hospital, but he wouldn't tell her. When they got to the room, he went to take a shower while Mom lay on the bed and cried. That was when Cait had called me, terrified: he must have found pills in that bathroom. I demanded to speak to Pat, but she thought it would make things worse. Maybe the shower would bring him down; it was so late, and they had to be in front of the judge in less than ten hours. I hung up, hating myself for not being there and hating Pat for everything he was doing to our family.

Mom lay awake, waiting for Pat to emerge from the shower. He finally did. He crawled into bed and softly apologized to Mom. She told him that she was sorry too. She was a stiff board, staring at the ceiling as she tried to rise above Pat's snores, repeating the Hail Mary over and over and over and over until she realized that he was no longer making any sounds. His breath had stopped. Turning toward him, she saw that his face was turning gray, now blue, now indigo, now purple. Foam was gurgling at his iridescent lips. She screamed and pulled his eyelids skyward to reveal white, white landscapes, framed by red.

As I sit on this bed now, these images feel like something conjured, as if I've made it all up. I thought that seeing these places and touching these objects that were part of the story of Pat's demise would flip that switch in my brain that insists it's not true, that Pat isn't gone. But they only make everything that happened seem even less true. Losing Pat seems just as impossible today as it did on that chilled afternoon in December when I answered my phone, yet again, to another story of my brother gone wrong.

✖

PAT'S FRIEND EVAN has agreed to meet me at a pizzeria near the San Diego State University campus to talk about their years of addiction to pills and heroin. He stares down at the table from under the frayed fold of his baseball hat and picks at the corners of his thin gray sweatshirt. His eyes, brown and distant, have the detached look that is characteristic of Suboxone users: slightly pinned, but not high. Medicated, but not numbed. Though it contains an opioid drug, buprenorphine, in combination with naloxone, an opioid antagonist, it doesn't provide the sweet solace of Evan's vices, OxyContin and heroin. It helps with the cravings, makes him believe he can stay clean, but it can't give Evan what he really wants: a respite from the pain.

Six months ago on February 4, Evan woke up around three o'clock in the morning. The moonlight struck his guitar, making him think of Pat, who liked to play when they hung out. Evan couldn't fall back asleep, so he went to school and later work, fighting his fatigue and a weird feeling that something was wrong.

Later that day, he had just gotten home when the sound of a motorcycle barreled through his off-campus apartment. Though Evan had no real cause to be disturbed, something about the noise shot straight to his heart and made him think of one person: Pat. Evan had only two friends with motorcycles, and one of them was close to Pat.

"Pat's dead," the friend said when Evan opened the door, and Evan couldn't believe it. He immediately reached for his phone to call another good mutual friend, Steve, who would surely be able to tell Evan it wasn't true—that it was all just a rumor, a story gone wrong. But the phone started ringing as Evan fished it out of his jeans. It was Steve. And Evan knew it was true. Pat was dead.

A week later, Evan walked into the church and felt sick to his stomach when he saw the open casket at the altar. He approached it as if in a dream, disbelieving that the body inside was his friend Pat. His friend who called him Ev-olution and who made him laugh about the stupidest shit, who brought out the best in him, who knew what it was like to feel like you were fucking up your whole life but didn't know how to stop it. Evan's struggle with drugs had made him feel so alone, but Pat had always been there, supporting him, even as Pat fell deeper into addiction.

"It was as if we were keeping each other afloat in the middle of the ocean while weights were tied to our feet, making us sink lower and lower, but one of us would help the other or be there in case we couldn't support all of the weight by ourselves," Evan tells me now.

The unending lines of people shuffling past the coffin also shocked Evan. He'd always thought Pat was just some beach bum. He carried around his few possessions in a shabby backpack, earning him the nickname Backpack Pat, and he couch-surfed and wore used clothes and barely went to class. Besides mentioning monthly checks from his grandmother to pay for his cell phone, Pat rarely spoke of his family. He'd told Evan once, while they were bombed, that his dad had died when he was very young. Beyond that, Evan had no idea why Pat would want to numb himself out to such extremes—he had guessed that the kid just liked to party.

Evan tells me this shyly, almost gingerly, as if he doesn't want to hurt me with the facts. And it hurts, to see him hurting for me, to think of how young he is to lose someone. With the din of the pizza parlor buzzing all around us, reality blurs, and it seems just as likely that there is an alternate universe in which Evan died and Pat is alive. It was a game of Russian roulette, and it had to end sometime, and this is the way it went down.

Evan has been feeling guilty. Even blurred by the drugs, he'd known that something was off about Pat. Everything Pat did, he did to the maximum limit: whatever drug he could get, and huge amounts of it. Someone was always telling a story about Pat, usually that he'd passed out at a party—one time he didn't wake up for sixteen whole hours. When Evan heard that one, he felt scared: clearly Pat had overdosed, and what if he hadn't woken up? Evan had thought many times about telling Pat to slow down, but he didn't know how to say it.

"How are you still alive, man?" he'd say, half-jokingly. "How can you take it? That shit's gonna start melting your brain." They'd be walking through campus to skip class and go skateboarding, and Pat would laugh it off, and Evan would put it all out of his mind.

There were darker times too: Evan was worried about his best friend back at home, who was struggling with his own addiction. He was also in love with a girl, and things were going downhill. When she broke it off with Evan, Pat came over with pills and dope. Through the smoky haze, Pat asked sleepily whether Evan ever felt really depressed and down, like being unable to climb out of a deep, dark hole. Evan said he did, a feeling they decided was probably due to the drugs. Then they promptly did more. The next day they woke up, drove down to Tijuana, and went to a restaurant where black tar heroin was sold under the table.

Now these memories claw at Evan. He'd hit his own bottom before Pat died, when his parents had found a needle in his truck and told Evan they were cutting him off unless he got help. They'd found him a doctor who prescribed Suboxone, and Evan was able to stay off drugs—he'd even told Pat that he should try it, that it might be a way out. Evan has relapsed twice since Pat died, but he wants to make it work so badly. He doesn't want to end up like Pat, or like the people all around him at parties, the ones he sees nodding off in the corner. Evan shakes these people, stays up nights with them, unwilling to let them sleep because he's terrified they'll die.

Sometimes Evan wishes he could just stop caring. When he'd called his best friend after Pat died, he wouldn't even give Evan the time of day. He was using, and Evan knew it was the drugs that were making him so selfish and self-centered, but that didn't make it hurt any less that his friend couldn't be there for him.

After Pat died, Evan felt abandoned by everyone: no one from the dorms freshman year, or even the apartment complex sophomore year, reached out anymore, much less asked him about how he felt about losing Pat. Most nights he came home from work after going to school all day and just sat in silence waiting to hear Pat come through the door and yell his name. He wondered what he should do now that Pat was gone and found that he had no answer. So instead he sat in his chair, alone, and thought about the last time he saw Pat. It was the day before Pat's court hearing, and Evan had been surprised when Pat ran up to him near Evan's off-campus house. Evan hadn't seen Pat for at least a month, maybe more, and he'd been really worried. But Pat was in a big rush; he said his mom and sister were waiting for him in the car.

"Be careful, man. I love you," Evan said to Pat. It is the same thing Evan tells his best friend now, even though he knows his words aren't being heard.

"Pat said, 'I love you too,' and that was the last time I saw him," Evan tells me, his dark eyes vacant.

After the bill comes, we walk to the parking lot and I open the trunk of my car. I've brought some of Pat's boxes with me, and I tell Evan he can take whatever he wants. My heart sinks when he picks up a right-foot Converse shoe with doodles etching the yellowing rubber; its mate must be buried in one of the other boxes. I hate to part with it. But maybe, in the hands of this young kid, so sad, so lost, it will be some sort of talisman, the thing that keeps him safe.

22 | LETTING GO

AS ELLIE SORTS the laundry, she wonders when her son Dale will die. The chilled night air filters through the slit under the garage door as she throws the whites into one pile and the colors into another, thinking about her oldest son's death. Her hands shake as she pilfers through the clothes; she has been so stressed out that she has been losing weight, and the fluorescent orange sweatshirt she is wearing tonight swallows her whole. Inside the house, her husband tools around on the computer while Dale's younger half-brother and half-sister do their homework in their rooms. None of them is thinking about Dale, and Ellie feels incredibly alone.

She misses Dale desperately. But as she pours the detergent into the washing machine, she admits to herself guiltily that since she kicked Dale out of the house, family life has been mostly peaceful. Immediately, she feels like a worthless mother. Late last year, during one of Dale's stints in rehab, the family moved into a new neighborhood, and although Ellie talks to her son whenever he calls and even visits him sometimes, she hasn't given him the address of their new home in Mission Viejo. She doesn't want Dale to know where they live.

Ellie slams the dryer door and starts to cry. As she does every night, she prays to God that Dale doesn't die, or that if he does, he'll go peacefully. As she does every night, she tells herself forcefully, *I will not fall apart. I have two other children to raise and a husband.* She feels like she is being ripped apart down the middle, split between two lives: her

Dale life, and her family life. She carries on, trying her best to look and act "normal," whatever that is—she can't even remember anymore what it feels like not to be constantly suffering from this gnawing anxiety. But inside, she feels like she will explode from the pressure.

How could her beautiful, dark-haired, baby-faced boy fall so far?

All of a sudden, an overwhelming heaviness overtakes Ellie, and she drops to her hands and knees. She looks up at the ceiling, stunned. She is not a religious person, and she whispers out loud, "What the heck?" A wave of something warm and unfamiliar washes over her: the feeling of relief, the feeling of her prayers being heard. She stands and her shoulders unravel, the weight that had crushed them before disappearing into the night. Without understanding how or why it has happened, she has given up Dale to God, handed over the burden of worrying about his struggle with addiction, which she knows she is powerless over.

She picks up the laundry hamper, feeling an inexplicable lightness, and walks back into the house, for the moment at peace.

✖

THE DRIVE TO Norco is flat and long, with not much to look at besides the occasional McDonald's or truck stop. It takes about an hour from Ellie's house. One hour of silence, one hour to not have to explain or justify her actions to the rest of her family, one hour to think about what to say to Dale when she sees him.

Ellie doesn't mind the silence; she just minds feeling so alienated from everyone—from her husband, from her kids, from her coworkers, even from her friends, who try their hardest to understand. Most of all, she hates feeling alienated from Dale, because he is at the center of the storm.

The problem is that mixed in with the love, there is just so much anger between them. Ellie knows lots of teenagers yell at their parents, and Dale's addiction has only exacerbated the normal tension between parents and adolescents. She has endured years of Dale screaming and ranting and getting in her face in fits of rage. But the one thing her son has never done is swear at her. Although she's sure he's done it behind her back, Dale has never used curse words to her face, and for some reason that makes Ellie believe that he's still a good kid. And that belief makes her all the more desperate to shake some sense into him, to make him believe in himself again, to force him to understand what's at stake in this battle: his life.

On days like today, Ellie feels so alone in the world. Her husband and kids didn't want to come with her to visit Dale at his sober living house—they never do. She clenches the steering wheel and tries to focus on the positive. For one thing, there's the fact that she's been able to scrape together the $500 due in two weeks if Dale is to stay at the sober living house beyond the initial thirty days: it was mortifying to call up all her close family members and friends and ask them to pitch in, but almost all of them had agreed to donate, giving Dale a real shot at staying clean. Today she's looking forward to telling Dale about the money and hopes he'll be grateful. Initially, Ellie had told him she'd pay for thirty days and no more, but she'd been so encouraged by his last conversation with her.

"I'm done with drugs, Mom," he'd said. "I hate them. I really want to get better this time."

For some reason, Ellie felt that this time something was different. After all, he'd had one hundred days clean the last time he was in rehab, the longest amount of sober time since he'd started using drugs at age thirteen. Yes, he'd gone out and screwed it all up again, but only for a couple of weeks, and thankfully the treatment directors had agreed to take him back, even though they have a zero-tolerance policy. They like Dale, and they believe in his ability to get and stay sober—and now Dale seems to finally be on board too.

But Ellie hasn't been able to revel in Dale's apparent change of heart with anyone—least of all those closest to her. Dale has become the wedge that is driving Ellie apart from the rest of her family, who are fed up with the constant drama of his addiction, the fights, the broken promises, the stealing, the lying.

She remembers a time last year, when Dale was still using. He'd moved out of the house after he turned eighteen and dropped out of high school seven months before graduation. He was kicked out for stealing after living with his biological father for a few months, and he was living on the streets, which killed Ellie inside. Everywhere she went, she searched the faces on the sidewalks, hoping she would see Dale's face, because then at least she'd know he was still alive.

Late one night, Dale called her, asking to come over. He said he didn't want to live on the streets anymore and that he needed help for his addiction. The next morning he showed up at her front door and begged Ellie to let him in. His skin was a sickly shade of green, and he was fidgeting with his stringy, unkempt hair. He was dirty, hungry, skinny, and tired. She didn't have the strength to turn him away, so she called her husband, who came home from work and told Dale to leave. As her homeless son walked away, his shoulders hunched in defeat, Ellie's heart broke.

Since then, Ellie has been unable to bring up Dale's name to her husband without a fight. Her husband—Dale's stepdad—is angry, and he accuses Ellie of being taken over by Dale's addiction. What Ellie wants to tell him is that Dale's addiction has affected the whole family; that they don't just have a drug problem but a family problem. She wants to tell him that addiction is a part of their lives whether they like it or not. At least she's trying her best to deal with it, whereas he and the other kids don't seem to care about Dale.

Recently, Ellie decided that she should try to be honest with her family and not hide the fact that she was taking Dale's phone calls—the only lifeline connecting her to her son. She explained to her husband that the reason she answered Dale's calls was that hearing his voice let her know he was still alive. Her husband became irate and told Ellie to pack her bags and leave the house if she couldn't agree to stop all communication with Dale. Ellie shook her head and walked upstairs, hoping distance would calm the tension. How could a mother be forced to choose between her son and the rest of her family? What was she supposed to do—abandon Dale? Leave her husband and kids?

She thinks of the words of another mom she knows, Diana, whose son Andrew, a pills and heroin addict, is now behind bars, but sober: *My son has a choice, but only one choice—for once he makes the choice to use, his will is no longer his own.* That is what people like her husband just don't understand, in Ellie's opinion. Dale is a good person who deserves to live. He needs help in order to do that, and finally, he seems to want that help. How can she turn her back on him now?

It is noon by the time Ellie reaches the sober living house, the sun pelting heat onto the barren parking lot. Dale rises from the stoop of his bunk room, where he's been smoking in the sweltering, still air. He's starving, he says, so Ellie takes him to lunch.

Afterward, she drives him back to the sober living house, where they sit in the front room to talk. Dale tells Ellie he's thinking of applying for a job at the Costco down the way—he used to work there, so his references should all check out, he says. Ellie's heart sinks.

"No," she tells him. "If you get a job, you'll get money, and you'll start using again. Work the program—focus on staying clean. Use the tools they give you."

Dale looks dejected and doesn't say anything, which makes Ellie panic.

"You have done everything your way for years, and it hasn't worked," she says, getting angrier. "Listen to me! Do it my way now. Not your way."

Dale jumps up suddenly, his face inches from his mother's. The program's director appears and tells Ellie to go home, to let the situation diffuse itself.

✖

ONE NIGHT A few weeks later, Ellie hears that Dale's ex-girlfriend Alyson is having a hard time. Ellie can't believe how close Alyson has come to dying at such a young age—she is only seventeen, but she's overdosed multiple times on pills and heroin, including the time at the local gas station, when Dale was thrown in jail for the first time. Like Dale, Alyson has spent the last year in and out of rehab, though she seems to have more consistent sober time. But she'd recently relapsed again, and Ellie learns through a friend that Alyson is back at the beginning, with just sixteen days clean.

When Ellie calls Alyson, the young girl immediately starts to cry. Her family is ashamed of her, she says, and it makes her hate herself even more than she already does without their embarrassment of her, the dirty junkie.

"Can I call you my new mom?" Alyson asks Ellie, half-joking. Ellie tells her yes.

"There are so many firsts ahead of you, and you deserve to live them," she tells Alyson. "Your first prom, your first wedding, your first baby. Children should bury their parents, not the other way around. Don't let it happen to you."

Alyson stays on the phone with Ellie for nearly an hour. Alyson says she talked to Dale a week ago and told him how lucky he was that his mom supported him and understood his struggle. Ellie laughs ruefully to herself: Dale would never say that to her, of course, but it feels so good to hear the words just the same.

But she knows that it could go the other way too. She hopes that Dale is beginning to see the reality of what could happen to him, because it's been happening to many of his friends—and just because they're in rehab doesn't mean they're not dropping like flies. Dale's friend Brady, for one. Ellie had heard that he'd been in a treatment center for weeks when one day he simply decided to leave and go get high; he'd ended up on life support after another kid shot him up with heroin in a supermarket parking lot and then left him for dead when he started overdosing. Dale himself was in rehab when Brady died a week later, and he had been crushed that he couldn't attend Brady's funeral, though Brady's family hadn't ended up having one.

Though Ellie hates to think about funerals, she's already gone over it a thousand times in her mind: what she would say in Dale's obituary, whom she would choose to speak at his service. She has even spent hours hunting through boxes of photographs, searching in vain for an appropriate picture of her son. If Dale dies tomorrow, she wonders, will she have a decent picture of him?

The answer is no. The last picture of Dale smiling was taken when he was in the fifth grade. In all the pictures since, he is unsmiling, unhappy, or strung out.

"Don't feel guilty about me using drugs, Mom," Dale had texted her before he went into rehab. "It's not your fault. Don't ever blame yourself."

It doesn't help. Ellie knows that if she gets the phone call, the one in which Dale is dead, she'll be the first one she blames.

The next morning she receives another text from Dale. He has walked out of rehab, disappeared into the world.

"I'm sorry, Mom, I'm so sorry," he texts. "Fuck Mom I'm sorry. I failed you. I don't know Mom I just can't do things right I don't know why. I'll call you tomorrow Mom."

23 | BROKEN

THERE IS A rhythm about grief: the way it moves through our bodies like waves; it just keeps coming. And if you are not going to lie down and die, then you are going to go on. And going on means succumbing to the tasks of living: the brushing of the teeth. The cleaning of the coffee-maker. The emails from the boss. The dinner dates with friends.

But even as you go on, you are changed, because you have been reminded of the bitter reality of life.

Our family has become obsessed with losing each other. No one admits this. But revealed by Pat's death, the inevitable truth hounds us: we are all going to die.

Brian takes the old family dog, Romeo, up to our cabin in the mountains, where Mom has retreated for most of the summer. He and Romeo walk into the woods where we played as children. He sees the hammock, where we napped and read the *Guinness Book of World Records* on lazy afternoons, swatting away mosquitoes and sucking on Otter Pops. The burnt ashes of the fire pit where we roasted hot dogs and marshmallows on long sticks. The crumbling fort we had built out of fallen pine branches and old logs.

The woods make Brian miss Pat. Reading the *Book of Mysteries* and thinking they saw Bigfoot near the fort. Following the creek as World Explorers in its winding course until the brush became too thick. Setting up booby traps in the clearing to keep away the robbers from the *Home Alone* movie.

Brian decides he will make a cross out of sticks and fasten it on top of a California redwood tree in honor of Pat, who always climbed to the highest point of every object, be it roof, rock, limb, building, bridge, or mountain. He fashions the cross, instructs the dog to stay, and starts climbing the tree. But just when the sky starts to become visible through the cracks of the branches, he realizes he can't do it—it's too high. His fingers shake as they clutch at the rough, soft bark, and he shimmies back down.

By the time his feet touch the mishmash of moss and twigs at the tree's roots, Romeo is gone. This is horrible, because Romeo is so much more than just our family dog: he's really Pat's dog, because Mom had adopted him after Dad died, for Pat, who was the only kid left in the house. And now that Pat is gone, Romeo can't go too. Brian is frantic, calling for Romeo over and over as he stumbles back up the hill to the cabin.

Back at the cabin, Romeo, his thick legs crippled by arthritis, lopes back up the stairs to the deck, where Mom sits in the quiet sunshine knitting a blanket. His tongue hangs like an elastic strip of bubble gum. There is no Brian. Only the dog. Something terrible has happened. She immediately thinks Brian fell into the river. He stumbled and broke his neck. He slipped on a jagged rock. He is impaled on a log. He is dead.

She panics, snatching a bottle of water and, for no good reason, a towel, and runs out of the house. But there is Brian, sweating and swearing at the dog for running away.

The story is later recounted among our family members as a sort of joke: the silliness of Brian thinking old, stubborn Romeo would obey his commands, and how Mom thought a towel would save the day. But really, it's something we tell each other to signal that we are terrified of falling off that gruesome edge, of having to again relive the moment of reckoning, the reminder of reality, the truth of our mortality: Pat is dead. There is no way around it.

Desperate in this knowledge, we grasp at each other—though we all pretend not to. That's because we are also fiercely saddened by each other, by the mere presence of others who loved Pat. I can't sleep at night for fear that the rest of my family will suddenly die too; at the same time, I don't want to see or talk to them right now.

So I become an outrageous spy. I walk through Mom's house looking for clues when she's not there. I am terrified that she will kill herself. In the pallid hours after midnight, I lie in bed and imagine her suicide note. Things she had said to me in the weeks after Pat died, things I hadn't been able to respond to in a way that reassured her. Well, why should she have believed me? I knew nothing; I was grasping at explanations.

"Pat's addiction killed him," I had said to her. "He made a stupid mistake. He loved you. You did the best you could. You are an amazing mother."

She had hugged me faintly and shook a little in my arms.

"As a person, I know I did enough," she had finally said. "But a mother fights forever to protect and save her child. So as a mother, I failed. I did my best, but my best wasn't good enough. I let him down."

I had told her again that she was powerless, that we were all powerless, but I could see in her eyes that she did not believe me, and I wondered if I even believed myself. She fidgeted for a minute, and we hugged again. Then she pretended to brighten, and went to make dinner.

The thought of Mom taking her own life has become a persistent fear among all of us siblings, though at first we only allude to our worries. Mom has always been fiercely independent, but now her solitude verges on isolation. She has taken to turning off the answering machine and unplugging the phone for days—sometimes weeks—at a time. We fill these periods with incessant back-and-forth chatter: *Have you talked to her? She emailed me on Wednesday. How many times have you called?*

Should I go over there? No, she's probably watching her soap opera. Let's call again in the morning.

After one particularly excruciating bout of unresponsiveness, I call my sister.

"This is crazy!" I say. "I've called her twenty times in the past two days."

Cait agrees. She's just as worried as I am. But we're both drained, and it's so late.

"She's probably out or in bed, really," she says, trying to convince us both. "I mean, look. Even if anything was wrong, we can't do anything about it right now."

"I know, I know," I say. "It's true. There's nothing we can do right now. Let's just go to bed and deal with it in the morning."

We agree and say goodnight.

Ten minutes later, Cait calls me in a panic. I answer immediately, convinced that she has just received news from whoever found Mom dead.

"I cannot believe I just said that," she says. "That even if anything was wrong, there's nothing we can do about it now. Do you think something's wrong? I can't believe we just agreed to not do anything when something could really be wrong!"

I have no answer. I also don't know why we just agreed to that. If we really thought something had happened to Mom, of course we wouldn't put it off until morning. But it becomes funny, and I start laughing because I suddenly see Mom's number pop up on my phone: she's calling. She's fine. We are being ridiculous.

But this communal trepidation persists, and our fears soon take on new urgency. When I know Mom is going to be out, I go to the house and search. I justify my reconnaissance by telling myself I am working on her behalf. What if I catch some crucial detail, some red flag, some warning sign that she is spiraling toward death? After missing everything with Pat, I would never forgive myself if I missed the thing that could have saved my mother. My sister too has taken to going room to room when she "stops by" the house and there's no sign of Mom. She catches herself only when she opens the basement door, looking for Mom's body hanging from a noose above the washing machine.

We finally tell each other that Mom would never do that.

Still, the secret expeditions persist. Today I come home to an empty house and find myself checking rooms. In her bedroom, the sheets are ruffled and unmade, and there is a box of pink tissues hidden under the pillows. I check her bedside table, which contains a stack of books. *A Season of Grief: Praying through Your Losses. Grieving with the Help of Your Catholic Faith. The Grieving Garden. Get Over It! A Guide to Understanding Guilt during Bereavement.* I find sticky notes in her handwriting, quoting advice from the books. "Be a survivor of grief rather than its victim," one note reads. "Rebuild a new life with new hopes and dreams," says another.

I am thrilled. Mom is clearly trying to work through her feelings— she is thinking, rational, in touch with reality—and therefore can't be suicidal. This mission is going exceedingly well.

Next up is the kitchen. The dishes aren't done, so I do them. The refrigerator is surprisingly well stocked. Encouraged, I proceed to the bathroom. It looks clean. The dining room table sports a fresh table-cloth and even has the lace overlay we used to use for special occasions, birthdays, Christmas. Now, especially without my mother, it is heavy and vacant. There are two candlesticks on the table, their waxen claws petrified by gravity. So she used them. Probably only once and for a very short time, judging by their height—but an encouraging sign nonetheless. Why would she set the table if she was going to, you know, do anything?

The wind howls. Everywhere there are pictures of Pat, radiantly alive. His chunky toddler cheeks, his blond hair, his eyes that were so large, even when he grinned. I wince, thinking of his gray and powdered face in the coffin, and the stitches on his skull.

The backyard is gleaming. It is almost summer, and the leaves of the cottonwood tree are luminous and plentiful. The potted plants, gifts from someone in the days after Pat's death, have wilted. I suddenly realize I have forgotten to check the basement. The Mary Engelbreit calendar on the basement door is up to date: a sign that she knows what month it is. For a moment I'm convinced she's hanging from a noose, and I know with complete certainty that if she's dead, I will die.

But I don't die, because of course there's nothing in the basement, save for a basket of clean laundry and the recycling bins, crammed with crushed soda cans and cardboard.

It's been nearly two hours since I arrived, and my probe has produced nothing but ghosts. How does Mom live in this empty house? Seeped in the memories of the dead, stewed in the juices of their abandoned things, she moves from room to room, doing what? Thinking what? Feeling what? I can't ask her; I don't want to set her off. My role is to be the opposite of weak, so that she, my mother, can be strong again.

I am out of my mind here; it feels like I am suffocating. There is nothing, only a pit into which I fall every time I open the door, which is now opening to reveal my mother. She is crying because she came home and saw my car, and every time my car is unexpectedly in front of the house, something must be wrong.

I hold her and she holds me back, and we sob without explaining to each other why. She trembles, her hair—the same color as Pat's—so silky, so fine, like a baby's. She has been at his grave all day long, while I snooped, smoothing the warm grass and writing him a letter.

"He broke my heart," she says, and I know.

24 | SECRETS

TREY DOESN'T KNOW his friend Brady is dead, and his mother, Julie, doesn't know how to tell him. In just a few more months, Trey will reach two major milestones: his "belly button birthday," as his treatment program calls it, when he will turn twenty-one, followed by his "sober birthday" a few weeks later, when he will have been clean for a whole year. If Trey makes it to that point, it will be the longest sober time he's had since he began using pills and heroin. Julie worries that if she tells Trey about Brady's death, it will knock him off course.

It will also be nearly a year since Brady died. Julie has felt guilty about keeping the news from Trey for so long—the two were close friends, and she knows Trey will be devastated.

She just hasn't been able to find the right way to tell him.

The strict rules of his eighteen-month treatment program have preserved her secret: residents are forbidden to even mention the names of people they used to use with, much less discuss their current whereabouts, and unsupervised phone or Internet use isn't allowed, so there has been little chance for Trey to come across the news of Brady's passing. Still, every Saturday, when Julie and her husband visit Trey during the program's weekly family meeting and potluck, she takes great care not to leave any evidence on her cell phone, which she sometimes lets Trey use briefly. She logs out of all social media and erases her call history so that Trey won't somehow stumble upon Brady's Facebook page, which is now filled with "RIP" posts, or see that Julie has called Brady's mother, Abby. That, for sure, would make Trey suspicious: Julie and Abby had never met before Brady passed away, when their two sons were still using together.

Nobody that close to Trey has ever died, and though her son is nearly a man, the mother in her wants to protect him from that pain just a little bit longer.

Julie still remembers when Trey's friend Sam called her to say that he was worried about Trey. Sam told Julie that Trey was doing heroin, and she was flabbergasted. She'd known things were bad—pills bad, but not heroin bad. Julie and her husband had agreed earlier that they were done helping Trey, but heroin was a game changer; what would they do if Trey died and they hadn't done everything in their power to throw him a lifeline? She kicked into high gear, locating Trey a spot at New Life House, a structured sober living center in Torrance that cost $2,500 per month—more than some mortgages. But the money didn't matter to Julie; what mattered to her in that moment was getting her son clean and keeping him safe, and New Life House boasted a 95 percent success rate for residents who stayed for the program's full eighteen months, which was much better than most rehabs.

When Julie and her husband approached Trey at a friend's house, they knew they had one shot at convincing him to get help. They tried not to let the shock show on their faces when they saw his six-foot-one, 115-pound frame, emaciated and trembling. When Trey found out why his parents were there, he started crying and pulled his shirt up over his face, revealing his sunken stomach—he'd never been able to look his mother in the eyes and lie.

"I don't need help," he said, the shirt shielding his face from his mother's gaze.

Somehow, miraculously, they were able to get him to agree to go to rehab on the spot, though Trey politely asked if he could run back inside before heading to detox—he'd left his backpack inside his friend's house, he said. With his parents waiting outside, Trey smoked heroin one last time. Then he walked out the door and joined them.

That was the thing about Trey: he was so charming that you just wanted to believe him. But ever since he was little, he'd been a pathological liar. Julie had first discovered this about her son in the first grade, when a friend accused him of stealing a stack of Pokemon cards during a play date. When Julie had confronted Trey, he'd avoided her gaze and constructed an elaborate story denying the accusation and had kept the ruse going even later that night, when Julie roused him at midnight in an attempt to startle the truth out of him. She finally marched into his classroom at school the next day, yanked him out of class, and demanded that he hand over the stolen cards. When Trey reluctantly produced them, it was a turning point for Julie: her child was both incredibly smart and incredibly deceitful.

A few years after the Pokemon incident, Julie discovered that Trey, now in fourth grade, had swiped candy from the counter at the local Starbucks. As a frequent customer, she knew the manager well, and she enlisted his help in what she hoped would be a learning experience for her son. She brought Trey to the store and made him confess and apologize to the manager, who made the situation seem more serious by telling Trey that he could go to jail for such an offense. Julie watched Trey's eyes widen and hoped that the lesson sank in: stealing and lying were wrong.

Unfortunately, Trey seemed to understand that, but his sticky-finger habit continued. And as he grew older, it became even more apparent that his mind worked differently than most kids'. Though both his older and younger sister were focused and well adjusted, Trey was the opposite. He was scattered and disorganized, and he often resorted to clownish antics to hide his low self-esteem. In his early teens, he was diagnosed with attention deficit hyperactivity disorder and began a regimen of Adderall. The medication seemed to work, but Trey hated it because it made him irritable and took away his appetite.

"It makes me not me," he had told Julie.

Julie wasn't exactly sure when painkillers had entered the picture. All she knew was that the downward spiral happened quickly. She was no longer the mother, the authoritative figure; she was the pawn. It felt like playing a video game: installing monitoring software on Trey's computer, putting a tracking device on his car, buying home drug tests in bulk at Costco without realizing Trey was still getting loaded every day—he was just buying synthetic urine to thwart her detective work. Julie would pull Trey close to her when he came home, hugging him in order to smell his hair and perhaps detect the drugs.

"I had no control from day one," she says. "I just thought I did."

It was on Mother's Day last year that Julie finally realized how out of control everything had become. The entire family was gathering for brunch at a restaurant in Dana Point when she received the text from Trey: "I'm so sorry, Mom, but I'm not going to make it." Within a few days, he'd sold his car and headed off to Hawaii, where his drug use escalated. When he finally came home at the end of the summer, he didn't even call his parents—he had a friend pick him up from the airport and then went on a three-week heroin bender. That was when Trey's friend Sam had called Julie about the heroin. She hadn't wanted to believe him, but she was forced to: Sam said Trey had done heroin right in front of him, and that was all Julie needed to crush any sense of denial about the trouble her son was in.

Sometimes, Julie feels like she has dreamed the past nine months of Trey's sobriety. Compared with the nightmare of the preceding years, it feels almost too good to be true. On Mother's Day this year, she was overwhelmed by the heartwarming speech Trey gave during visiting day, about the many things a child owes to his mother. His words washed over her, encompassing and tender—and such a far cry from his words the year before. Then, she had been so angry with Trey, the addict who just didn't get it, who refused to get clean for her. Now she is proud of her son, the way he is learning to live life in a healthy way despite its obstacles. The way he looks people in the eye and extends his hand. The way he is trying so hard at sobriety, for himself, for his mother, and for their whole family, even though she knows it is the most challenging thing he has ever done.

And Julie knows she is lucky. So many others, like Brady, have died. Maybe soon she will find a way to tell Trey about his friend, to let go of the immobilizing fear that makes her want to keep everything stable and positive. She has had so little control for so long, and she dreads being the bearer of news that could throw Trey off track and launch the nightmare once again.

"We are all just trying our best," she says.

25 | MAKE IT NOT SO

PERCHED ON A sticky leather bar stool, I fidget nervously, wishing I were alone. It is unlikely that the only other patron in this dive bar, a grizzled gentleman reeking of freshly smoked marijuana, will notice anything, but I still feel oddly watched.

I am debating whether or not to delete Pat's number from my cell phone. I sit and stare at the wall, at my hands, at anything but my phone. I am thinking of the punch to my stomach every time I come across his number. It no longer works; Pat's phone has been thrown away, and he no longer exists, so there is every practical reason in the world to erase the number assigned to "Bunny."

And yet I hesitate.

I had called Pat from this same sticky bar stool a few weeks after his San Diego overdose. Ben and I were planning on hosting an after-party following our wedding reception at a nearby restaurant, and we'd come here to scout the scene. As Ben reviewed the jukebox selection, I told Pat about a recent nightmare in which he'd committed suicide by drinking too much red wine. We had laughed in the sickening way that you laugh when things aren't really funny, because they're not true but could be. We both knew that even though his drug of choice wasn't alcohol, he had flirted with death in other ways. I'd stared down into my own glass of dark liquid, racked by waves of guilt: for imbibing when my brother was struggling so agonizingly with substance abuse, for being so utterly unable to help him or relate to him or get through to him.

Then his phone had died, and I was left on the bar stool in abrupt silence, his last words echoing in my head: "I can't believe you're getting married, Ern, it's so awesome!"

In the blurred weeks that followed his death, I would stare at my phone and hope that "Bunny" would appear. I scrolled through my contacts and missed calls, searching for his digital ghost, replaying his voice mails over and over. I even found Pat's phone, buried in one of the boxes in Mom's garage. Although it had been disconnected soon after he died, I called it repeatedly. I'm mostly a skeptic, but part of me is a dreamer: I imagined that instead of that tinny computerized voice telling me the number was no longer in service, it would ring. Then there would be a nearly imperceptible click. Then him. Of course that never happened.

Now I sit again on the bar stool, thinking of Pat, while the stoned gentleman looks on. The basic tasks of life, impossible in those first grief-clouded days, have become bearable: brushing my teeth. Making the coffee. Walking the dog. But I can't delete Pat from my phone.

Deleting Pat means that I go forward without him. Deleting Pat means we won't grow old together. Deleting Pat means he is really gone.

Finally, I push the button. Deleted. I look over my shoulder furtively, like I have committed a sin. It feels wrong because I don't want to comply with this reality.

Or maybe I balk because I feel like Pat is watching me from wherever he is. I want to tell him just how much I don't want to let him go.

✖

I HAVE STARTED seeing Pat everywhere by the time summer hits. Although it has been four months, his death has not sunk in.

One day I see him coming toward me while I'm jogging with the dog in Golden Gate Park. The afternoon sun is setting in the west, illuminating the sweat that seeps down my eyelids and blinding me in flashes through the dangling arms of the eucalyptus trees.

Because of the sweat and the sunspots, I can't see him very clearly at first. I can tell that he's on a skateboard and that he is blond. There's a whole group with him, teenage kids wearing Converse shoes and shabby T-shirts, barreling through the park. The dog is terrified of skateboards and starts to strain at the leash. Although I'm running and the dog is pulling, my feet suddenly feel like they're pounding the pavement backward. The pit sucks me down, spiraling. My throat closes.

"It's not Pat," I say to myself desperately. "It's not Pat. It's not Pat."

Rationally, I understand this. But I want it to be him. I begin to imagine the possibilities: it's one year ago, and he has made an unannounced trip back home. It's three years ago, before he dropped out of the private high school in the city, and these are his new friends. It's five years ago, and he has cut middle school to escape suburbia, to find a better skate run. It's ten years ago, and he's here visiting me at my first apartment, before we head to the Mission for burritos.

The kid bolts toward me, surrounded by minions. He's obviously the leader, because he is the best, poised on the moving board with his hips slung forward and his arms dangling back. The resemblance to Pat is staggering. His slouch, the set of his jaw, his dusty blond mop and his dark eyebrows. I can't see his eyes; mine are full of stinging tears. He's coming closer and closer and closer, and I hate him and I love him and I want to hit him and embrace him and feel the warmth of his cheek. He is right there: I could touch him. I could hold him. I could kill him.

"Cute dog," the kid says, and he is gone.

I choke and stumble. He looked so real. Fumbling with the leash and my feet, I make my way into a shaded glen with a steep hill. I climb it, heaving. The sobs clog in my throat, a polluted mass that can't be expectorated. I am not an irrational person, but I find it especially cruel that this kid decided to skate through the park on a Wednesday afternoon, looking like Pat, and remark on my dog.

I look skyward, searching for some sign of him. There is none. I wipe my nose and turn up the music in my ears. I want to fall into the ground and never get up.

I will myself to think terrible thoughts about Pat: I want to hate him. I want to look down on him. I want to hurt him. But just as easily, I could love him. I would give anything to hear his voice again. To hear him calling me "Ern." To see his stupid grin and envy him as he jumps off the precipice of some phenomenal cliff, unfazed by heights, fearing nothing, the abyss below him paling in comparison to the unfathomable, peaceful sky.

✖

LATER THAT EVENING, there is a timid knock on the door. Our across-the-street neighbor, a ragged man who appears to live in his mother's garage, has a request. He wants to borrow $15—only $15, nothing more. He'll pay it back tomorrow; he'll even give us his cell phone as collateral. We see his desperation, the itch in his eyes, but we gently refuse. He back-steps quickly into the night, apologizing, moving on.

I see my brother in him now, so it is difficult to say no. I couldn't draw the line with Pat, and drawing it now with a near-stranger seems silly. But I can't do something that would further this man's path of destruction.

Then again, I am doing nothing to actively help him. Nor am I doing anything to help the swarms of street kids lingering under the flaps of their military-style tents in the shady glen, their faces slack, their hands outstretched. Or the ones that have fallen even further, the stick figures stumbling along city streets, alive but also dead.

A wormhole happens. It can be anything: one of these sorry wanderers, an object Pat once touched, a song he hated but put on a mix tape for me anyway because he knew I loved it, a shift in the wind, someone's smile. All of it makes me tumble back to the day he died.

"In the space between what we didn't say, my stupid hope and his sickness flourished," Thomas Lynch writes of his addicted son. "I wanted to remember him the way he was. And wanting it so bad, I welcomed him, half-hoping some of the lost months of his lost years would return. But they are gone."

The realization of my denial, my unwillingness to face the truth of Pat's addiction, sits on my shoulder and taunts me. I beg it to stop; I'll give it anything it wants. It is a child's wishing game, like when I was four years old and plagued with jealousy after my sister was born: her big blue eyes, her beautiful name, her status as the baby of the family at the time. I wrote imploring letters to the authorities—Santa Claus, the Tooth Fairy, the Easter Bunny—to not leave me any gifts. To please just make it so that when I woke up, I would be Caitlin and she would be me. My petitions went unanswered, and I was left to stew in the sour juices of my reality: Mousy brown hair. A dumb name. Freckles.

Now I throw my prayers to the universe, to an unknown God, with the same childlike zeal. *Please just make it so that those lost years will return.*

Nothing happens.

✖

IN THE DREAM, Pat calls me from a pay phone at a gas station. He has been on a run for weeks, and I've been so worried.

"I'm a heroin addict, Ern," he admits. I tell him I know.

"I love you whether you're a heroin addict or a saint," I say. "I can't lose you. You are my sweet baby, my Bunny."

I start to cry, and Pat becomes upset. He says he needs a hit, and I beg him not to, but he says he has to, so I wait on the other end of the line while he shoots up.

"Please come back to San Francisco," I say when he returns to the phone.

"No, never again," he says. "No more rain, no more fog, no more broken-hearted people."

"Aren't there broken-hearted people everywhere?" I say, but he doesn't respond.

"I want to come see you," I say. "Please, just let me see you."

He finally agrees and tells me to meet him in the parking lot behind our old middle school, at 3:00 AM a week from now.

I wait for a week, then go to the parking lot. When I arrive, there is a crowd of people and an ambulance.

"There was an accident," says one of the bystanders. "It was Pat. He's dead."

I run into the science classroom, full of posters of the periodic table, frogs in jars, a plastic model of the human skeleton. Pat lies on one of the Formica lab tables; he has already been embalmed and prepared for the casket. I touch his skin gingerly, terrified the makeup will rub off and the seams along his head will unzip, causing his insides to burst out.

He opens his eyes suddenly and says, "I told you so."

I lurch awake. I look at the clock: 3:00 AM.

It is always 3:00 AM when I dream of Pat. I think back to the autopsy report: "Decedent reportedly smoked heroin with his girlfriend at about 0130 hours; they subsequently watched television, going to bed in separate rooms at about 0300 hours."

Three o'clock in the morning: a still, silent time when the world is supposed to be asleep. I rustle out from under the covers and grope my way to the door, trying to open and close it softly, but it creaks. I walk to the kitchen and pour a glass of water, the quiet unmoving trees shining in the moonlight. I remember what the autopsy said next:

"At about 0920 hours, decedent's bedroom door was found locked. With no response at the door, the family used a tool to allow access into the bedroom; upon entry, decedent was discovered down on the floor with an uncapped syringe nearby. Responding Burbank PD/Engine 016 paramedics pronounced decedent at scene at 1013 hours."

I wish for the morning, for it not to be 3:00 AM when Pat is dying. At least in the morning, he will already be dead, his suffering over, his spirit gone.

26 | TOO LATE

WHENEVER THE DOCTOR hears the familiar sound of screeching tires outside the wide glass windows of the emergency department, he has the same disheartening thought: *Our kids are dying. Here comes another one.*

By now, the doctor has become so accustomed to the sound that it registers in his mind as something completely normal—the ringing of a doorbell, say, or the dog's bark. At Mission Hospital in Mission Viejo, the sound is so frequent that he and his colleagues refer to it as a "positive screech sign." A car pulls up to the roundabout, a back door opens, and a body is pushed onto the hospital's walkway. The door slams shut, and the car screeches away, driven by someone with enough clarity to seek medical help for a friend but not enough courage to face the authorities and potentially get in trouble for drugs. (In January 2013, California became the tenth state to implement a so-called Good Samaritan overdose fatality prevention law—designed to encourage people to seek help for overdose victims by providing limited protection from arrest, charge and prosecution—but many still fear repercussions.) The nurses come out and load the body onto a gurney, and the doctor begins to work.

Over the past few years, the doctor has seen a marked increase in heroin use accompanying the dramatic rise in prescription opioid abuse among young people in Orange County, where the painkiller epidemic is particularly pronounced. When OxyContin was reformulated in 2010, some addicts began turning to other powerful painkillers instead: that year, fifteen people younger than twenty-six died of Opana overdoses, up from three deaths that were attributed to Opana in 2009. Others transitioned to heroin, which accounted for nearly 40 percent of accidental overdoses in that age group in 2011, as compared to 25 percent in 2007.[61]

Doctors who practice emergency medicine generally go into the field for a reason: they live for these kinds of cases, in which patients are straddling the line between life and death and there are only minutes or seconds to decide what to do. The doctor doesn't fear such situations; he knows that his adrenaline, training, good sense, and years of experience will kick in to guide him. He also knows that sometimes, for some reason, everything is on his side and seems to work out, while other times there's not much he can do. The problem is that often, by the time he sees the screech-sign patients, the drugs—most often heroin, prescription opiates, benzodiazepines, or some combination of all three—have already taken over. They're already in respiratory arrest or have suffered irreversible brain damage. It's too late.

As a survival mechanism, the doctor has to desensitize to a point. Most of the time, he doesn't remember the faces or identities of the young overdose victims who come through his doors, their heads thrown back, their abdomens thrusting up and down, their eyes rolled so far skyward that only the whites are visible. But he tries to treat them with respect and dignity, to see them for who they are beyond their drug use: athletes, cheerleaders, straight-A students. Somebody's brother or sister, somebody's child.

Not everybody in the hospital sees them that way. In one recent case, the doctor recalls, the paramedics dropped off a young man who was near death—he was cyanotic and was quickly losing brain function. Though the doctor suspected an overdose, it was unclear if drugs were involved or if the cause of his distress was something like a brain hemorrhage or an aneurism, so a toxicology screen was sent up to the lab as the young man was stabilized. But before the results came back, an internist discovered a square of blackened foil in the young man's pocket: the telltale sign of a heroin user.

"Well, at least if he dies, it's his fault," the internist said offhandedly. The remark sticks with the doctor even today.

"This internist is a wonderful person, and a tremendous doctor," he says. "But it's so disturbing to me that, as a physician, she found that comment acceptable. It was the opposite of compassion. It was judgment."

So the doctor tries not to judge his screech-sign patients as he navigates through the labyrinth of decisions, each one with the possibility of saving, or failing to save, a life: can a vein be found for IV insertion, or have the patient's veins collapsed due to intravenous drug use? Can endotracheal intubation be performed and a breathing tube placed to administer paralytic drugs to stop possible thrashing due to hypoxia? Is the patient aspirating on vomit or other fluids? Can the patient be oxygenated with a bag, then a ventilator? Does an EKG reveal evidence of acute dysrhythmia?

On the good days, the doctor is able to save these kids, like the young man with the burned foil in his pocket, who was eventually transferred to the ICU to recover. The doctor went to visit him in his new room, where his parents and brother had rushed to be by his side.

"I hope you'll live a long and healthy life," the doctor told the young patient. "I'm going to be honest with you—I'm astonished you survived. I was certain you wouldn't make it."

Everyone in the room cried as the young man hugged the doctor and promised he'd never put himself or his family through that situation again. The doctor wanted to believe him, but he wasn't born yesterday: all the time, he saw repeat patients cycle in and out of the hospital's doors, young kids—like this one—who started abusing painkillers in their early teens and had been treated for multiple overdoses by the time they were in their twenties, after they had moved on to heroin.

On the bad days, the doctor isn't so lucky. On those days, he has to have a much different conversation, as he did recently with the parents of another screech-sign patient—also a young man—whom he and his team had attempted to resuscitate for over an hour. His parents, who had arrived at the hospital and were in the room as the team worked, whispered encouragements to their son: "You can make it. We love you. Please don't die." A pulse and heartbeat were finally restored, but the doctor knew it was pointless. There were no brain waves, no pupil activity. He had to explain to the parents the pros and cons of continuing care for their child.

Four days later, after the parents took their son off life support, they came back to the ER to thank the doctor for taking the time to explain everything to them so thoroughly and compassionately. They had made the decision to donate their son's cartilage, corneas, bones, and skin and felt that at least some good would come from his death.

These are the faces that chip away at the doctor's survival mechanism. The ones for whom it is too late.

✖

ABBY STAYS AT the hospital all night long, holding her son's hand. For nearly seven days, Brady has been in a coma, and Abby knows it is time to make a decision.

Abby is exhausted; she has barely slept since Brady's overdose. When she'd left for England a week ago to visit her eighty-two-year-old mother, Brady was safely settled in his latest treatment center and had fifty-four days sober. The next thing Abby knew, a friend was calling her about a disturbing post she'd seen on Facebook: Brady was in a coma. All in all, it had taken Abby forty-eight hours to get herself back to the

United States; the entire flight home, she hadn't known whether her son would be alive or dead when the plane landed.

At first the doctors had left open the possibility of hope, though they told Abby and her husband that it was impossible to predict Brady's prognosis. After all, no one knew how long he'd been unconscious, passed out in the backseat of a car in the parking lot of a local shopping center. The kid he'd shot heroin with had finally shouted for help, and a nurse had come running out of the bank nearby. She'd done chest compressions on Brady, who was blue and had no heartbeat, while instructing another young man, a bystander, on how to give mouth-to-mouth resuscitation. By the time the paramedics arrived, Brady's pulse had returned faintly.

Over the last four days, the doctors had tried everything to save him, preserving his body in order to give his brain a chance to recover. "Stay positive," they said to Abby, her husband, Brady's younger brother Jeff, and Brady's best friend Catherine as the family gathered in a circle around Brady's bed, searching his face for signs of life. Brady could hear them, the doctors claimed, so they talked to him as they held his hand, and sometimes they felt a faint grasp back.

When they shouted at Brady to open his eyes, he could do it. But there was no recognition, no connection, only a blank stare as he gazed just past their shoulders, crying.

Brady started having seizures, which steadily worsened. An MRI showed a devastating amount of brain damage, and at one point he coded and had to be revived. His lungs were full of fluid, and he was struggling on the ventilator. He began yawning and making guttural noises, then posturing: his arms and legs went rigid and turned inward, and he arched his head back and clenched his teeth. Tears rolled down his cheeks.

Now Abby touches the trails left behind by his tears. She thinks back
to Brady as a toddler, during the early years, when they were still living
in London. Bringing him to the States was a death sentence, she thinks.
Maybe if they hadn't moved here, he wouldn't have had such easy access
to the painkillers that took over his life: Vicodin, Xanax, OxyContin. If
he hadn't become hooked on the painkillers, maybe he wouldn't have
said yes when a high school friend—the same high school friend, ironi-
cally, who later abandoned him in the parking lot to die—offered to
show him how to smoke heroin for a cheaper high. If he hadn't gotten
wrapped up in smoking heroin, maybe he wouldn't have had to go to
rehab, where he'd met the young woman who'd introduced him to the
needle. And if he hadn't become an IV drug user, maybe he wouldn't be
lying here now, a shell of the lovely boy he once was—her lovely boy.
Her brilliant, loving, free-spirited, articulate twenty-year-old boy, who
can no longer speak, move, see, or breathe.

A nurse who has been on duty for much of the duration of Brady's
coma comes into the room while Abby is sitting with her son. The nurse,
who sees many young overdose victims in this state, cries with Abby,
saying, "You don't understand what it's like to keep somebody alive like
this." Brady is struggling, and it is excruciating. All night long, Abby
prays that her son will die so that his suffering will end and she won't
have to make the decision before her.

Abby wants something beautiful for her son—not this. Brady would
want the suffering to end and the beauty to begin. She feels distinctly, as if
Brady is whispering in her ear, that someday, something good will come
of this loss. She hears him telling her that a beautiful story will unfold.

By morning, Abby knows what she must tell her family: they can't
keep Brady alive.

After Brady is taken off the machines, he is given his last rites. Then
the family sits with him, talks with him, smoothes down his hair. For

six hours straight, his brother holds Brady's hand, falling asleep on the crumpled white sheets. And just like Brady said, it is beautiful, because the room is full of love.

"You can go," Abby tells Brady.

At 3:15 PM on October 18, 2012, Brady goes.

27 | THE GOD STORY

"HEY YOU!!"

The cartoonish character, a bespectacled, spiky-haired boy with three eyes and a lolling tongue, sits on a skateboard and points his finger at me from the crumpled sheet of binder paper, torn from Pat's school notebook.

> Yes you. The extremely beautiful, awesome, nice, excellent, utterly cool, hip, best, cutest, well-dressed, good mannered, awesome, cool, cool, cool, person I can call, talkative (in a good way) positively excellent, adventurous, great tasted, insuperable, smart, intellective, great, nice, coooooooooool x infinity person. I LOVE YOU!!!
>
> Love
> Pat
>
> P.S. Just so you know, "insuperable" means "impossible to overcome." In other words, you are strong!! I love you!

It is this kind of thing that makes me want to believe in God, and here is why: if God exists, then the person who wrote this note is safe, because God keeps all good people safe, and the writer of this note—Pat—is clearly good.

As a child, God was always told to me as a beautiful story. Heaven was a glittering wilderness in the sky, an infinite ocean of clouds like the ones you see from an airplane when it rises above the horizon. If you were good, when you died you got to go live there forever with the angels and rainbows and fluttering doves.

I still want to believe that story. I consider other compelling alternatives: reincarnation, spirits existing in another realm of consciousness, the notion I read in a book once that "perhaps our lives spread out around us like a fan and we can only know one life, but by mistake sense others." But the God story of my childhood is the one I wish I could believe, because it is the better story, the best story. I know that Pat was good, and if God exists, then Pat is with God, and Pat is still Pat, and there is the chance that I will see him again.

Jen, a childhood friend of Pat's whose family has been close to ours for years, writes me a letter: "I pray for you every day and have faith that you will be brought joy when you think of all the memories. I know you aren't strongly affiliated to religion, but I truly believe in God's power to heal the broken-hearted and bind our wounds."

If only I could believe. Believing in the story of God would not only mean that Pat is safe but that there was a reason for his death, some divine plan that would make sense out of all the chaos. If only I could trust that a higher being would heal the pain, like ripples of sand being smoothed by an unseen hand.

I wish so deeply that I could believe these things.

I do feel joy, as Jen hopes, when I think of the memories. But the warm rush is tinged with shadows, a hungry hollowness. I remember Jen's eulogy at Pat's funeral, how out of place the sweetness seemed as Pat lay there in the casket. I had been unable to look up at her as she spoke. Instead, I stared down at the black heels of my shoes, which I hooked onto the pew below me, the light from the stained-glass windows reflected in the patent leather. In my hands, I held the program open to the page of pictures of Pat through the years: Hiding in a dresser drawer. Wearing a suit and tie. Pole vaulting. Dancing with Cait. Wearing two backpacks, one on the front and one on the back, for a camping trip. Playing with the dog. Playing the guitar. Laughing, hugging, smiling.

The Pat in these pictures matched the Pat in Jen's speech. "I was in preschool and my mom was going over to her friend's house to quilt," she had said.

I tagged along and met Pat. Our first encounter was that of two outgoing, obnoxious little kids who started a game of jump rope with the sewing machine cord, which led to a game of pretend. We imagined we were orphaned kitties performing in a circus, mostly for Pat's benefit so he could do flips off the front porch. And for the next decade or so, we were pretending to be kitties, or puppies, or bunnies, but always something together, something fun.

The times when Pat would come over to play were always the best, and we eventually invented a game, creatively titled The Game. It was an Indians-and-cowboys-themed adventure in which the older boys, Brian and my brother Justin, would go off to war while my sister Juliann would keep Pat and I at home, usually locked into the rabbit hutch my dad built in the backyard. Once we tired of The Game, we would Rollerblade down to the elementary school, or play laser tag around the cottonwood tree in Pat's backyard.

The greatest vacations I ever had were with Pat. There was the surprise trip to Disneyland during which we ate breakfast with the characters from Pinocchio, who talked to Pat by writing in the sugar he spilled on the table. And the summers and winters at the Daly cabin: eating Charleston Chews by the pool, sledding in the snow, and putting on plays for the adults—the most memorable one being a reenactment of the Lion King in which I was Nala and Pat was, of course, baby Simba. That was how it always was with Pat: the baby lion cub everyone adored.

At that point, I remember, Jen had started to cry.

"Pat, I keep trying to imagine what I would say to you if you were here right now," she finally said. "It's hard to say goodbye. Whether it was a weekend sleepover with waffles in the morning, or my dad explaining to you and I how our new electric toothbrush worked, or you and Juliann arguing over who got to sled down the hill first, Pat, you always knew you were one of us, one of the kids, our brother."

The Pat in the casket didn't match Jen's description. How was it possible that such sweetness had ended in such sorrow?

The juxtaposition of all the goodness in Pat with all the bad makes no sense to me—plus it fumbles the way the God story plays out. I wish that the goodness had never existed; if he'd been bad from the start, his descent wouldn't have felt so wrong, and maybe then I'd be able to square all this away in my head. Maybe then the concepts of peace and healing and God wouldn't feel like such a stretch, the memories wouldn't sting so much.

Another friend of mine writes to me: "Love is stronger than death, even though it can't stop death from happening. But no matter how hard death tries, it can't separate people from love. It can't take away our memories either. In the end, life is stronger than death." She adds, "remember the love and the memories, and be hopeful that though you feel such grief, once again you will be able to make more wonderful memories and Pat will be with you, watching from above, sharing in all of those too."

I can't bring myself to believe in God just yet, but I become desperate to bring myself to at least believe that Pat still exists somewhere. Take one baby step forward. All the rationalizations and justifications that swim around in my head when pondering God's existence are getting me nowhere; leaving God as an unanswered question allows me to think in more simple terms: where is Pat now?

"He is with you," says an energy reader. Specifically, she says, he is hanging out on the left side of my body, down by my knee, tugging on my sleeve as if he were a needy child. According to her, he is battling a great depression, and one of the reasons I haven't been feeling his presence is because he has been working through his guilt: "He is still a karmic mess," is the way she puts it. When he heals himself, he'll get in touch with me, she says.

"He is waiting for you," says a psychic. Our souls are very close, she says, because we were together in a past life, and there was some sort of pact, a beautiful sacrifice that was made. It is time to break that pact, she says.

"He is hovering over you, seeking forgiveness," says a medium. "He is sorry he couldn't stay. He couldn't get free from the drug, or the girl, and he says it wasn't your fault. It wasn't anyone's fault but his own."

But, like the God story, these are all just stories too. Sometimes I like to let myself believe them, to pretend for a little while that I feel peace. Just for one moment, I can ignore the question that smolders faintly in the back of my mind, a charcoal-colored ember that illuminates when blown upon: five months ago Pat was here, and now he is not.

How can this be?

PART IV

DEPRESSION

I BURIED MYSELF THAT WARM JUNE DAY.
IT WAS ME THOSE GARDENERS LOWERED
ON SQUEAKING STRAPS INTO THAT HOT
DRY HOLE, CURIOUS NEIGHBORHOOD
CHILDREN LOOKING DOWN IN AT ME,
EVERYONE STILLED, WIND RUSTLING
THE OAKS. IT WAS ME OVER WHOM WE
SLID THAT HEAVY SLAB, MORE THAN
I CAN LIFT. IT WAS ME ON WHOM WE
SHOVELED DIRT. IT WAS ME WE LEFT
BEHIND, AFTER READING PSALMS.

—NICHOLAS WOLTERSTORFF, *LAMENT FOR A SON*

28 | BLACK TEARS

THE BATHROOM TILES are hard against my skin. I am ten and you are one. The damp air smells like bubblegum. You smash your fists against the water and you are happy, but then you start to cry. I try to cheer you up by jiggling your hands back and forth, but I am too rough and you just cry more. You cry even after Mom takes you out of the bath, even after your pajamas, even after your bottle. You cry so long into the night that Mom takes you to the doctor and he says I dislocated your elbow. Then I cry too, but I don't get in trouble because I didn't mean to hurt you, and you are smiling again.

The sun and colors are bright and loud. I am nineteen and you are nine. It is Christmas and we are in Disneyland and everything is hollow and raw. We are far away from the vacant wheelchair and abandoned bedpans and the striped bathrobe hanging inside Dad's closet. You are spinning in oversized teacups and shouting down Splash Mountain and eating cotton candy, and I think of everything you have seen. Your cheeks are flushed with heat and sugar, and you grab my hand, begging me to join you, "one more time," you say, "one more time."

From downstairs I hear the crash. I am twenty and you are ten. I run up the carpeted stairs of the cabin. It is July and blisteringly hot. You are standing at the top of the stairs next to a big hole in the wall where your skateboard has pierced the plaster. You are crying and Mom is yelling, and she cancels your birthday party at the pool because you rode your skateboard in the house for the hundredth time after she told you not to, and she will take you to the hardware store to get supplies, and you will spend the afternoon fixing the wall instead of swimming and eating cake, and you are begging for forgiveness and she says no.

In the mornings you ride the bus to school. I am twenty-five and you are fifteen. You hate the private school it takes you to, but you'd ride the bus all day if you could. You strike up conversations with the bums, the old ladies, the alcoholics, the disabled adults from the assisted living center, the war vets. You even talk to the rat-haired woman, the one we're all scared of, who walks the streets wearing only an oversize T-shirt, mumbling about prophecies. "She's really nice," you say cheerfully, and I think of you coming home from kindergarten crying because the other kids were teasing your friend with Down syndrome and you had asked, "Why?"

You are fading in and out. I am twenty-seven and you are seventeen. You are applying for summer jobs at Pizza Hut, Baskin-Robbins, the taqueria downtown. You ask me to help you fill out the applications because you can't remember anything. You sit next to me at the computer and laugh when I poke fun at your forgetfulness. You don't know your Social Security number, your reference's address, your place of birth, and is it because you're seventeen or is it because you are giggling and buzzing and strange and your eyes are twitching and I want to ask you what you are on but I'm too scared, so I say we'll finish later and watch as you walk sideways out of the room.

Sometimes when I see you, I think you are fine. I am twenty-nine and you are nineteen. When you smile, I forget the things that make me worry about you. I don't know how fast you are falling. I don't know that you are writing alone in your room. I don't know that you write:

I don't give a damn
If I live or die

I'm gonna get
Drunk get high

Hit it one more time
One more to numb the pain
Who knows what happens next
Just the black tears running down the foil

Last time, last call, late night
Turned to early afternoon
Every day turns to every week
Off and on turns to constant electrocution

Black tears, running down the foil
Since I cried when my father died
Small bumps enclosing my body
Every morning around sunrise

My chest explodes with my adrenaline
When's the time to stop
Who decides what I do with my life
Not me

My father
My lips form words to curse
My father, my lips, my chest, my body
Scratch away the skin

Twenty scars to count the years
The guilt, anger, and fear
Terror and my brain are the same
I'm not alive, I just feel this way

One thing that I really know
It feels so good, when I let go
Every day just to numb the pain
I kick back and I live away
And those black tears keep running down the foil

I try to imagine you at peace, nestled in the violent and smoky sky. I am thirty and you are gone. I run underneath this sky, cursing your black tears and wondering where you are. My feet pound out a rhythm on the rough waves of the pavement and seem to disconnect from my body, taking me nowhere. There are always so many people out under this sky, running, hundreds of people with their legs and arms moving in the very same way, their breath swarming on the cold wind, and none of them are you. At night, in my dreams, I run too, searching for you among the passing faces. The flashing neon signs hit the corners of my peripheral vision and give me vertigo, but I keep running, furiously, endlessly. A tidal wave is behind me, roaring high above my head, going much faster than I am or could ever hope to, and I know it will overtake me, but still I look for you. People float by me in the flooding waters, some of them screaming and flailing their arms, others mute. I recognize friends, coworkers, people I passed by on the street at midnight on a Tuesday: none of them are you. I am floating too, getting caught up in whirlpools of slime and debris, now being propelled uncontrollably toward a giant, yawning waterfall.

✖

I WAKE UP again and run. I run, and run, and run, and still you are gone.

29 | YOU WITHOUT ME

"I REMEMBER THE first days of our relationship. I remember dreaming that I could make you mine forever. Looking back and seeing my dreams coming true is a wonderful thing."

Catherine traces the words Brady wrote to her with her finger. The sun, setting through the trees in the park, reminds her of a time when he sat beside her on this bench, alive. She remembers dreaming that she could make Brady hers forever too.

That was before she lost him, before he slipped, inch by inch, into addiction. She thinks of the words of a song by Joy Division, one of Brady's favorite bands: "I tried to get to you." The words that are now tattooed on the arm of another young man, the one who'd helped the nurse who ran out of the bank and tried desperately to pump life back into Brady's body. Brady changed that young man's life forever, as he changed so many other lives.

Catherine doesn't come here much anymore. Somewhere along the way, Florence Joyner Park in Mission Viejo had become their haven, mostly because it was roughly halfway between their two houses, but also because they loved it, and loved being in it together. They called it Flo-Jo Park for short. After school, Brady would drive Catherine there in his truck. They'd park under the wide canopy of trees with purple blossoms shedding in the wind, roll the windows down, and listen to music. Sometimes they'd walk along the winding stone pathway, past the ebbing shouts of children on the play structure, onward toward to the fountain, circled by neatly trimmed hedges. Or they'd cross the small wooden footbridge into the flower garden, where they'd sit on the bench where Catherine sits now.

Today she reads through Brady's journals, found by his mom after Brady died and given to Catherine. She reads them today without crying. She looks up intermittently to gaze into the distance, her eyes faraway and blank, dazed by the impossibility that Brady no longer exists in their little world.

"Where did the happy Brady and Catherine go?" he had written, and she wonders the same thing.

Brady and Catherine were happy once—so happy. They were best friends long before they were a couple, although if they were honest about it, they had been in love with each other all along. They were young and unbroken then, experiencing all their firsts together: neither one of them had ever been in love before and thus had never been hurt before.

"Maybe that's what made it so hard in the end," Catherine says. She stares off into the rosebushes, bathed in the dying light. She recalls one time Brady brought her here practically jumping out of his skin with excitement and nerves.

"Let's walk over to the flowers," he said, and when they got there he pulled a box out of his pocket. Inside was a promise ring.

"I can't wait to marry you and have a life with you," he'd said. "You without me is no life."

Catherine was scared, but she accepted the ring. She decided to give him a shot because she believed he'd never hurt her.

She was wrong, of course, although Brady didn't mean to hurt her. She knows that. But he did. His descent into drugs left her flailing and helpless.

"I need you to trust I will never hurt you," he'd said, but he'd lied.

When Catherine graduated from high school and moved to San Diego for beauty school, Brady came to visit her almost every weekend, and they were solid. It was just the small changes she noticed at first, little things that at the time were easily explained away. Catherine has blurred out many of the pieces, because now that he's gone, she doesn't want to remember the signs she may have missed. There was the bottle of Vicodin she'd been prescribed for a dental procedure that suddenly went empty. Then Brady broke his arm while skateboarding and an ER doctor prescribed OxyContin, and suddenly there was a tiredness to him that didn't go away.

Then the signs became bigger and more disturbing. One day, after Catherine had moved back home, she was lying cradled on Brady's chest in the space between his arm and neck, the place she called her nook. From where she lay, she could see Brady's phone as he held it in his hand, and the text message that came through mentioned something about heroin. Catherine became flustered, but Brady told her he'd tried it only once and was never going to do it again.

That wasn't true. Brady's drug use was spiraling out of control, and soon he couldn't hide it even from the person he wanted to protect most in the world. "Please don't tell Catherine," he'd plead with his mother whenever she found him rocking back and forth in his bedroom, high, but Catherine knew.

She had a theory about life: anything good in life that ends must end badly. Brady hated this theory. "If you lose someone you love, where's the good in that?" Catherine would ask him, and Brady would say emphatically, "You would still have all the memories of the good times, and that would make it all worthwhile."

Catherine did not want the best thing in her life, her relationship with Brady, to end badly. She never wanted to break up with him. But finally, thinking of his theory that the good memories would sustain her, she forced herself to do it. They could be together when he got sober, she told him, and he agreed. There were a series of detoxes and treatment centers, and along with them some fleeting hookups with other girls, which upset Catherine, but then Brady would tell her they meant nothing.

Then he went to a rehab where he got involved with a girl who was an IV heroin user. Prior to meeting her, Brady had snorted and smoked heroin, but now he started using a needle. The pair left the treatment center and began bouncing between motels, doing nothing besides shooting up.

"She gets me in a way you don't understand," he told Catherine, who was infuriated. She just wanted to move on. She couldn't stand watching her best friend go down, but she couldn't do much to help him either. So she continued responding to his texts, whenever they appeared on her phone: "Thank you for always being there for me," he wrote. "You will always be my best friend. All I want is for you to truly be happy, with or without me in your life."

Sometimes Brady seemed to be asking her for help in his texts: "I miss you. I want out. I want to put my life back together. This is all a bad dream, and I need to wake up."

One night he was so high that he couldn't string together a sentence when he called her. His parents had done an intervention, telling him he had three options: rehab, jail, or death.

"I know it's true," he slurred to Catherine. "But I want to know how you are. I just need to know you're happy."

The last time they spoke, Brady was clean, living at a treatment center, and Catherine was relieved he was safe. She could finally breathe.

"I'll spend the rest of my life trying to make up what I've done to you," Brady told her. "I'll never stop trying. I'm never going to leave you again."

The next day, Brady kept calling her, but she didn't pick up—their conversation had felt so good, and she was so emotionally spent that she felt like it would finally be okay to let herself rest for a bit. The horror of the last year felt surreal, like a dream from which she had been struggling to wake up. She decided she would do something healthy for herself and go to an Al-Anon meeting with a friend—but when she showed up at the elementary school where it was scheduled to be held, it turned out the meeting was canceled due to back-to-school night. She and her friend walked to a shopping center across the street, through the very same parking lot where she didn't see Brady, a needle piercing his skin for the last time.

That night, Catherine couldn't sleep. Her mind was disturbingly blank, as if someone had wiped away all her senses, and she was screaming from the inside in a voice no one could hear. She started browsing through Facebook to distract herself from the weird sensation and saw a post that said Brady was in a coma. Panicked, she called the hospital, where a nurse in the ICU was finally put on the line.

"I need to talk with Brady," Catherine said, and the nurse said gently, "Sweetheart, he can't come to the phone."

In the small hospital room, crammed with tubes and machines that beeped and bags of things that dripped, Brady lay unmoving in the bed. Although Catherine, in frustration and fear, had said the words to him many times when he was using—*You're going to die*—she couldn't believe he might die.

She squeezed Brady's limp hand and whispered to him, "I can't live life without my best friend. There is no me without you." She was startled when she thought she felt him squeeze back. Was it their old sign—three squeezes of the hand when they were in public, just to let the other know that you loved them? Or was it just a reflex?

Catherine wondered what it would be like if Brady woke up and was permanently disabled. It would be terrible, she thought, but hadn't Brady always fought against her theory that good things don't end unless they end badly? He would want her to see the positive: that even if he ended up confined to a wheelchair, he would be surrounded by love—and he wouldn't be able to use heroin anymore, so life might actually be easier.

A nurse came in and removed one of the tubes that was keeping Brady sedated to test the strength of his lungs and to determine whether the drugs were the reason he wasn't waking up. In a while, she said, Brady's body might start to panic, and they shouldn't be alarmed if his limbs started flailing. Catherine hoped this meant he'd be okay.

She waited with the rest of Brady's family.

As the minutes and hours passed, things became hazy and confusing. The internist apparently believed there was hope in the fact that Brady was opening his eyes and making movements, but the neurologist thought the absence of brain activity indicated that Brady wouldn't recover. Then it was apparently determined that if there was a chance for Brady to come out of it, he'd wake up within seventy-two hours, and Catherine wanted to tell them that Brady was notoriously late; what if he needed more time? But then it was apparently determined that he was not going to come out of it, and then the tubes were pulled out, and then the machines stopped beeping, and then the bags stopped dripping, and then came the long hours of Brady struggling and lurching and rasping, and then came the final throes, the death rattle racking his chest, and then, apparently, Brady died.

When it was Catherine's turn to say goodbye, she shut all the curtains and crawled into the bed next to Brady, nestling herself in her nook. A man came in and started unplugging all the machines and wheeling them out of the room. For the first time, Catherine felt that Brady was really gone, that the body she was snuggled against was just a shell. She held Brady's hand in her own, touching his nails, stroking the tiny hairs on his wrist, thinking to herself: *This is the last time in my whole life I will have this. I will never be able to hold his hand again.*

She wanted to ask if they could cut off his arm and give it to her, so that she could still have his hand to hold.

She wanted one of two things to happen: to stay in this moment forever, or to no longer be twenty-two. To fast-forward through her whole life until the day she was an old woman, ready to die herself. Everything in between now and then seemed too terrifying without Brady by her side.

Or maybe she just wanted to go ahead and die next to him.

Catherine went home and sat in the bathtub. She felt paralyzed, as if even the simplest movements—hand to face, foot to floor—were impossibly complex.

"Do you want to go to dinner?" her mother asked her, and Catherine didn't understand what that meant, to go somewhere, to eat dinner, to move.

To go on with her life.

All of it seems so far away now to Catherine as she sits on the bench. And yet it could have happened yesterday: a part of her still expects to look up from Brady's journals and see him walking toward her down the stone pathway, where an old woman walks a downy white dog, who comes sniffing around Catherine's feet.

"He wants to study too," says the old woman kindly, but Catherine does not respond. Another line in one of the journals has caught her eye. "When you were falling asleep, I was trying to tell you how happy I feel."

Though she knows her whole life is ahead of her, right now she feels like she will never be happy again, now that she is without Brady.

30 | LITTLE BIRD

THE LITTLE BIRD comes to my grandmother's window and weeps. Its tears are white, and it smears them on the glass.

"Hello, Patrick," my grandmother says to the bird. "Happy birthday."

When she was given the news about Pat's death, she laid her head on the kitchen table and sobbed. She hadn't cried like that, she tells me, since our grandfather passed away thirty years ago. It all came out. She cried, and cried, and cried. Her little Patrick was gone.

Then she raised her head and said, "Thank you Lord." *Thank you for taking him early and soon, before he had kids, responsibilities, before life got complicated. Thank you for taking him peacefully, instead of letting him get wrapped up in the streets, having him die a violent death.*

The little bird comes to her window every now and then. It started in the first few weeks after Pat was buried. The same thing had happened after Grandpa died, she says. There was a clock that had to be wound up twice a week, a task that had always been his. The first week after his funeral, on the day the clock was supposed to be wound, a little bird came and pecked at the window. My grandmother said to my uncle, "That's your father, coming to tell me to wind the clock."

Patrick's little bird first appeared at the window above her kitchen sink while her hands were immersed in suds. She wiped them on a dish towel and reached toward the sunlight. She imagined the bird was telling her it was sorry. She accepted the apology. And the bird told her it was safe. It kept coming back. Soon her neighbor noticed it too, saying the bird was impossible to ignore because it pecked noisily at the glass.

As my grandmother tells me this, I look out the kitchen window behind her. I try to imagine the little bird appearing there and saying to it, "Hello, Pat." But the window remains empty.

The desire to believe he isn't gone. The ache to know that death isn't the end. These things can make you crazy.

It is July 15: Pat would have been twenty-one. One year ago, he was here. Now he is not.

For my grandmother, this bird is the story of God. She looks to the little bird and sees Pat, telling her he is at peace. She also believes that God's decision to take Pat was a kind one; Pat's future was grim, and because he died young, we were all spared the heartache sure to come. This is the way she thinks in order to reconcile Pat's death and her faith.

My mother has settled on a different story of God: he is not all-powerful, she has decided, and by accepting this, she can forgive God for not saving Pat and can still keep her faith. And her faith assures her that she will be reunited with Pat and Dad. So she goes to their graves and tries to find comfort in the knowledge that she will one day be together with her loved ones again.

As for myself, I do not know which story to believe, or how to distinguish signs and dreams.

After visiting my grandmother, I head to the Cedar Street house, where everyone else is gathering. On the way there, the Beatles' "Blackbird" comes on the radio, and I wonder if *that* is a sign. I decide it is not.

At the house, we bake Pat birthday cupcakes, not only with extra fudge but with peanut butter and chocolate chips and butterscotch chips and mini-marshmallows and caramel drizzle. It makes us all sick, but his taste for sugar was something we can laugh about. We drive to the cemetery and put the cupcakes on his grave, where they quickly melt in the sun. The heat feels inescapable, the same way it did on the day Pat was born twenty-one years ago, on the hottest day of the year.

"I can't remember him the way he was. I can only see him in his coffin," my sister says to me as we leave, and I find I am suffering from the same amnesia. His face floats before me, frozen and emotionless, forced into place by the mortician's hand, little boy nowhere to be found.

I remember my sister coming to me after Pat died, frantic, sobbing, wanting to know why his body was smashed up against the door, whether he had fallen in pain or, even worse, if he had been in pain when he died.

"There was no pain," I had told her. "He just fell asleep and slowly slipped away." It was, and remains, the only comforting thing I have to say about Pat's death.

We decide to hike through the woods near the cemetery to escape the heat. For awhile, we share some of the better memories of Pat, before his fall. Pat reading a Christmas story about the quick-running Gingerbread Man, whom he began to impersonate, running off as he called to us behind him, "Run, run, as fast as you can, you can't catch me, I'm the Gingerbread Patrick!" Playing the part of a street urchin in the play *Oliver!*, doing a little dance with the orphan girls, bowing to his partner and grasping her hands, his pixie face tilted up toward the stage lights, beaming. Sitting at the long wooden table at our cabin, eating saltwater taffy and folding colored origami paper into intricate designs: animals, boxes, flowers. After a childhood surgery, clutching the rubber examination glove blown up to look like a rooster that had been given to him by the nurse, toddling over to the diaper bag at Mom's feet and pulling out his little white shoes, saying one word: *home.*

Take me home. Home, the place where Pat was there with us.

Eventually, we begin to talk of not-Pat things. Our togetherness is meant to be unifying, but I still feel as though I am drifting away, just barely fastened to the ground.

Our togetherness, his neverness. I cannot reconcile the two. I wish that I could take comfort in some of the things my grandmother said this morning, but I can't.

✖

IN THE DREAM Pat walks ahead of me. He is shirtless, and the muscles move along his spine, the taut slickness of his young skin glowing in the early morning sunlight. The little hairs on his arms stand on edge in the cold.

We are at the border of the woods near our cabin, passing the side of the house that gave Pat the scar above his left eyebrow. He had been three years old, and Sam, the neighbor's overly excitable dog, had come barreling toward us as we played. Pat had run to me, screaming in terror. I'd reached out my arms to catch him, but it was too late. He'd fallen headfirst into the house, an avalanche of blood dripping from his forehead.

The scar winks in the sunrise now, reminding me of my failures: I could never save Pat, even from the beginning. He turns around.

"Please tell me you would never try to hurt yourself," I say to him.

"No, no, Ern, I'd never do that," he laughs, his eyes shining, and he runs deeper into the forest, the trees devouring him in their lacelike shadows.

These dreams leave me desperate. He is always just out of my reach, and though I try to save him I fail, again and again. I wake up and pace through the moonlit halls, rehashing the things I said to him as he spiraled down. I sit on the floor of my office in my pajamas, sifting through the boxes that hold the papers he left behind, the brutal account of his addiction. Every sentence, every word assaults me, and though my hands tremble, I force myself to take them in, to really read them, to understand the whole truth, as noxious as it is. "In the beginning of me shooting up heroin, I only told the people I did it with how much I actually did," Pat has written.

> When I could no longer hide it from my other friends and girlfriend, I think I was pretty honest with the amounts I did. Everyone knew I shot up, and everyone knew I shot up a lot. I often tried to stop and was successful for a few weeks, or sometimes even months. But I always seemed to go back. I even told my girlfriend to hide my passport from me so I could not go to Mexico, a place where I often got drugs, but I would always find it and go back. I would also tell my dealers who were my close friends not to sell to me anymore, but I would always convince them otherwise.
>
> Almost every aspect of my life was affected by my addiction. I would often call in sick to work with fake excuses of why I could not be there in order to recover from the night before or to get high. I completely stopped going to my classes because I wanted to get high. Before I started getting high, I used to skate competitively, but I stopped because I was so wrapped up in getting loaded. My relationships with my friends, girlfriend, and family also suffered and sometimes even crumbled. I was a complete dick to everyone when I was high. I would start fights in order to "get angry" and have an excuse to use. I would use in order to cover up my depression, anxiety and anger, and as I used, these feelings all got worse.

Page after page, my brother tells of the forces that pulled him down. "Will this make it right?" he has scrawled in the margins. "Will this take it all away? Just one more cut to feel . . . just one more shot to live." I remember one of Pat's friends, a girl who'd known him since childhood, telling me how blindsided she'd been by his death—she knew his partying was getting out of control, but the weird thing was that his personality never changed.

"He always seemed so happy," she had said. "Maybe it just goes to show you that a person doesn't have to turn into a total monster to be really fucked up."

But the monster was there all along, living inside of him, eating away
at him: we just hadn't seen it, or hadn't wanted to see it, or saw it and
looked away.

We wanted to see Pat in snippets, to isolate his behavior, because
then it was more believable, more palatable. He was a risk taker, we
thought, a typical young kid doing typical risky stuff. We refused to
see the big picture: a young adult with a significant drug problem that
was interfering with his relationships, his employment, his education, his
finances, his health.

The whole picture of Pat provides one explanation for his death:
given his risk-taking personality, his denial of his drug problem, his feeling of invincibility, the power of his drugs of choice, and his addiction
itself, he couldn't resist taking one more run. That run turned out to be
his last. In other words, he did not intend to die.

But the words he has written in these pages ignite another explanation in my mind. "In the midst of life, we are in death," it was once said,
and I wonder if this is what happened to Pat. The worse his addiction
became, the farther down the well he fell, until finally the light all but disappeared. Inch by inch he had fallen, his death drive—in Freudian terms,
the unconscious desire to die—finally overtaking his desire for life. Not
exactly suicide, though his actions were certainly self-destructive; more
of a slow giving up, a surrender, a weakening of the compulsion to live
and a strengthening of the compulsion to be at rest.

Or as Mom said to me in the weeks after Pat died, "I don't want my
life to end. I just want the pain to end."

I don't think my brother explicitly wanted to die. But I do think
he knew that he was being drawn toward death, and at some point—
whether consciously or unconsciously—he yielded.

But what do I know? Perhaps, in the absence of the God story, I am
simply making up another story to quiet the agonizing fear inside me, the

thought that he was so broken that he didn't see a reason any longer to live, that he willingly left, that he put the needle in his arm and thought, *I hope this is it.*

I am analyzing a ghost, chasing a dragon, digging in the ground for skeletons I will never find, because they have already turned to dust.

Like my grandmother, I cry, and cry, and cry: at the pain my brother suffered, at all the ways I failed him. I had stood on the sidewalk with my sister, talking about how selfish Pat was, how he just needed to pull it together. I had told him to quit partying, as if "partying"—fun, enjoyment, pleasure—described his state of mind. I had shown him little compassion; I had refused to believe him or to believe in him. I hadn't listened; I had only spoken. I did not want to hear what he had to say or see what he had to show me. I did not learn about the disease of addiction because I did not want to believe that my brother was an addict. I wanted only for everything to be as it was, for the world to be righted again.

"The illusion of infinite time clouds our understanding of the preciousness of one another," writes Elisabeth Kubler-Ross. "That value grows in death as we realize all that was lost." I have lost Pat, and I feel that I have lost myself too. I want to sink downward, into the scratchy fibers of the carpet, into the floorboards, into the foundation and mud and bedrock, into the very center of the earth, where I can vanish like him.

31 | IMPRISONED

BEFORE BRYCE'S GRANDMOTHER had a stroke, he would sit and talk with her for hours. Though the fog of Alzheimer's had descended by then, she still loved reminiscing about life during the war in the 1940s, and her mind was still sharp enough to throw out the answers to *Jeopardy!* while the two of them watched TV. Leigh would linger in the doorway, watching her mother and her son as they laughed together. In those moments, she could see that the son she once knew still existed: the loyal, kind boy who helped his neighbors carry their groceries upstairs and eagerly rode his skateboard to the Pacific Coast Highway to catch the bus downtown to his dishwashing job in Newport Beach.

Leigh's mother is gone now, and things with Bryce are different. He is still that compassionate, earnest boy, the one who takes out her trash, tidies her kitchen, hugs and kisses his mother whenever he sees her. The goodness in him is not gone. But when he is on drugs, a nastiness and a harder edge descend.

"There is nothing I would change about my son, other than the drugs," she says.

Small things still give her hope. The fact that Bryce still calls and texts her just to tell her he loves her reminds Leigh of standing in the doorway and watching Bryce laugh with his grandmother. She reminds herself that these moments are not just glimpses. They are not just blips on a screen. They are not just fleeting bursts of memories from another time, before she was locked inside this prison her life has become. No,

Leigh tells herself, these moments are evidence that the real Bryce still exists, somewhere outside these prison walls.

But for now, both she and her son live inside the prison, which Bryce has unwittingly created. Slowly over the years, he has constructed it, bar by bar, block by block, until finally they have both become completely ensconced.

Bryce has tried to let her go free many times. Once, while Leigh was at work, he filled himself with pills and heroin and wrote a suicide note to his mother: "I am so sorry I cause you so much pain and sorrow. I am so sad and hate myself so much for where I have gone with my life. I love you more than anything, and I am so sorry to disappoint you. You deserve better." He placed the note inside a book on the coffee table in the living room and stumbled down the hallway to his bedroom. Leigh came home before it was too late.

Bryce was trying to escape his own pain, but he was also trying to save her, to lift her out of the pain his addiction has caused her.

"He sees what my life is, and my life is lost," she says.

Leigh knows the conventional wisdom, the advice given by all the therapists and self-help books and people at addiction support groups: at some point, you have to let your child go. You have to stop enabling, you have to stop rescuing, you have to stop obsessing. And she has drawn some boundaries. Bryce hasn't been allowed to sleep in her home for months—he now mostly lives out of a backpack and stays with friends—and she very seldom gives him money; when she does loan him cash, he always pays her back, no matter how long it takes him. Sometimes Leigh takes him out to eat, just to make sure he's getting a good meal once in awhile. But these are tangible restrictions, far easier to enforce than walking away emotionally.

In her early twenties, Leigh spent summers picking huckleberries in the Montana mountains. Sometimes she would see a mother bear trailed by a litter of baby cubs wandering through the bushes. Leigh was taught that the one thing you were never supposed to do was get between a mama bear and her cubs. Now, as a mother herself, she feels that animalistic protectiveness toward her child, the urge to rip the head off anything that tries to harm him.

But, Leigh wonders, how do you rip the head off drugs? During the times when Bryce is clean, even if it's for just a few hours or days, Leigh feels like she's won against the monster. *You're not going to steal my son,* she screams, *I've got him. I've got my boy back.* But then Bryce goes back out again, back into the arms of the monster. He wants sobriety so badly, Leigh knows it, but he just can't hold onto it, and she can't do it for him.

How do you let your child go, Leigh wonders during these dark moments, when all you want to do is grab him closer to you and protect him from all the evils in the world, which is the singular mission of a mother? So she retreats back inside the prison of his addiction, the prison of her mind. All she can do there is cry at her lack of control, her utter inability to save her son from his addiction. Her inability to save Bryce from himself.

She knows Bryce never wanted to be this way. No child dreams of growing up and becoming a junkie, sticking a needle in his arm. And no mother thinks she can't save her child.

"But even if I gave up everything for Bryce, he wouldn't be able to pull himself out of it," she says. "I'd sell all my possessions, sleep in a tent the rest of my life if it meant he could be free of drugs. But even if I handed him a million dollars, it wouldn't work."

Leigh knows it will take more than this for her son to achieve lasting sobriety. He can't just will his addiction away; he can't simply say *I'm not going to use anymore* and have it be true. He needs to totally surrender. To realize that his addiction is bigger than he is, that it is controlling him completely, and that he is utterly powerless over it.

But surrendering is easier said than done.

It seems impossible to Leigh that Bryce is still alive. From the day he came into this world twenty-seven years ago, she has lived a life of facing his death: he was born with a congenital heart defect and had open-heart surgery at just nine months old. Then came his addiction, first to pills—Soma, Vicodin, Oxy—and then heroin. For nearly as long as he's been addicted, he's been trying to get clean. Often he is so desperate that he'll deliberately overdose just to get into treatment. He will get on his bike or the bus and ride to the parking lot of a nearby hospital, where he'll take as many pills or do as many shots of heroin as he can. Then he'll walk into the emergency room and tell the doctors he's overdosed and needs help. Before he does this, he takes Leigh's number out of his phone or obscures it under a name other than "Mom" so that the hospital won't be able to contact her: he doesn't want to worry Leigh. "If I'm gone for a few days, don't go looking for me," he'll tell her, hoping that he can go in and come back out clean, freeing them from the prison.

But Leigh always finds her son. Sometimes she finds him lying unconscious in the ER; one time she found him hooked up to a ventilator in the ICU, where he remained for four days.

It helps that she has access to Bryce's cell phone activity. When she sees his outbound calls and text messages, she can breathe, because she knows her son is alive. But when they cease, Leigh knows something he is wrong, and she begins the hunt. She becomes laser focused, obsessive. Her son has become addicted to drugs, and she has become addicted to her son. She needs her fix: she needs to know that Bryce is still alive. She starts calling the hospitals, one after the other, until she finds him. Usually it takes her less than twenty-four hours.

Bryce's phone is the only lifeline connecting Leigh to her son, and he knows it. Though the phone is in Leigh's name, Bryce pays for it, and he could easily switch to another plan or take his mother's name off the account. But he allows this lifeline to remain.

Perhaps he wants to be protected by her, even as he tries to be the protector himself, by shielding Leigh from the things that make her hurt and cry: shielding her from him.

Bryce wonders why he can't get clean, but he also wonders why he doesn't die. Either outcome, he thinks, would end his mother's suffering, and his own. But he is like a cat with nine lives: he simply refuses to die, or God won't let him.

"Mom, I've overdosed so many times. Why don't I ever die?" he asks her sometimes, and Leigh struggles to answer. As much as she suffers, she sees that Bryce is suffering even more—and unlike Leigh, Bryce doesn't have the luxury of simply walking away. Although she knows that when he gets clean, his cravings will eventually diminish, they'll always be lurking inside him. He will have to remain ever-vigilant; he will have to choose, over and over again, not to feed his addiction.

So she tries to make Bryce understand that he has a purpose, that there is value to his young life. "There's a reason you're here," she tells him. "You could be so effective in helping others. You have a gift; you're here to teach us something." She thinks back to the early days of Bryce's life, when he was a newborn struggling to survive with a defective heart. Leigh had decided then that if her son died during the surgery, she would take her own life too: she couldn't imagine going on after losing him. Now she doesn't know which is better: to lose her son or to keep on living this struggle as she watches him straddle the line between life and death and can do nothing about it.

Would she take her own life if she lost him now, she wonders?

Like most nights, tonight Leigh sits alone in her home. The air is still and dark, and the only sound is the muffled laughter from a sitcom playing on the neighbor's television. All day long, she had gone through the motions at work, the paperwork and phone calls secondary to the ongoing voices in her head: *Where is Bryce? Is he alive? What is he doing right now?* In the evenings, her fourteen-year-old old dog snores under the coffee table while she plays detective, monitoring Bryce's outbound calls and texts. She stares out the window and thinks about telling Bryce she's done. But she's so afraid that if she cuts herself off from communicating with him, it will send him over the edge, that he'll be so angry and hurt that he'll shoot up and die.

She has accepted the fact that her son's addiction may kill him. That scene plays in her head all the time. But if he went down because of her, if she said goodbye to Bryce and then couldn't take it back, she'd never be able to forgive herself.

Sometimes Leigh thinks about dating, maybe even getting married again. It would be so nice to have a partner, to be supported, not to feel so alone all the time. Her life is flying by her, she knows that, and she believes she deserves to have joy and happiness, the same as everybody else. But the other night she saw who she has become: a person incapable of that kind of life. She was sitting in the dark, afraid of the worst-case scenarios that were running through her head: *Where's my son? Is he dead? Will I ever see him again?* Suddenly, she started taking pictures of herself on her cell phone, and she was shocked by the woman who stared back at her from the screen.

"I saw myself for the first time in seven years," she says. "I'm just lost. To think that this is what I've come to: the emptiness in my eyes, the fear. There is no joy, no hope. These drugs have got him by the balls, and there is no hope."

I ask her if she thinks there's really no hope.

"I'm starting to think that," she admits.

She explains to me that Bryce's addiction has taken her over so completely that whenever someone talks to her about any other subject, they interrupt what's going on inside her head. She feels crippled, unable to function, a stranger in the normal world. She doesn't know how to function outside these prison walls.

Which is better, she wonders, *life in this prison or death?*

"It is hell," she says quietly, her toenails curling inward, clenching at the soles of her sandals as she scrolls through Bryce's most recent texts. "Most of the time, I think I want to die. Wouldn't it be nice to just be in heaven?"

32 | HAUNTED

THE SIDEWALK STRETCHES flawless and gray in front of the Cedar Street house. You would never know it, but a magnolia tree used to grow there, its roots bursting through the concrete, its branches obscuring the view of our front porch.

It was Pat's favorite tree growing up. When he came home from school, he'd scurry up the knotted trunk and perch in the highest branch, where he could see to the end of the block, to the corner where Cedar Street met Manzanita Avenue. There was a church on that corner, and a five-way stop sign with a curbed island in the middle of the intersection that marked the farthest Pat was allowed to ride his bike. It terrified Mom whenever she found Pat up in that tree, and she would gently coax him down.

Once he was safely on the ground, she would grab his arm and reprimand him, saying, "It's not safe to go so high! Don't ever do that again!" Words that sounded angry but were really simply fear, that were truly meant to say, *I love you. I don't want to lose you.*

"Why did you climb that?" she would say instead, shaking a little, and he would answer, "Because it has the best view."

The magnolia tree has been gone for years now. By the time Pat turned seven, the tree had started sprouting roots that erupted through the sidewalk, and the city arborist had recommended fully removing the tree rather than simply destroying its roots; even if the tree survived the severance, it would die slowly over time.

Pat was at school when they took away his tree. He came home to find only a pile of rubble and some fallen leaves, and he was inconsolable. He climbed up into his bunk bed and burrowed in his sea of stuffed animals. There were so many of them that Pat could barely fit on the bed, but that was the way he liked it: surrounded by soft, familiar things.

Years later I still notice the tree's absence, which only further confirms the nonsense of loss.

✖

MOM DISAPPEARS AGAIN in mid-October. I call and email her obsessively, but she's turned the phone off and doesn't reply to my messages. I vacillate between practicality and paranoia, respecting her need for solitude but crazy with fear.

She finally emails me:

I'm doing okay but have to admit this month has been difficult for me. Halloween was one of my favorite holidays when you kids were little. Today I'm not so sure. I loved making your costumes, decorating the house and carving our pumpkins. I loved stuffing our baby scarecrow with newspaper and straw each year and sitting him out on our porch steps. I loved taking you out to trick-or-treat, coming home and watching you kids divide up and trade your treats.

Halloween was always special for your grandma, too. Grandma used to take Pat to Safeway to buy pumpkins. And Pat always came home with multiple pumpkins, the biggest ones he could carry. When the boys got older, Grandma took them to the "Spirit" Halloween store where Pat would choose the scariest mask he could find. I think of Halloween as Pat's holiday. I think he was my child who trick or treated the longest. His love of candy drove him to trick or treat in high school! Today these memories stop me. I get locked in sadness realizing again the neverness of Pat. No more new memories to be made. Halloween just emphasizes the fact for me. Tomorrow will be a better day.

There is nothing really to say in the face of someone's neverness. I think of Mom in that big house, filled with reminders of neverness. Our whole lives, we never expected anything like this. We sat on the rug in the family room in our waxy makeup as we gleefully dumped the night's treasures from hand-sewn trick-or-treat bags shaped like pumpkins. I hated licorice and loved coconut, so Red Vines were my trading tools in my quest for Almond Joys. My sister hated gummy bears and loved Snickers. Brian hated Skittles and loved 3 Musketeers. And Pat loved everything, of course.

After the trades, we'd run around the house, cracked out on sugar and excitement. The rule was that we could eat as much candy as we wanted on Halloween night; after that, we could choose two pieces after dinner every night for dessert until it was gone. But we always snuck into the stash when Mom wasn't looking. She had to have known.

All those memories are so long ago, though. We are grown. Pat is gone. But reading Mom's words, I can smell the brown carpet and feel the itchy costume and taste the glossy chocolate, and most of all I see Pat, his little face, his crystalline eyes, as I cradle him in his polar bear outfit and tell him he's my Bunny.

In the face of neverness, there is only despair.

I wish I could dive into my mother and tap into her deep pool of pain. To drain it into a bucket and sap her of everything that makes her hurt. But I am helpless. I can only write back to her that I understand.

✖

WE MOVE, ALL six of us, like grainy phantoms across the screen. The rainbow Christmas lights and the blaze of the fireplace move in zigzag patterns behind us, leaving trails that fade as the camera moves, slightly wobbling, from face to face. An unintended trick of the early 1990s home video camera has lent an incandescent cast to our figures. We look like wayward ghosts, like apparitions that are partly of this life and partly of the next. Pat shouts in delight, "Thanks Santa!" The sight of his cherubic face, his chubby five-year-old cheeks and Superman pajamas, makes me want to throw up.

How is it that we were once all so unknowing? How did this little boy turn into a drug addict right before our eyes?

It feels like self-sabotage to watch this video on Christmas Eve, when Pat and Dad are gone and there is no way to bring back the joy we once felt, when we were all together. I should be trying to make myself feel better, not worse. But I can't tear my eyes away from this nostalgic happiness. It sparks memories of a childhood that felt so safe, so unending, so unbreakable. Everyone in this video is happy: me in my teenage awkwardness, bumbling around the Christmas tree in my poofy pink slippers and sweatshirt from the thrift store downtown. Cait in her Strawberry Shortcake nightgown, her hair pulled back with a plaid scrunchie. Bri, the official present distributor, sitting under the tree in his Teenage Mutant Ninja Turtles sweatpants, calling out the names on the gift cards like an auctioneer. Mom in her turtleneck and reindeer sweater, sipping her tea and beaming. Dad, asking us questions from behind the camera: "What's that there, Pat? What did Santa get you? Hold it up for the camera."

And Pat, holding up his brand-new glow-in-the-dark sleeping bag, his eyes shining as he joyously yells, "It's just what I always wanted! I love you, Santa!"

Mom runs a pair of scissors along the seam of the box and helps Pat unfold the sleeping bag as he hops on one foot around her. She unrolls it on the floor, and he crawls inside of it, giggling with delight so tremendous that you'd think he had just been given the whole world.

This year, there is no Christmas tree, and very few presents. We go through the motions; we light a candle for Pat and Dad and eat dinner.

There are Christmas carols playing in the background, and the dog wears a jingle-bell collar, but there is little joy. We do not speak of Pat or Dad.

Later that night, Mom lies next to me on my bed as I hold her and she cries, wordlessly and hard. I think of a quote I once read: "Sorrow is no longer the island, but the sea."

Do Pat and Dad still move through our lives like they did in the Christmas video from long ago? Shimmering, camouflaged, barely there but not fully gone?

If they do, it is with stealth. I do not feel them—either of them—at all.

�֍

WHEN NEW YEAR'S arrives, I feel only dread. At this time last year I was still reeling from Pat's brush with death in the San Diego motel and our Christmas Day confrontation. I was too emotionally exhausted to be much fun, and Ben and I had decided to quietly celebrate with close friends. Only one picture of me was taken that night, leaning against Ben's leg as I sat on the floor, a glass of champagne cradled between my feet. The Christmas tree lights shone in the background, making the look in my eyes seem even more lackluster. Pat had almost died, and I was stunned.

Stunned, stupefied, immobile: then, as now.

A month from now, we'll be standing in the grass by Pat's grave, and it will be the one-year anniversary of his death. The headstone is already in place—a surprisingly quick move by Mom, who let years go by after Dad's death before deciding on a marker. We hadn't minded; the space for Dad's forthcoming stone was covered by a wooden board that could be flipped up, allowing us to leave things in the shallow compartment underneath, wrapped in a plastic bag to prevent them from molding.

We had an agreement that no one was allowed to read any letters placed there. At the time, I believed Dad could see them, that in some form or another he was watching down on us. I'd go to his grave, write to him, and nestle my thoughts in the dampness of our secret space.

Today I do not believe that anything about Pat exists. The thing is, I try very hard to convince myself otherwise. Who wouldn't? It's nicer to say that Dad and Pat are together now in heaven, waiting, watching, protecting. No one wants to say that actually, the putrefied remains of their organs and bones and skin have rotted into their caskets, one on top of the other. That a little bit more of Pat is discernible, because he's been dead for less time. That none of us can answer the question, *What happens next?*

Because, like everyone else, I can't definitively answer this question, I turn to the physical. Proof, actual and obvious. Reality. What we see. Not what we want to believe but what we know.

If we dug into the earth, what would we find? I exhume their bodies nightly in my head. It's as if I have the shovel itself in my hands, tearing into crusted layers of dirt and wood and satin and then, finally, skeletons, brittle and with tiny bits of flesh, blackened and spongy, falling apart at the whisks of my brutal attempts to find them again.

This imagining has become a frenetic exercise, a way to feel that I somehow still know them, that I can be near to them, even if only physically. I need to see them because I do not feel them, despite my best efforts.

Without fail, it becomes 3:00 AM, when Pat probably stopped breathing. I startle upward, bathed in a hot sweat that chills at the shock of the cold bedroom air above the covers. I know it is coming. I can't avoid it by thinking pleasant thoughts. I can't escape it by deep breathing or by touching Ben's back or by snuggling the warm dog or by drinking hot milk or by counting sheep or by trying on different stories about the possibility of life after death. It always comes. I am there, at their graves, picking, prodding, stabbing. Desperately trying to get back to those who have left me.

✖

SOON FEBRUARY LOOMS. Hanging above my head, it nags like a mosquito. Tomorrow the month of Pat's death will be here.

It is January 31, and Pat is the opposite of me. Here I am, on a couch in the sun. The dog sleeps next to me. Because it is California, it's already getting to be spring, and the air is warm. Steam lifts from my tea. Birds flutter to the rooftop and warble. I smell dew and grass and the earth where he lies. There he is, miles away, but if I could find him and brush away the dirt, what would I find?

My obsession with picturing Pat dead is only getting worse. The effort causes hours to leak from my days. There he is, in a box over our father and under the earth. Dad is only a pile of bones by now. Pat still has flesh and organs, though they are rapidly falling away. There are holes that grow ever wider, and maggots. Black spots whose decay spreads outward.

I am life and he is death. I am here and he is there. I breathe and he decomposes. I ache and he . . . ?

33 | ATONEMENT

JOEL'S BROKEN DREAMS lie scattered all around him, petals dislodged from a flower. In the mist that rises from the bay, they dampen and wither while he looks on, useless to reverse the course of fate. He digs into his pocket for his phone, and although his fingers are shaking, he is able to type out a message: "the obvious truth is that I'm killing myself. I'm not sure what I should do Erin. I hate how I've become. I've been up for 5 days now, and I wish I could just stop Erin, I hate myself right now."

My heart sinks when Joel's text appears on my phone, because I know I am powerless.

"I'm sorry to hear things have been rough," I type back. "Let me know if you need a ride to rehab."

He doesn't respond.

✖

WHEN I FIRST met Joel, he was a twenty-six-year-old client at the Henry Ohlhoff House, a San Francisco residence for men dealing with substance abuse. The program director had arranged for me to interview a few young men about their opiate addiction, and I sat waiting in the entrance hall of the old Victorian where the program is housed. Roughly half the residents—most of them white males between the ages of nineteen and twenty-eight from the Bay Area suburbs—were addicted to painkillers and heroin, the director had told me. Joel was one of them.

In his wrinkled flannel shirt and tattered sneakers, Joel looked like any other twentysomething kid as he was led down the staircase for our interview: he would have fit in perfectly as the barista, the indie band leader, the deejay. It was hard to believe that there could be anything dark behind his sincere gaze. He shook my hand eagerly and settled onto the stiff velour couch in the visiting room, shuddering off the last of the morning draft and running his fingers through his rumpled hair. He launched straight into his story: He grew up with nurturing parents, attended a prestigious arts school, and dreamed of becoming a digital audio producer or writing and performing music for movies. Pills and heroin, which he got hooked on at age fifteen, killed those dreams. When he checked into Ohlhoff, he was forty-five pounds underweight and violently sick, praying to God every time he picked up the needle that he would never wake up.

"I felt like I was just a piece of trash," he told me. "I lost my will to live."

Joel's eyes were pinned as he talked, the telltale sign of Suboxone. He said it quieted his cravings and that even though it hadn't worked for him in the past, the quietness made him feel like maybe, this time, he could stay clean.

Before I left, he grabbed my hand. He wasn't much of the praying type, he said, but he did pray here and there, and my family and Pat would always be in his prayers, when he did say them.

"If you ever need help for anything else or just to talk, I'm down," he said. He was so genuine that I wanted to hug him, but I did not. "Stay strong."

✖

A FEW MONTHS later, Joel relapsed. After Nate, his roommate and best friend at Ohlhoff— another twentysomething hooked on pills and heroin—decided that he was dropping out of the program, Joel followed suit. And the relentless cycle began once again. Only this time it spiraled even further out of control: since Joel was still taking his Suboxone in the hopes of resisting heroin, he couldn't get high. So he began filling the void by slamming speed. He hated being spun, because it made his brain whirl even faster than usual, but he became addicted to the rush. It felt like the ultimate antidepressant. And "depressed" didn't begin to describe the depths of Joel's low once he was back on the streets.

Now he lives day to day, hour to hour, bouncing between the motels that line Lombard Street in the Marina district, where he is just another easily forgotten ragged face. That's the way he wants it: he's been badly struggling these days, and he doesn't want anyone to know. But for some reason Joel lets me in. He begins sending me rambling text messages, sometimes writing to me for hours at a time. While I kick myself for crossing the sacred journalistic line of keeping distance from one's subject, I can't help myself: I care about Joel, and I fear for him, and I worry constantly that he'll die. I keep my responses as short as possible but try desperately to make him feel heard, to let him know that his life is important.

His communications become an unwitting obsession for me. When he disappears for days or weeks or months, I am hypervigilant; I don't stalk him exactly, but I check his Facebook page for clues. When driving through the city, I keep an eye out for a lanky, shaking kid in a flannel shirt. I am navigating uncertain waters: I'm not his guardian or his friend. In reality, I don't know what I'm doing in allowing myself to be drawn in by Joel and his struggle.

Sometimes I think I am trying to atone for my sins against my brother.

Jan. 9, 2012, 2:56 p.m.
Nate called me the other day. He didn't sound well . . . I wanted to help him but I haven't been top notch myself lately. I don't know if me hanging with Nate would be a great idea right about now. Hope you're well Erin.

Jan. 9, 2012, 3:04 p.m.
I actually just got off the phone with Nate. I'm sorry to hear you are struggling. I wish I could help you in some way. Anything I can do, let me know. I believe in you and Nate both.

Jan. 9, 2012, 3:16 p.m.
Thanks Erin. I'll never forget that thing I read that 85 percent of heroin addicts never stay clean for good, or 2 percent of heroin addicts will stay clean for life, horrible odds regardless.

The reminder of how brutally the odds are stacked against Joel—and the fact that he knows this—makes me want to convince him that he can fight the path he's on and turn things around. I have a sinking feeling that he is falling hard and fast, and I know there is not much I can do about it. But I want to believe too that Joel can be saved. He doesn't have to be just one more life wasted or lost. How do I persuade him this is possible? What would I have said to Pat, and will it make a difference if I say it now to Joel? I consider my response carefully.

Jan. 9, 2012, 4:12 p.m.
I know it's so hard but remember people rise above statistics all the time. I'm happy to listen, I just wish I could do something but you know as well as I do, that the person has to want help. It sounds like you need to get into treatment. I don't know if this helps or hurts, but I can tell you how your family is probably feeling right now based on what I felt with Pat. They just want you to be okay and are terrified of losing you. I know it's fucked up now, but it's more fucked up if you die.

Jan. 9, 2012, 4:14 p.m.
Seriously Erin, just you not minding me telling you what's really going on in my life is all that I need. Years of relapsing, and then you start finding yourself in a corner with absolutely no one you can tell what's going on. With the people that know I'm using because I have to see them from time to time, I find myself minimizing what's going on because a) I'm either afraid they will stop talking to me or b) I just don't want to hear how I'm fucking up again. I push a lot of people away, I ended up making

my ex-girlfriend leave me because, well I fucking love her and she can do way better, but also I don't have to feel bad for disappearing. And the worst part is when I realize that I'm alone again all because I wanted to get loaded, without even consciously wanting to use . . . I just never expected that it would become like this. In all honesty Erin, I hate myself, and not necessarily because of the drugs, it's because I really want to be a good person and hold on to things I love, but I feel like I can't help it anymore. I start to become scared because all I can imagine is that they'll eventually not love me anymore. And trust me Erin, you have no idea of how much it hurts me to even fathom what it will do to my family if I accidentally went too far, it makes me sick to my stomach, especially since I've witnessed many friends die and seen what it's done to their families.

As Joel writes these words, things start to get blurry: it's hard not to mix him up with my brother, to think of him as a separate person from Pat. Had Pat hated himself too? Had he worried about dying even as he found himself unable to stop doing drugs?

Jan. 9, 2012, 4:50 p.m.
I get it. I found Pat's journal and it was full of exactly the feelings you just said. And you know Joel it just made me so sad because he judged himself so harshly. That's what I hear you doing. You ARE a good person, no one hates you . . . they may not understand, but they love you.

Jan. 9, 2012, 4:51 p.m.
You found Pat's journal?

Jan. 9, 2012, 4:52 p.m.
Yeah I did. It about killed me. I had no idea how much he was hurting.

Jan. 9, 2012, 5:12 p.m.
I used to journal until someone read it and after that was never able to write exactly what was really going on. I was always afraid someone would read it and think I was crazy, especially since I can pull normal pretty well when I'm sober. I do find myself writing notes to my family at times when I'm using too much and I feel like something may happen, I freak out and make sure they all know how much I really loved them

and that I'm sorry. But then I usually rip them up because the thought of someone finding them kinda freaks me out.

I tell Joel I think he should keep the notes. It had hurt to read my brother's writing, I say, but it also helped me understand him better. To know that he had felt remorse, because most of the time he hadn't acted sorry for hurting us. To learn how much pain he was in, because that helped explain his actions. To remember that he had so much goodness inside of him that had been forgotten amid his addiction.

I remind myself that Joel is high right now, but—as with my brother—I find that in some sick way the conversation feels more honest than if he were sober. He's letting his guard down and being truthful with me—at least I think he is—and it feels like I'm getting closer to him. And even though this closeness may be false, I want to trust it.

I failed Pat. I will not fail Joel, I think to myself. Then I wonder again what I'm doing, but suddenly he is texting again.

Jan. 9, 2012, 5:49 p.m.
Well I do know this, getting sober you realize how dangerous the road you were just on was, but you push all that to the side because you never actually think it's gonna get you, and then once you have a habit, you become desensitized to the thought of dying. The part that drives me crazy is that I've witnessed people going out over exactly how I use, but I always tell myself that I can escape. For years I made myself think that most people ended up going out because they lost their will to live, but then I started realizing that the majority of friends that went out still had a light in them. But you eventually find yourself having pushed everyone away, and taking your life seems less painful than having to tell people you need help . . . again. And that's when I started to freak out that it's a possibility, Erin, especially since I'm not exactly living like a person that is really trying to make the most of things. Thanks again for being there for me.

Jan. 9, 2012, 5:58 p.m.
I'm glad to be here for you Joel. You're smart and thoughtful and loving. You deserve to make it. I hope you want to make it. Is there anything I can do in terms of helping you get help? A phone call, a ride?

Jan. 9, 2012, 8:17 p.m.
I appreciate the offer, my problem at the moment is that I have a decent amount of money, and I have a car. And in my case I'm thinking that I'd be better off without it all, but I've already tried asking people to take my shit away from me and I always end up getting it back from them. Last week I asked my friend to take my truck and hold my money I've earned, and I lied saying I was done with drugs, but then I got it back and disappeared again. My sponsor is trying to get it into my head that there's only three ways this will end, choosing to go to rehab, or just keep going until that moment where a cop sees me driving completely whacked out of my brain and I'm off to prison, or I'll end up dead. But I've been thinking of that elusive fourth option, but it dawned on me that I'm trying the fourth one at the moment and it's not working. I'm having a problem accepting that I need a rehab again. I can't figure out why I hate myself so much, because I've always been someone that tries to put others before me. But there is something that has always been killing me inside in regards to how when I first got strung out on heroin. I ended up stealing everything from my family, all my mom's jewelry, wedding rings, anything I could sell and I ran away from home too terrified to admit to my mom that I was hooked on heroin at 15, all because I saw this gorgeous girl look like she was in heaven and then after I found out it was heroin she was on, I thought wait a minute, a girl this beautiful uses heroin? And I convinced myself that it couldn't be that bad. I didn't realize that it would make me steal things from my parents, and that's one thing I have never ever forgiven myself for. My mother is by far the most important person to me in the world.

Holy shit, I'm really spun out, I can't even make myself stop texting right now, I'm shutting off my phone for sure.

I tell Joel not to feel bad, that I'm happy to listen to him. I say I'm worried about him and that I hope he's okay. But he suddenly stops responding, and I become panicked.

Jan. 9, 2012, 8:58 p.m.
Joel . . . are you there?

Jan. 9, 2012, 9:15 p.m.
Hey Joel just let me know you're ok.

Jan. 9, 2012, 10:01 p.m.
Hey sorry I had to shut my phone off to break my addictive pattern of typing. God I'm in Walgreens and I feel everyone's looking at me because there's no hiding my drug use . . . that's probably one of the things I hate the most. Heroin makes me feel confident and charming, I ended up calling my heroin dealer tonight and met up with him, I'm hoping I can equalize myself out, I'm completely spun and I can't stand that.

Jan. 9, 2012, 10:19 p.m.
Hey by the way how's Nate doing? I feel bad not wanting to hang with him but I'd probably end up being a worse influence and I don't get high with friends anymore, there's something really dark about slowly killing each other together. I've become a strictly isolated user . . . anyways I hope he's alright.

Jan. 9, 2012, 10:25 p.m.
He sounded ok. Are you safe tonight?

Jan. 9, 2012, 10:41 p.m.
Yeah I think I'll be ok. I am driving to Safeway to force feed myself. I haven't eaten in four days, and I try to avoid looking in the mirror but I peeked tonight and I kind of freaked out but I hope fixing a shot of dope knocks some sense into me. I need to eat and sleep for a couple of hours, or else I'm really asking for problems, and once I get more drugs I'll disappear again for a few days.

Jan. 9, 2012, 10:50 p.m.
Don't disappear for too long Joel.

Jan. 9, 2012, 11:11 p.m.
I won't. Thanks Erin.

I decide to let Joel choose whether to pick up the conversation again. But even though I'm anticipating the silence that follows, I'm surprised by how much it bothers me. I wonder who Joel is turning to, which friends still care about him, whether his family knows where he is. I feel driven to make him know that he is important and worthy and loved, as if doing so will make up for all the times Pat felt insignificant and worthless and rejected.

Jan. 28, 2012, 11:08 a.m.
Hey Joel . . . just checking in . . . how are you?

Feb. 2, 2012, 2:23 p.m.
Hi Joel are you there?

March 7, 2012, 8:59 a.m.
Hey Joel it's Erin. Just checking in. I know it was your birthday this week, hope you're doing ok.

As the months go by with no word from Joel, I try to remain hopeful that he's gotten the help he needs, though I know it's just as likely that he's still out on the streets. Sometimes I wonder if he's dead. I feel helpless and pathetic and angry: for caring about him, for not being able to make a difference for him, for waiting and thinking and hoping for a resolution that may never come. But finally Joel writes.

April 13, 2012, 4:48 p.m.
Hey Joel just wondering how you are. Doing a story on heroin in LA. It's rough. Hope you are doing ok.

April 13, 2012, 7:14 p.m.
Hey Erin, I'm good. In New York visiting my family. Went to treatment for a little before I came here. Hope you and your family are well. I probably know most of the bad junkies in LA. Had to get away from that city. I've stayed clean. I feel like I'm in a better place, but I'm in the process of dealing with all the wreckage in SF. I used to tell my sponsors that I should do the steps while strung out on heroin. You feel the desperation in real time, and have a tendency to open up more. It seems more difficult after being clean for a few months because that's how sick we are, we forget. The only down side to opening up while using is that you don't go through the healthy motions of processing it and feeling it. Hence my

million texts to you. And that's my exact problem, I'll open up high, and then when sober, I'll only trust one or two people.

April 13, 2012, 7:27 p.m.
So are you in NY for awhile? When are you coming back?

April 13, 2012, 7:29 p.m.
I'm actually on a plane right now heading to Berlin to see a friend and I might stay a week or two and then I'm heading to LA for a few days to see my ex-girlfriend, and then I'll be back in SF.

April 13, 2012, 7:31 p.m.
That's awesome. That will be good for you to see her, I know how much you love her. Well safe travels and keep me updated on how you're doing.

April 13, 2012, 7:37 p.m.
Ok just boarded and bout to take off, I'll be in touch. Yeah I love her more than anything in this world, so much so that she was dating a guy and she broke up with him, and I contacted him and told him how to get her back. And I said I wanted him to marry her. This didn't go over well with her. She asked me why I wanted her to get married to someone else, and I said sometimes when you love someone so much, you have to let them go.

That is the last I ever hear from Joel. His final words linger in my ears, a reminder of one of the most difficult lessons I face: *You have to let them go.*

34 | DESPAIR WITHOUT HOPE

THE MOTHER SITS across from me, twisting a gingham dish towel in her hands. It curls over and around her fingers, absorbing her pain, soaking it in, just like on the day she is telling me about right now.

She already knew her son was going to die, she says—had known it a few days earlier, when she and her husband had gone to visit him in rehab, just before his twenty-fourth birthday. They'd sat at a picnic table with him, trying to talk, but he was flat and depleted.

"I stopped praying to God to cure him and started praying to let him find peace," she says, twisting the towel.

When the police knocked on her door, she hid in her bed, pulling the covers up to her ears to block out the sound. Finally, she forced herself to answer the door. Her son had been found dead of a heroin overdose on a park bench, where he was sitting in the pouring rain, his feet submerged in a puddle of water. She listened. Then she walked calmly through the kitchen, grabbed a dish towel, and stuffed it between her teeth. She went out into the garden, the cloth muffling her screams.

Her son's worst nightmare was that he would become a "puddle junkie"—when you're so desperately dope sick that you use puddle water to dilute the heroin you're shooting.

"I will never stop loving him," she says, blotting at her tears with the towel.

I don't acknowledge my own tears as I write furiously with my right hand and grip her other hand with my left. I am losing it, and I want to

stop the interview—I *should* stop the interview, seeing as I can't maintain my distance—but I cannot. Her blond hair, like my mother's, is
graying at the temples and shaped like a bell; her hand, like my mother's,
is thin as it grips the towel and twists. I am thrust down into a vortex,
back to that February morning, hearing my own mother's screams.

It's always the same story. Before the death, there was the heroin;
before the heroin, there were the pills; before the pills, there was a child
whose eyes shone clear and bright, who went to school, who did his
chores, who played in the backyard. A child who loved, and whose parents loved him. Tiny fluctuations in words, miniscule differences in turns
of phrases. But always the disbelief, the incredulity of a life extinguished
by something so simple as a needle or a pill. And always the pain, the
endless pain.

"One day he went to take the garbage out, and he never came back,"
the mother says, shaking her head in disbelief, and I finally have to put
down my pen.

Of all the interviews I have been conducting, the mothers are the
hardest. I think of my own mother, alone in the Cedar Street house,
time passing in a haze. Every morning she wakes up and thinks of Pat.
She can't remember what day it is, how long it's been since he's been
gone. Her thoughts are jumbled. She goes to bed late on purpose, so that
she has little time to think. Yet the thoughts come, racing, bombarding,
overflowing.

The question of why burns in her heart, like a pilot light in a furnace
in an unlit closet. When I say to her, "Because Pat was an addict," she
looks back at me blankly, and I realize that she doesn't mean "why" in
the literal sense but existentially: *Why did Pat have to die? Why didn't
God save him? Just Why?*

The doctors never figured out why Dad got cancer. At first Mom and
Dad spent lots of time asking why: he was healthy, young, a good person

who made the world a better place—a person who deserved to live. They never came up with an answer, so they gave up the question of why and settled on the sentiment "shit happens." Released from the question of why, they could focus on the question *Now what?*

In the end, Mom tells me, letting Dad die was a good plan of God's, one she supported. It was horrible for us, but Dad had suffered too long, so it was a blessing for him. The unanswerable question of why no longer needed an answer.

But letting Pat die was not such a good plan, Mom thinks. Like Dad, Pat was young, healthy, a good person; unlike Dad, he had a future ahead of him, the possibility that he might get better. She feels that God chose to not let him have that future.

No one can answer why.

People tell my mother to focus on the good memories. They say those memories will keep Pat alive for her.

But Mom doesn't want the memories of the past. She wants a future with Pat. She will never see him graduate from college, get married, become an uncle, become a father.

Her grief books instruct her: "The true work of grieving is that of imagining, and thus recreating, your life. List all the things you want out of life now—despite your impulse to give yourself up to despair, exhaustion, and pain. You can remake your life once you can imagine it."

But my mother does not want to invent a new future. She wants Pat.

"You deserve happiness," we say to her, with Kathy as our backup. "You deserve to find love again." We start a campaign to convince her to try online dating; she hasn't been on a date in twelve years. She finally agrees to let us post a profile, and we explode into action. I interview her, journalist-style, and help her write up a bio. Kathy takes her shopping, and we spend an afternoon taking pictures of her modeling her new outfits against the backdrop of the juniper bushes on the patio. The sunlight

shines in her hair, and she laughs as we ham it up, telling her to *work it,
work it!* She is beautiful without trying, but her bright new clothes hang
on her bony frame, and in her eyes I see only darkness.

My mother is broken, and I cannot fix her.

She berates God: Why did he choose to take Pat, who was good in
so many ways? She had prayed to God, begging him: *What I want is
reasonable; I'm not asking for a miracle. Help my son. Stay by his side.
There isn't a mean bone in his body; he's a good person, he's just on the
wrong track. Help him get the help he needs.*

Why bother praying at all?

She berates Pat: He was on the right path, doing the right things.
Going to meetings, putting out job applications, participating in family
life. Everything was going his way. Why did he choose drugs?

She berates herself: She had called him an addict, but in her heart it
was only a word. *How did my son become an addict?* she wonders. *Why
wasn't I there to help Pat? Why didn't I accept that he had other inter-
ests beyond college and that he needed guidance in finding a new path?*

These thoughts hammer at my mother relentlessly. She is a shell, and
I see her emptiness. She is surrounded by loving friends and the rest of us
kids, who keep her busy, but it's simply motions. All the commonplace
tasks of life suddenly take on a desperate urgency, because these tasks
will fill the emptiness: The basement needs to be cleaned out. The family
room needs to be redone. The house needs to be painted. The couches
need to be replaced. The backyard needs to be weeded, and while we're
at it, why don't we tear out the concrete patio, replant the lawn, maybe
even install a pool?

My mother nods at these suggestions and smiles weakly. But I know
she is just humoring us; I know what she really wants: solitude. She
wants all of us to leave, so that the house is finally quiet and she can
decide whether or not to come back to life again.

I am scared that she will decide not to.

I know that what she wants is the one thing she cannot have: for Pat, the little boy, to come back. The little boy who slept next to her one night a few weeks before he died, after he'd fallen in the upstairs bathroom and knocked his head against the toilet. Maybe a part of her believed his story that he was disoriented because he was tired, or maybe she didn't want to think about the reason he fell. It didn't matter. There was still everything that made him her son, and everything that made her his mother. She'd made him crawl into bed beside her, to make sure he was okay, and as he fell asleep he became her little boy again.

But the little boy is never coming back.

35 | BLINDSIDED

"LIFE IS CRASHING down hard," Brianne's friend Mark wrote on his Facebook page the day before he died.

Brianne thought it was out of character for her friend since elementary school. He was the type of person who could have had his own TV show: the short black-haired kid with the big personality, the one who always made everyone around him happy. Even if she thought back all the way to the days when he'd come over for PlayStation marathons and backyard birthday parties, she didn't have one bad memory of him.

Of course, Brianne knew that Mark had problems in his life: his parents had split up, and his older brother, Andrew, was always getting in trouble for partying too hard. Mark had always been the fixer, the giver, the class clown—but lately Brianne had noticed that he was partying a lot too. Then again, lots of kids at Dana Hills High School were pretty into partying: it wasn't called "Dana Pills" for nothing. Brianne was never really into that scene though. She'd always been afraid to do something that was so risky, although the kids who were super into pills were so knowledgeable about the science behind the drugs they were using that they were basically chemists. But it just seemed like a waste of time, like something that turned you into a completely different person—especially people like Andrew, and like Mark's friends who messed around with drugs like heroin whenever they couldn't get their hands on the pills. So Brianne hadn't been hanging around Mark much these days.

That was why his Facebook post alarmed her: she didn't know things had gotten that bad for Mark, so she thought she'd better check in the next time she saw him.

At school the following morning, Brianne was confused to see kids sitting against the walls in the hallways, looking stunned. A bunch of football jocks walked past her. Big, beefy guys, and they were all crying. "Mark is dead," Brianne heard one of them say, and she couldn't believe it.

How could Mark be dead of drugs—an overdose of Opana, which was what everyone was saying? Her sweet friend, the one who'd dragged her out of her shyness when she was little, telling his mom, "Mom! Did you know Brianne is not only the prettiest but the smartest, most talented girl in the whole wide world?"

At his funeral, Brianne felt like she was in an alternate universe. It was in an enormous church choked with incense, and it was so packed that people crowded into the aisles and spilled out the doors. Mark's brother, Andrew, sat stone-faced next to their mother, Sylvia, who wore a black veil. Andrew had been the one to find Mark, Brianne had heard, which was even more surreal since everyone had sort of secretly thought that if anyone was going to die, it would be twenty-one-year-old Andrew, the one with all the run-ins with the cops and overdoses and stints in rehab. Not his kid brother, who was only seventeen.

When Mark's casket was wheeled out into the center of the church, Brianne almost threw up. The body inside didn't look at all like her friend. It was dressed in a tuxedo, and its skin looked all pasty and waxy—not like a real person at all but more like a mannequin. Plus, it didn't have Mark's signature faux-hawk.

Brianne watched Sylvia walk up to the casket, sobbing, and wondered if it was all a joke. It would be just like Mark to jump out of the casket and scare everybody for a good laugh.

✖

THE GOOD SHEPHERD Cemetery in Huntington Beach is mostly silent on a Saturday morning. The lush, flat grass spreads outward toward the traffic on Talbert Avenue, interrupted by the bursts of pink and yellow blooms sprouting here and there from graveside flower holders. A lone white-haired man stands motionless beside one of the plots. After a long time, he crosses himself and clasps his hands to his chest. A helicopter cuts through the clouds, miles overhead, and the wind rustles gently through the trees. The man starts to leave but then shuffles around again and resumes his trancelike watch over the grave, his hands in his pockets, crying.

Near Mark's grave, the statue of the Pietà cries too, a mother shedding eternal tears for the loss of the son in her lap, gone too soon.

Mark was too young to die. Too young to be forever confined underneath the shadow of these stone tears. Today it has been three years, and already it feels like a lifetime ago to Sylvia.

Sylvia still has Andrew, and she almost can't believe that he will be here today with her—the third anniversary of Mark's death and the first time since Mark died that Andrew won't be in prison or rehab and can actually come to the grave. The irony of the whole thing is that for years she'd been preparing herself to lose Andrew, but she had never once worried about losing Mark. After all, Mark had seen the turmoil Andrew's addiction had caused, even saying to her one time, "You don't have to worry about me, Mom. I'm okay. I would never do drugs. I swear on my life."

When Andrew had said to her, "Mom, why don't you take a good look at Mark instead of focusing on me all the time," she had dismissed it as a blame-shifting strategy, an addict's twisted way of getting away with things.

Plus, the notion of two addicted children was just inconceivable. Her boys had always been so different. Andrew, even at four years old, when his little brother was born, was the troublemaker; Mark was the little angel. But despite their differences, they were always close. These roles persisted as the boys grew older together. It seemed that the deeper Andrew fell into addiction, the more Mark tried to protect him. Which is why in the end, it made no sense that Mark was the one to die.

Maybe Mark had to die to save Andrew, Sylvia thinks. But if that's true, then why can't Andrew manage to stay clean? Isn't it enough that he was the one to discover his baby brother, head buried in his hands at the kitchen table of his father's house, as if he were sleeping, vomit coming out of his stiff blue lips?

Sylvia thinks back to that night, when she was alone at her own house, up late doing the bills. She came across an old file folder and out fell a school picture of Mark—he'd hated it, so he'd crumpled it up before Sylvia had rescued it from the trash. "My cute, good boy," Sylvia said to the picture, kissing it. "I hope you're not in any pain, sweetheart. Go to sleep."

All through the next day, Sylvia had a terrible headache. She struggled through work and a Lakers game in Newport Beach, feeling all the while that something, somewhere, was wrong. When her sister walked in the door later that night, Sylvia's first thought was that something had happened to Andrew.

"This is the hardest thing I'll ever have to tell you," her sister said, crying. "Honey, Mark died."

Then Andrew was there too, saying, "I'm sorry, Mom, I am so sorry."

Sylvia was the last to know about Mark's death. Or was she the first to know, she wonders, when she kissed his picture the night before, right around the time he died, and told him goodnight?

Today, three years later, Sylvia tends to the grass around Mark's gravestone and arranges flowers in the little cup holder. Brianne and some of Mark's other friends are coming to the cemetery, as well as her family and Andrew. A group of other moms she's met in the support group SOLACE will also be here, and Sylvia is grateful for her new group of friends. Though they are bound together in sadness, they hold each other up in times like these, and there is a lightness in that. Sylvia will read a poem, and then they'll all take butterflies into their hands, the tiny wings tickling their fingers before they release them into the warm, changeless wind. They'll release balloons too, which will float heavenward, disappearing behind the clouds.

Sylvia does not want to live the rest of her life in sadness. Mark had such joyfulness, and she knows he'd want her to be happy. She has started volunteering at a hospital that overlooks the beach where Mark surfed, and she thinks of him then, trying to fixate on the good memories. But it's hard to keep the sorrow at bay, especially as she comes to know more about the darkness that had crept into Mark's life, the darkness that still haunts his brother.

She wishes she had opened her eyes more to Mark, that she had seen more of the warning signs. The bottles of pills easily pilfered from Andrew's stash or bought from other kids at school, the burned foil, the tiny packets, the needles. When it came to Andrew, that was all Sylvia had seen, but for some reason when it came to Mark, she had been blind.

And now that Mark is gone, Sylvia wonders, will Andrew make it? Or will she lose two sons?

Today Andrew is clean, and Sylvia is grateful for that. At least in grief, there is just the sadness to deal with—not the constant, unending state of fear that goes with addiction. Unlike some of the other mothers in her support group, for Sylvia the nightmare of addiction hasn't ended with one son's death. She has had to grieve Mark's death and Andrew's life simultaneously. And while she has reached the point where she can say of Andrew, *I cannot control him; this is his journey; he must live it on his own terms,* she can't help but fear that one day the other shoe is going to drop, and both of her sons will be gone.

Today she consoles herself with the thought that Mark had always wanted to be with God.

"Mom, God is really smart, and I can't wait to meet him so I can learn everything about all the planets and the universe," he'd told her once when he was little.

"Don't say that. You're freaking me out! You'll meet him in time," Sylvia had said.

"No, Mom, really, it's okay," Mark replied. "It's a good place, where God is. I want to go be with him."

You are finally with him, sweet boy, Sylvia thinks as the cars begin their slow crawl through the cemetery gates and toward Mark's grave, full of butterflies, and balloons, and tears.

36 | FALLING APART

THE NIGHT OF the one-year anniversary of Pat's death, I dream of him as a toddler. His pudgy cheeks, his little toenails, his flaxen hair. I am holding him, as I used to, like a doll. Playing house, playing mother. But as I cradle him, he starts hemorrhaging from his nose and eyes. I ask him, "Sweetheart, what's wrong? Tell me, Bunny."

He answers, clearly enunciating: "I. Am. Falling. Apart."

I am outside on a crowded city street; I shout frantically for someone to call an ambulance. Everyone ignores me. Somehow I find my way to a pay phone and call our mother. She tells me I'm overreacting and no medical intervention is necessary. I look down at Pat, at the crimson rivers now pouring down his chin, and tell him I will save him.

Of course I can't. I don't need a dream to tell me this. I couldn't.

The next morning I am the first to arrive at the grave. It's a Thursday and very quiet. Everyone else is off in the world doing whatever it is that people do on February 4, no matter the year. A member of the cemetery staff is walking from grave to grave and row to row, plucking flowers from the small cups in the markers. He throws them—quite violently I think—into a canvas bag as if they were refuse, not the offerings of loved ones to the lost. A second worker follows, riding on a motorized lawn mower and slicing the greenery into neat, thin lines. I watch this process from my car and marvel at the insensitivity of it all, the monotony of the daily chores. Of course they have to tidy up, but must it be today?

Then again, why are we so special? How many other tragic stories float in this air?

A flock of black crows—or are they vultures?—sweeps across the rolling hills. There are butterflies too. I want to close my eyes; I am so tired, but it's only 9:30 in the morning. At this moment one year ago, the paramedics were pronouncing my brother dead.

My mother and sister arrive; Brian has decided to stay in Santa Cruz for the day with Elise and Romeo, whom they've adopted as their own. Earlier today, Elise had sent us a group email: "I am still sad and angry and confused and incredulous. Pat was full of kick and love. It seems impossible that someone so incredibly alive could so easily die."

There had been another message too, from Brian:

Today, I'm doing my best to picture the Pat I knew and loved, and not speculate on the side of him I didn't see until the very end, the side that led to his death. When I close my eyes, I can see him in front of me as we snowboard down the backside of Bear Valley. He darts in and out of trees, me following close behind. We come to a drop off a small boulder. He takes one look, doesn't hesitate, and takes the jump. I wait a little longer, thinking it over: is it safe? Will I land? What's below? I see Pat's blue helmet in the distance as he continues down the mountain, and know he landed it perfectly. I take the drop, finish the run, and find Pat waiting for me at the chairlift. "That was a sick run!" he says, face red, snot dripping from his nose, smiling. We hop on the lift and sit side-by-side, riding back up the mountain to do it all over again. I'll always be thankful for the good times we had together, sad when I think about the difficult ones, and angry as hell that we can't spend more time together.

I want to stop speculating too. The story of Pat's downfall will always just be a theory. And even if this theory led to some sort of understanding, Pat would still be dead. But the unanswerable questions remain inside my head. Poking, prodding, maddening.

Mom has brought a bouquet of daffodils from her garden; like the flowers I brought, they are yellow: a cheery color, one that reminds us of Pat. We place them on the grave, along with bags of Hershey's Kisses. We try to remember some of the good things, the funny little quirks that made us love Pat: the way he made a wallet out of duct tape; his habit of climbing out the window of the upstairs bathroom when Mom wasn't home so he could hang out on the roof; his signature homemade gifts, cobbled together from whatever he found lying around the house. One year for Christmas, I received an old peanut butter jar filled with yarn and crumpled-up green construction paper, topped with a tinfoil ball—an alien holding a sign that said I COME IN PEACE. For Cait's sixteenth birthday she got a silver wire box filled with love notes: "Every time I see you, I smile! Any guy with brains would want you to be his girlfriend. How can you be having a bad day, you're beautiful. Pat loves you, and so does the rest of your family, so that's all that matters!"

We talk about Costa Rica, about the way Mom's host family had celebrated El Dia de la Muerte, the Day of the Dead. Every year on that holiday, they'd travel together to their loved ones' gravesite, bringing a picnic lunch and special gifts for the deceased. We'd decided to bring Pat a magnolia tree to climb, a skateboard—forget the helmet and knee-pads because he wouldn't wear them anyway—and candy. Mom recalls the night we all took dance lessons from the young girls of the family in her village, crowding into the neighbor's cleared-out living room as salsa music blared from an old CD player in the corner. All the girls were smitten with Pat and fought over whose turn it was to dance with him. Pat laughed and laughed as his feet moved awkwardly, his light brown hands intertwined with their dark brown ones. Every time he laughed, the girls went wild. Mom remembers how Pat finally pulled himself away from the gaggle of giggling girls and asked her to dance. She'd been surprised at first, and then so proud, so happy. *My son wants to dance with me!* she'd thought, glowing.

We polish the granite marker with a special cleaner. Dad's name is listed first, there is a space at the bottom for Mom's name, and Pat's name is sandwiched in between. Down the way, two women are also cleaning a headstone and snipping the grass along its border with a small pair of clippers. They light sticks of incense and let them burn inside the flower holders. Before leaving, they stand and bow three times.

"Should we bow to Pat?" Mom wonders.

"Shouldn't we know why we are bowing first?" Cait laughs, to which Mom improvises: "We bow once for how we loved Pat in the past, second for how we love Pat today, and third for the future and how we'll always love Pat in the days to come."

"Good enough for me," I say, and we all bow our heads three times.

It all suddenly comes back in a rush: the velvet cloth lining the rectangular hole in the ground, the casket perched above it that is slowly lowered, wobbling precariously. I worry it will fall and break apart, revealing my brother inside. But it holds. The roses we throw into the hole make a sickening, hollow thump. My mother throws hers in last, and it is the loudest, longest sound I have ever heard.

"There has never been a tunnel so long that it did not ultimately emerge into daylight, or a night so dark that it did not ultimately yield to the dawn," I remember reading once. At this moment it seems so untrue.

I leave my family and drive down the California coast, wanting to get as far away as possible from the vile place that houses my father and now Pat. A storm hits in Pescadero, and I pull off onto a road that leads to the beach and park in a gravel lot. The rain is too heavy to get out, but I can see the foaming, angry waves.

In the back of my car is a bag with some of the things I pilfered from the boxes in Mom's garage: mementos of Pat's short life. I climb over the front seat and open it. Here is a bracelet he made out of rubber bands.

Here is his left-foot Converse sneaker with doodles all over the side. Here are his leopard-print slippers, flecked with gold glitter.

I put on the slippers, which don't smell very fresh. But they evoke him. I read some of his letters, fingering the pages he once touched.

> I like telling you all my problems. Thank you for being there for me. You are so cool. Just so you know, I am always here for you and you can tell me ANYTHING! You are one of the BEST things in my life and I love you sooooo much. I am going to make you some origami, but I can't afford to send you a package, sorry. I am sooooo poor. I think I have like, one dollar. Hey! I just got a great idea. I'm going to send it to you right now. I got it at school. It says if you keep it, you will become rich and powerful. I want to pass it on to you. I hope it works.

The dollar falls out of the wrinkled envelope. Written in hot pink ink around its edges: "If you keep this dollar you will grow to be rich and very powerful!"

A wave breaks against the sand. In another letter, he has written: "On the subject of being high, I have never been high. I don't think I will EVER do drugs. I might just try once but not anytime soon. I think it is gross. WOW!! Where did that come from. I guess you can't hang this up on your wall of cute letters from me. Haha."

And then, just as quickly as it came, he is on to the next topic.

I search for a date, a marker in time I could use to pinpoint when it was that he started to fall. At the top of the letter: "I don't know the date, sorry!!!"

The dunes in the distance, through the muddled misty heat of my breath in the car, seem vacant. It all seems pointless. There is a part of me that has been carved out—he was not my child. He was not my friend. He was not my responsibility. Toward the end, he was not the brother I knew.

He was my Bunny, and he is gone.

In the gravel near where I've parked, a seagull lies in a large puddle, its wings folded awkwardly, like the underside of a broken umbrella. I think the bird might be sleeping until I see it flex and flutter one of its legs. It twitches violently, and I do not want to see it die. I take off Pat's slippers and put on my shoes. I leave the car and scale the craggy cliff down to the sand, where raindrops are falling along the crest of the tide, thousands of tiny bubbles popping all at once. As I walk along the shore, the wetness and tears blur my view of the horizon. I come across a wilted carnation that has washed up in the sand. I pick it up and toss it into the churning waves, where it quickly disappears. *For you Pat,* I think. As memorials go, it is pretty pathetic. I feel nothing: there is a total absence of emotion, different even than numbness, just a complete vacancy, a fissure with nothing below it.

I wonder why Pat didn't come to me when he was hurting, why he didn't reach out for help. Then again, why would he have? I had always thought of myself as a supportive sister, but why didn't I try to understand what it meant to have the disease of addiction and learn what I could do to help him? Why had I thought that yelling at Pat to "grow up and be a man" or "just stop using drugs" was in any way productive? My words flood back to me, choking my throat with the failures of my past. Of course Pat didn't come to me; he didn't want to be judged, and I would have judged him—I did judge him.

I think of the night Pat sang as he played the guitar in Dad's armchair; his fingers were buoyant as they strummed the strings, the melody deceivingly light. I had focused on the music, but I hadn't heard what he was saying, as if the notes filtered out the lyrics themselves. Only later did I come across his brutal words, etched in red pencil inside one of his notebooks:

In your powder lips, in your rolling hills of white
I see the future fade in and out

And then I'm on the ground
In my dreams I'm hiding
In my dreams I can fly
Swim through the sky into a tree
To never be seen again
All my dreams are bad
Ones where I die, so sad, too bad
It's just not enough, I need more
I say I don't want it
I just need it
To breathe, to feel, to know I'm alive

His cry for help was so obvious, and I had done nothing but nod. I had seen what I wanted to see; heard what I wanted to hear.

"Great song," I remember saying to him. "You're an awesome guitar player."

The wind lashes around me, making my ears burn. The storm is getting worse, and I start heading back to the car. The gull lies motionless in the puddle now, its wings frozen in the throes of death. Once the storm is over, it will be swept away and forgotten.

PART V

ACCEPTANCE

IN MY BEGINNING IS MY END.

IN MY END IS MY BEGINNING.

—T.S. ELIOT, *FOUR QUARTETS*

37 | A TERRIBLE TRUTH

AT FIRST THE movement is barely visible, a delicate shift of shadows and light. I follow it clumsily, unsure of where to look. But slowly it falls into a rhythm that I can follow, a wave, an infinitesimal pulsing. A heartbeat, a new life. A baby girl.

Ben turns from the glow of the ultrasound screen to face me, and we laugh, because it's magical and unfathomable and real. The wand pushes across my stomach in a sea of coldness, Ben holding my hand tight and reassuring. The tiny heart beats rhythmically, knowingly. It goes about its work, relentless and mechanical, without instruction or prodding.

I've anticipated this moment all my life: becoming a mother. The little figure on the screen will be our child. The world shifts again, the dim room filling with the warmth of our exhaled breath. Tears slide down my cheeks and tickle my neck, pooling on the table where I lie amazed and thrilled and terrified.

Someday I know this child will break my heart. All children break their parents' hearts at some point in their lives, in some way.

But what if this child breaks my heart like my brother?

A biting fear takes hold deep inside me. The fear that history will repeat itself. The fear that—like my mother—I could do everything in my power to protect my child and still she will slip away.

In that tiny smudge on the glowing screen is the promise of a whole person. How can I know all the joys and sorrows, all the things wonderful and ugly, that are to come as a result of her young life?

And knowing that I can't know, how can I possibly move forward into the fearful unknown?

My brother has gone away these days. Absent from my dreams, a faraway spot on the horizon that can't be reached, only seen flickering faintly through the haze of the sun's heat waves. I throw a rope toward him to try and tether him closer; I want to ask him, *Is this baby like you?* As if having that knowledge would somehow change the outcome, blockade the heartache that might be to come.

And what if he said yes? What if the tiny smudge is to grow into a baby and then a toddler and then a child and then a teen and then a young adult, only to die of addiction, like he did?

How would I bear it?

✖

ON THE WAY home from the doctor's office, driving along Van Ness Avenue, the streetlights slice the darkness like ships on an ocean, the pavement rising and falling like waves. From deep inside me, there come tiny flutters, and I unlatch the seat belt to press into my belly with my hand.

"Baby girl," I say out loud, making it true. I look out the window at the craters on the full moon; it is a sharp night, and the air smells of ice. Patches of gray dot the luminescent disk, the edges of one side imperfect, like a stone cradled by creek waters. It is so far away that its powdered mountains and crevices seem like something out of a fairy tale.

At a red light near city hall, a young man wearing a flannel shirt and Chuck Taylors steps into the crosswalk. His feet slop in the oily puddles riddled with the trash of life, soggy newspapers and cigarette butts. There's a childlike quality to the way he walks, something simple and open in the way he turns his face to the night sky with a slight open-mouthed grin. He evokes Pat like a punch to my gut that has come out of nowhere. It makes me blur my eyes to continue the dream, to indulge in the life that could have been, had fate taken a different turn.

For a moment I let myself believe that I can roll down the window and call out to him, "Pat! You're going to be an uncle to a little girl!" He'll turn back around and laugh in disbelief: "Ern! What? No way!" And then he'll hop into the passenger seat and we'll drive through the softly falling fog. When the time comes, he'll hold the baby girl in his arms, lumbering and gentle. He'll hoist her onto his shoulders as we walk along the beach while she grabs the bridge of his eyebrows from behind, and they'll face the windy ocean together.

Then comes the realization that this can never happen. Four years later, all it takes is seeing a glimpse of Pat in a stranger, and the impossibility of losing him comes rushing back. I ache to grab this imposter and hug him, to learn it was all a mistake and that Pat has been living on the streets. But the young man fades into an alleyway, his shadow swallowed by the headlights of oncoming cars. I whisper to the baby, "He would have been such a great uncle," as if this will help somehow. How am I ever to convey Pat to her? She'll know of him in the way of legends, a story passed down from another time, but she won't really know what's missing from her life with him gone.

I am sad that he took this from her, and from me. That he took this away from himself. I know he didn't mean to. But I grip the steering wheel and cry for the loss of the uncle my child will never know.

✖

OUR GRANDMOTHER IS getting old. Her skin lies creviced and papery on her form. Touched, it crinkles and warms and cannot be smoothed. For almost a hundred years, it has woken and breathed, soaked and purged. It is immeasurably changed from what it was at birth.

I kiss my grandmother's cheek, feeling the rose-petal softness. I watch as she opens the gift I have brought her: a baby bib sporting a pink monkey who declares, "I love my great-grandma." When its meaning sinks in, she looks up at me and shines.

"Well, well!" she exclaims. "Well, well."

As old people do, she talks often of death these days, and it makes me sad. I do not like to think about the moment her heart will stop beating. The thought makes me feel like a child again, the little girl untouched by death, who thought she had the ability to transcend the natural order of life and make all her loved ones live forever. But my grandmother brushes away my tears and winks.

"It's all right," she tells me. "It's as it should be. I have lived a wonderful life, and I have no regrets. Now have another brownie."

She talks of Pat often too: the younger Pat, her sweet little grandson, and the objects he left behind. The hard red suitcase he carried when coming to spend the weekend at her house as a toddler, the one that said GOIN' TO GRANDMA'S. The mess he made with his toys on her living room floor and refused to clean up: "I can't clean it up, Grandma," he said. "I'm Harry the Cat. I don't have any hands, only paws." The lawn chair he'd make her sit in while he showed her his tricks on the tire swing in our backyard, his blond hair blurring in the breeze of the cottonwood tree.

Sometimes she talks of the older Pat, trying to put together the pieces of the puzzle his life became to her, where he went wrong. She has always had a near-photographic recollection of dates and events, but some of the details have started to muddle. So she falls back on the memories that are still clear: "I kept telling him to join some clubs, get involved in new activities, run for student body president," she says, "and he just laughed and said, 'Oh, Grandma.'" She laughs a little too as she says this, as if to throw up her hands at the impossibility of the situation, the silly little things she once thought might save Pat.

But she says Pat is where he should be. The more she reads in the newspapers about the growing numbers of painkiller addicts overdosing on heroin, the more she believes Pat's fate was imminent, because he suffered from the disease of addiction and always would. She misses him, but she believes he is at peace now, and she says she will see him again soon. She sets the tea water to boil and asks me to hang the bib in the doorway of her kitchen with Scotch tape so she can see it every day. I tell her how scared I am that my baby will break my heart like Pat did.

"Don't ever allow yourself to get caught up in thoughts like that," she says. "You can't think about what might happen tomorrow or the next day. Just treasure every moment."

I walk through her dining room to get the tape to hang the bib. Pat beams from his high school graduation picture on the piano next to the bay windows. Someone who didn't know him might look at it and comment on his handsome features, his brilliant smile and broad shoulders cloaked in cobalt polyester. But those of us who knew him well can see the teasing trickster, the way he is hamming for the camera, poking a little bit of fun.

My knees go weak, and I feel there's something over my head or behind me perhaps: a presence or a thing. I open the drawer of the antique writing desk and search for the tape. There is a pause in the air, a stillness in which the whole world freezes. On my shoulder I feel a pressure so light that it is barely noticeable. I close my eyes and think of my brother.

"Pat?" I whisper into the sudden stillness, but the pressure on my shoulder has already disappeared.

The tea kettle whistles. I look again at Pat's picture on the piano. I remember the way he sat there, that last Christmas, after our fight. He was goofing around, making faces as Brian sat on his lap. I had looked at him with my swollen eyes and thought, *I love you.*

If there had been a way to know from the beginning of the sadness Pat would bring into our lives, would I rather that he had never existed? If I could know the price I might have to pay for loving my unborn child, for the heartbreak that might be ahead, would I choose not to have created her at all, never to have her be a part of my life?

No.

"If I were going to begin practicing the presence of God for the first time today, it would help to begin by admitting the three most terrible truths of our existence: that we are so ruined, and so loved, and in charge of so little," writes Anne Lamott. My grandmother is right: I cannot let the fears of my past overtake my future; I must take each step as it comes. I can't save anyone: not Pat, not my future child, maybe not even myself.

It is indeed a terrible truth, and I am learning to admit it.

✖

I AM BEGINNING to lose count of the time we have spent without Pat. It is another year; winter is fading, spring is approaching, and soon it will be summer, and his birthday. I find that I have to count: one, two, three, four, almost five years gone; this year he would have turned twenty-five.

This process of forgetting is natural—maybe even good, I know, but still sometimes it feels shaky and uncertain, perhaps forbidden in some way. I do not want to forget Pat; nor do I want the world he lived in to forget him. But I realize I need to loosen my grip. We will always be tied by that invisible thread, but I must let it grow longer and let him go.

I think he would want me to let him go. If I had died and he had lived, I would want him to loosen his hold on our thread. Not all at once, and never completely, but centimeter by centimeter, slowly over the years. No matter what terribleness had transpired between us, whatever pool of regrets and guilt had been left in my wake, I wouldn't want him to be weighed down forever by this heaviness. I would want forgiveness, and I would forgive him. I would want him to hold me always in his heart but to be happy and free.

Is this what you want for us, Pat? I ask the grinning blond boy in the picture on my wall. He is hugging me tightly, our faces lit from the glow of the birthday cake candles below us, and though he gives me no answer, I feel that he says yes.

38 | I SEE YOU

BRENDAN WAS THE first friend Alex lost to heroin. He looks down on her from where he sits on a stoop clutching his Yankees cap, immortalized in his youth on a poster tacked to the wall in her office at a harm-reduction non-profit in downtown Oakland. Emily is there too, her youthful eyes facing the camera, unflinching. "I need to get this under control," she'd told Alex the day before she OD'd, frustrated with herself for relapsing after three years clean. Corey squints into the sunlight in the picture next to Emily. The evening of Emily's memorial service, he couldn't take it anymore: the pain of losing his friend, the unseen wounds of war from the time he'd spent fighting in the U.S. Army, the sickening feeling that he was never going to be free from heroin's grip. He'd gone out that night and overdosed too.

There are others on the wall: hundred of names etched in Sharpie on construction-paper flowers—mostly strangers to Alex, but somebody loved them. Pete. Hailey. Amber. Danny. J.D. Lola. Every day, Alex is reminded of these losses, of the fact that she is swimming upstream while the river bears down on her.

I ask Alex if it makes her sad to be surrounded by these constant reminders of death. She says that it does, but it also motivates her to keep going back out on the streets, where there are so many people who need help.

"It reminds me why I do what I do," she says.

She gestures to an Oscar Wilde quote written on one of the posters: "We are all in the gutter, but some of us are looking at the stars."

✖

FIRST THE FACE pales and turns colors: blue if the person is light skinned, gray if the person is dark. Then the nail beds go purple. The breath comes in short, shallow gulps and slows until it is nearly imperceptible. Foam forms at the edges of the lips. A gurgling sound wrenches from the throat: the beginnings of the death rattle.

Time stops in the midst of an overdose. For Alex, there is always a moment of panic. Not all overdoses have to end in death: there is an antidote that can reverse the effects of an opiate overdose—naloxone, sold under the brand name Narcan—and Alex is trained to use it and to teach others how to use it. But it's all a matter of getting to the person in time.

Alex, who is thirty-six, has been doing this kind of work since she was twenty-four and living in Massachusetts, where she ran a needle exchange and helped develop the state's overdose prevention program. Though Alex herself never got into drugs, lots of her close friends did, which was what motivated her to work in the field. Back then, she was constantly getting emotionally tangled up in the lives of the people she was trying to help. During the day she could put up a strong front, but at night she'd go home and cry, overwhelmed by the infinite cycle of sadness, the suburban kids she'd been working with since their early teens, when they were hooked on pills, who were now homeless heroin addicts with hepatitis B and end-stage liver disease.

That was before she'd learned that no matter how hard she tried, she didn't have the power to save those she cared about. It was a tough lesson, but it has helped her set better boundaries with her clients, to labor under the pretense not that she might be able to save them but that she might be able to help them save themselves.

One of the first overdoses she witnessed was behind city hall in Cambridge. Tim, one of her clients at the needle exchange, had been on a weeklong bender of booze and benzos and dope. His limp body was surrounded by government employees, some of whom had called the paramedics. Gripped by the fear that they wouldn't get there in time, Alex fumbled with the Narcan applicator in her shaking hands and shot him with the antidote twice. As she rubbed Tim's sternum and administered mouth to mouth, she screamed at him in her head, *You cannot die in front of me right now. You can't.* Alex's coworker, a former addict, stood unmoving beside her: she'd seen plenty of overdoses in her time, but this was the first one she'd witnessed sober, without drugs to dull the fear.

Even when the ambulance finally pulled up, Tim still hadn't woken up. But the Narcan had worked, and Alex breathed a sigh of relief as he was carted away to the hospital.

After the doctors released him, Tim overdosed twice more that week. Alex believed he was trying to kill himself, though she didn't know for sure. She'd figured out that sometimes there was no rhyme or reason to an overdose. Some people, like Tim, were on a suicide mission every time they used; others just wanted to get high because they were bored or depressed or wanted to get out of their own heads. Nor was there any predictability as to who avoided death, other than the fact that sometimes, like Tim, they happened to be in the right place at the right time when the overdose occurred.

A few years later, she heard that Tim had gotten clean: he ended up living the life of a soccer dad, married with two kids.

She still thinks of him sometimes when things get tough.

Of those who don't make it, it's easy to think about the what ifs. What if that person's life hadn't been snuffed out? What if she'd been saved, grown up, gotten clean, had a career and a family? What if he'd had the chance to turn his life around?

What if Pat were still here?

I'm not naive enough to believe in the inevitability of happy endings. I know that even if Narcan had saved my brother from death in the early hours of that February morning, he likely would have gone down another time.

But that's the thing: he also might not have.

✖

THE YOUNG WOMAN standing in front of Alex tonight gazes down at her feet when Alex beckons toward the folding chair beside her. She sits, one hand gripping her only belongings, a tattered black sweatshirt and a backpack full of books. All day long, she rode the bus from one end of the city to the other and back again, trying to read. But her mind wouldn't stop spinning.

The night before, she'd spent three hours walking the streets with her male companion, supporting the weight of his body, his face crushed into her neck as he babbled. The heroin had been so potent that he'd fallen face first into the pavement after he shot it, and she was sure that if she didn't keep him moving, he'd overdose and die. So they walked. Tonight, she's brought a paper lunch bag to Ladies Night at a drop-in center for homeless drug users in San Francisco—her "just in case" bag—and is filling it with clean needles and Narcan. She's not naive: she was a medical assistant before she became a homeless drug addict. But she is ashamed of her sun-reddened skin, of the bumpy scar on her neck from shooting heroin that curls like a dead worm decaying on the pavement, of the paper plate leaking fluids from a lump of chicken chow mein, her only food of the day.

Alex knows she can't save this woman, or the other women shuffling around the community center smelling of urine and damp clothes, or for that matter any of the dozens of people she encounters on any given day in her work on the streets. But she can give them one of the tools they can use to save themselves. She considers every Narcan training a success, because it has the potential to save someone's life—and she believes that even the lives of addicts are worth saving.

That is Alex's reward; that is the thing that keeps her coming back, despite the tidal wave of hopelessness she fights against: no guarantee, simply the possibility that one person's path might change course, averted away from death and back into life, giving him or her the opportunity to someday, maybe, get clean.

If you die, you don't get that chance.

"We're not God," she says. "We can't control everything that happens. We just want to give them the chance to stay alive long enough to change."

While prevention programs focus narrowly on reducing the risky behavior—drug use—itself, harm-reduction programs like Alex's operate on the principle that the risky behavior is the end result of many other factors that lead people to a place of ambivalence, the mind-set of not caring whether the next pill or shot will kill them. Alex's program accepts that—for better or for worse—licit and illicit drug use is a part of the world, and the program works to minimize drug use's harmful effects rather than ignoring or condemning the problem.

There is evidence that efforts to educate the public on Narcan are working: since 2003, when San Francisco became the first California city to publicly fund naloxone's distribution, the antidote has saved more than eleven hundred lives—reversing 274 overdoses in the city in 2012 alone; nationally, more than ten thousand lives have been saved since 1996.[62] But much of the time, for Alex, the battle feels like it will rage on forever. As in many other urban areas, heroin has long had a foothold in San Francisco, and the recent rise of opiate painkillers has fueled the problem. The people Alex works with are rarely one-drug users, and almost everyone abuses pills.

Most of the time, Alex can handle the day-to-day stresses of the job:
the degrading details of the tricks her clients turn to feed their habits,
the weeping abscesses on their battered arms, the news of yet another
relapse, overdose, or death. She tries to focus on the small successes of
human survival: the young woman who finds childlike joy in filling out
coloring books while passing time on the streets; the kid from Boston
who likes to share silly YouTube videos with her between needle swaps.
But as her career path has evolved, and she has scaled back on her direct
service work to tackle more big-picture challenges, she is facing a different kind of strain. The feeling that no matter how many trainings she
conducts, no matter how hard she lobbies state lawmakers or how desperately she seeks more funding and resources, she's up against Goliath-
like forces.

For one thing, there is constant pushback from people who seem to
view Narcan education the same way they look at needle exchanges, as
if such programs are somehow encouraging and enabling drug use rather
than warning against its dangers. There are essentially no downsides to
Narcan: it isn't addictive, and you can't take too much of it. Moreover,
the idea that Narcan might be viewed as a get-out-of-jail-free card, as
permission to use a bunch of drugs, is illogical, because Narcan instantly
wipes out a person's high. For those who have a habit, it throws them
into the hell of withdrawal. Still, at a recent prescription drug awareness
event in a wealthy suburb of San Francisco, not a single parent came up
to her table to learn more about naloxone—in an area where painkiller
and heroin addiction among the youth population is rife. Learning about
naloxone first requires admitting that there's a problem, and Alex is at
a loss for how to break through this wall of denial. She knows for a
fact that Narcan has made a positive difference for some parents, who
have realized that even if they are powerless over their child's addiction,
they can take some steps to provide a way out of death. Though it's

unimaginable for many parents, some have used Narcan to take a break from the frustrating cycle of threatening to throw the kid in jail or send him or her to rehab, only to have the drug use continue.

"It's a different kind of conversation; it's telling the kid, 'I don't want you to use, but I don't want you to die,'" she says. "It's the hardest kind of reality to swallow, but it's reality."

Basically, it's hoping that a singular message will break through: *I love you. I want you here with me.* Simple words, but ones that can be difficult to say in the midst of active addiction.

Unfortunately, parental denial is just the tip of the iceberg when it comes to the roadblocks Alex faces. There are also corporate forces working against her. The manufacturer of naloxone has considerably jacked up the price of the antidote in recent years, threatening the sustainability of overdose prevention programs nationwide. Alex's program, for example, pays about $15 for a 1-milliliter vial of injectable Narcan—a 1,500 percent increase since 2008; it is currently hoping for a "compassionate pricing" deal from the manufacturer or some of the Narcan distributors. Indeed, the past two years alone have seen almost 10 percent of the nation's distribution programs close their doors as a result of Narcan's high price tag.[63]

There are other barriers too. Just last week, Alex was on a conference call with a representative from a major pharmaceutical company that manufactures a widely abused opioid painkiller. Like other manufacturers, the company had recently reformulated its painkiller to include an antiabuse feature that turns the pill into a gummy mush when broken, making it more difficult to crush and snort or inject. When Alex noted that one effect of the company's highly addictive original product—and subsequently its reformulated abuse-deterrent product—was that abusers were making the switch to heroin, the rep seemed almost pleased. It was actually a good thing, he said, because law enforcement was better

equipped to deal with the "bad guys" anyway. The "bad guys" being the
druggies, the scummy addicts, the dirty junkies who were of no concern
to him, never mind the fact that his company's product had, in many
cases, fueled their addiction.

Alex muted the call so that she could shout out in frustration.
Although she encounters the stigmatization of addiction on a daily basis,
it still stings—and it gets her down if she lets herself think about it too
much. She has to remind herself why she continues to fight, and of the
small triumphs that make her job worth it. She remembers the words of
a heroin-addicted friend who told her he hung out at the local needle
exchange because it was the only place where people treated him like a
human being, where he could drink coffee and chat about the latest movies and not feel judged for being a junkie.

"There is something very profound about being seen and heard,"
she says. "When someone makes them feel like a real person, they
have a reason to stay positive about things; they might not want to die
anymore. You'll hear them switching from the mind-set of 'I'm just a
worthless junkie' to 'Maybe I'm not so bad after all—maybe I'm worth
saving too.'"

The message Alex wants to get through to the kids she works with
is simply, *I see you.*

*I see you as you are. The drugs you do, the tricks you turn, the stuff
you steal, the pants you're wearing that smell like piss: none of these
matter. Even though you're addicted, and you do all these things, I care
about you. I give a shit if you live or die.*

I believe your life is worth living.

39 | ANOTHER LIFE

Almost everyone who has had a limb amputated will experience a phantom limb—the vivid impression that the limb is not only still present, but in some cases, painful. Phantoms are more vivid, and persist longer, after traumatic limb loss. This may be due to the greater attention paid to the mutilated or painful limb before it is lost, or it may represent the survival of pre-amputation "pain memories" in the phantom.

In many cases the phantom is present initially for a few days or weeks, then gradually fades from consciousness. In others, it may persist for years, even decades.

— V.S. RAMACHANDRAN AND WILLIAM HIRSTEIN, "THE PERCEPTION OF
   PHANTOM LIMBS"

WHEN THE QUESTION comes, innocent and simple, I do not know what to say.

Someone asks, "How many siblings do you have?" and I am stumped.

Do I have two brothers and one sister, or one sister and one brother? Is Pat no longer my brother because he is dead? No. But then if I say I have three siblings, how do I explain the absence of one? The easy answer is that I have two siblings, but it seems unfair to Pat. It leaves him out, erases him, implies he isn't worth mentioning. The difficult answer is that I have three siblings, and one of them is dead.

Pat is dead. But in many ways, at least to me, he is not. He is my phantom limb: there, but not there. An illusion, but one so insistent that the perception feels real.

When I see him in the face of a boy waiting at a bus stop, I stifle the urge to drive around the block for one more look. I can now leave the phone in the other room at night and tell myself that any bad news will have to wait until tomorrow. I feel the tug, the slight ache, when I do these things, my phantom limb reminding me of what once was there, and now is not.

But Pat is still alive in many places. In the pictures on my wall, kissing Mom, smushing his cheek up against me, laughing with Cait, his arm thrown around Bri. In the origami book on the shelf at Cedar Street, and in the cottonwood tree, and on the rope swing where he used to play. In the notes he wrote to me on scrap paper and crumpled into balls, to be opened when I had moved away from home and missed him: *Thank you for loving me!!!*

He is alive in a cardboard box under his bunk bed at the cabin. The box is papered over with Homer Simpson gift wrap and cutouts from magazines. Inside are Pat's prized possessions from the summer he was twelve. There is a hacky sack, a friendship bracelet, and a broken yellow shot put. A miniature stuffed penguin. Birthday cards from Kathy, from Betty and Tom; a note from Grandma telling Pat she is proud of him. A beaded wooden necklace and a caterpillar fashioned out of purple pipe cleaners. A postcard I'd sent him while traveling abroad.

Next to the cardboard box is a bag filled with plastic water guns and a basket of our flippers and sandals, in various shapes and sizes. The pair on top is Pat's and is still covered in sand from the nearby creek.

He is alive there too.

✖

"I'M NEVER GOING back to that life," the young man tells me. "I don't want to be a loser."

He fidgets from across the sticky table at the Chinese restaurant, making the veins on his skinny arms stick out. He is so young—Pat's age, just twenty—and he is earnest and searching and lost. His heart-shaped face is bent downward as he defiantly rubs an errant tear away: man enough not to cry, boy enough to still be vulnerable. I want to comfort or reassure him somehow, but I keep my distance, letting him talk.

I also want so badly to believe what he says, that he is done with painkillers and heroin for good. He's been clean for nearly seven months, and he's on the right track: he has moved far away from his home in Orange County, which he calls "the realm of temptation," and he has lots of people who want him to succeed—loving parents, a supportive girlfriend, sober friends. He's looking to enroll in a community college and get a job, and hope lights up his eyes, bright and clear.

But by now I have learned the harsh truth. He says these words to me now, in this safe place that feels like it is a lifetime away from the madness of before. He believes them; I want to believe them. But in the end they are just words, fragile and fleeting.

With the exception of just a few, nearly every young addict I have met over the last few years has relapsed. Some, like Anna, have gotten clean again. Some, like Joel, have claimed to have gotten clean again and then disappeared. Some, like Ethan, have ended up in jail as a result of their addiction, while others have vanished completely. Over and over, they say to me: "I am really done this time. I don't know what it is, but something feels different. I never want to go back to what I was before." And then, suddenly, they do.

There is a small part of me that feels betrayed every time it happens, though they owe me nothing. I'm only a fleeting part of their lives, someone they open up to briefly before moving on—and I don't know them well enough to justifiably worry about them. But I want to ask them why they lied. Why they throw it all away again and again.

They don't know why, of course. Relapse is often a part of the process of recovery, and because addiction is a chronic illness, the possibility of relapse looms in the background even after the addict stops using. There is a physiological reason for this: drug use can cause measurable deficits in levels of dopamine—a "feel-good" neurotransmitter that helps control the brain's reward and pleasure centers—and it takes time for the brain to repair this damage; in the meantime, the brain craves drugs to compensate for the flatness, depression, and anxiety that characterize dopamine deficiency. There is also a psychological reason, which is that in sobriety, the emotional challenges that may have driven the user to self-medicate are no longer being numbed out by the drugs.[64]

And there is a third reason I have come to know: the "fuck it" reason.

"Take a moment to write some thoughts that you have had that led up to a relapse or using/drinking episode in the past," instructed one paper in my brother's rehab file, to which he had responded: "I've been clean for a month. Hell yes, I'm stoked, I'm gonna get fucked up. I'll stop tomorrow. Fuck it."

As simple as that. *Fuck it.* And all of a sudden, everything tumbles downward once again.

Sometimes a relapse is simply that: a setback, a reversion, a backslide. But sometimes a relapse is the end. There are reasons for this too: overdose is most common when an addict's tolerance is down due to not using—whether the addict took a break, was incarcerated, or, like Pat, was in treatment. Mixing drugs, going to a new dealer, or getting stronger drugs than usual also heighten the risk, as does using alone, because no one is around to help if the addict goes out.

And maybe there is another factor involving fate and luck and chance. Maybe for some unknowable reason, some people just don't make it out alive.

Across from me, the young man holds his head in his hands as he chokes up. He remembers the day last year when he randomly ran into one of his using buddies. Thirteen months of sobriety, and his first thought was, *What the hell. I'll just do it one time. Fuck it.*

That was all it took to be thrust back into the nightmare. He doesn't know why he survived the next few months, or why, when his parents forced him into rehab this time, it seemed to work. Neither do I.

As we leave the restaurant, he hands me a little cellophane packet.

"Don't forget your fortune cookie," he says. "It's bad luck!"

He gets into his car and drives away, waving. I am saddened, thinking of the way he described one of the last times he used, loading the needle with a big shot, not caring if he lived or died. The way he looked just a little bit guilty when he said he'd gone online recently to research the new tamper-resistant feature of some of his favorite painkillers; he'd heard you could break through it by soaking the pills in rubbing alcohol for ten minutes.

"Is that true?" I had asked him.

"Oh, I don't know, I haven't done it," he'd said hastily. "I just looked it up because I was curious."

The fortune reads: "Do not be overly suspicious where it is not warranted." It's advice I'd like to take, but I need to be realistic too: his chances are as good, and as bad, as anyone else's.

✖

IN MY IMAGINATION, on the night my brother dies, he loads the needle with a big shot and thinks, *Fuck it.* He ties off his arm with a shoelace and flexes his vein. Afterward, he sinks to the floor, alone behind the locked bedroom door. His breathing slows, his lungs fill with fluid, his heart stops.

In another life, the door isn't locked. His girlfriend stumbles down the unlit hallway. She is also high, but not too high to open the door, though she has to thrust all her weight against it to push aside his body, lying heavy and still. She screams and tries to rouse him; he won't wake up. Her parents come downstairs and call 911.

In that life, the antidote reaches Pat before it's too late. His breath returns, his blood starts flowing again, and as he's loaded into the ambulance, he's confused and sick and pissed off that his high has been wasted. But his body is sent to the hospital, not to the morgue.

Maybe it's still not enough for Pat, in that life where he gets saved one February night. Maybe he leaves the hospital filled with rage and guilt and the *fuck it* feeling and goes straight back to his dealer. Maybe he hurts everyone more: Mom cuts him off completely, I won't take his phone calls, Cait and Bri refuse to speak to him. Maybe he starts living on the streets out of his backpack, maybe he begins stealing from convenience stores and breaking into people's cars, maybe he gets thrown in jail. Or maybe his body just gives up one night and he overdoses and dies, just like he did in this life.

But maybe, in that other life, he survives. Maybe he finally gets some serious clean time, maybe he starts to really want it: the death wish overcome by the wish to live. Bit by bit, piece by piece, his brain rebuilds itself, and it isn't easy, it isn't the life he wanted for himself, but he's here, he's alive.

There are so many things I want to say to him in that life. Lots of it is just the little stuff, the random details. There's a new shop in my neighborhood that sells only Belgian waffles, their dough laced with pearl sugar that melts into a caramelized shell. Pat would love it. The baby just kicked and flipped; I think she might be taking after her monkey uncle. And has he heard about the twenty-year-old skateboarder in

Pennsylvania who just topped the Guinness World Record mark for the most 180-degree ollies in one minute?

There are bigger, more important things I want to say to him too. Things that might not have changed the outcome, that may have fallen on deaf ears, but that may also have sparked something in him that made him certain he was loved and wanted, drawing him closer to life and away from death.

I believe in you, I say to him in that life. *Every minute is a chance to turn it all around.*

I say other things too. In that life I am less angry, more straightforward, and better able to draw boundaries and be honest about them. *Because of your addiction, I have stopped living my life,* I tell him. *I can't do that anymore. I can't live my life waiting to get the phone call that you're dead. I will always be here for you if you want to talk, I'll always help you get help. But I am releasing you in my heart, acknowledging the fact that you may die, and I can't save you. I have to allow myself to move forward. I forgive you for everything you've done to hurt me. I know it's because of your disease, and I know how much you suffer. And I forgive myself for not knowing more about addiction sooner, and for all the hurtful things I said to you because I was angry and scared and felt you slipping away.*

I love you, Pat, I say to him. *I loved you then, I love you now, I will love you always.*

40 | TAKE HIM HOME

BAILEY IS LATE for her waitressing job, and she can't find the knives. Her red high-tops squeak on the tiled floor as she hunts through the drawers in her family's sun-drenched kitchen, racing against the clock. A glass of iced tea sits sweating on the countertop, next to a silver-framed picture of her with her older brother Asher. In the picture, the two towheaded toddlers hold hands on the beach, their bronzed backs to the camera, facing the ocean. They are only a year apart. So they are nearly the same height, like twins. As Bailey sifts frantically through potholders and measuring cups, she glances at the picture and says a silent prayer for Asher, who called earlier this morning from the rehab facility where he's approaching his one-month sobriety mark. He was threatening to walk out, and it made Bailey mad.

Or was it sad? Or frustrated? Or hopeless? Or all of those emotions mixed together?

As she knife hunts, she chastises herself in her head: *Do not judge. You don't know the storm God has asked one of his children to walk through.*

She finally opens a bottom drawer and locates the knives: a whole stash of them mixed together, anything sharper than a butter knife, the jagged edges searing against each other in a tangled mess. Bailey shakes her head—what family keeps knives in an out-of-the-way bottom drawer where no one can find them?

She slices through the rough green skin of an avocado and thinks, *My family*. The kind of family that lives in a perfect big house in a gated community overlooking the San Clemente coastline, the kind of family that is shining and blond and beautiful but is crumbling underneath. The kind of family with an addict like Asher, whose drug-fueled rampages have left holes in the wall and a kitchen cleansed of potential weapons, a secret drawer of knives.

As Bailey washes the knife and returns it to its hiding place, she wills her brother to stay strong. She thinks, *God gives the toughest battles to his strongest soldiers.*

✖

THE FIRST TIME Bailey betrayed Asher was when he stole her needles. Well, it felt like betrayal at the time, although now that she's studying to be a drug counselor, she knows that what she was really doing was loving him by refusing to enable him.

It was two years ago, when she was home on a break from Bible college in Maui. Bailey knew that Asher's addiction was out of control. He'd been smoking weed and taking pills since he was a freshman in high school, but things had really gone downhill when he started smoking heroin. Then his two best friends died, one of suicide and the other in a car accident, and their deaths had thrown Asher into a tailspin of depression. Nothing seemed to help: he'd been to jail, he'd been committed to a psychiatric hospital, he'd been through a series of treatment centers. But he just kept getting worse.

Bailey had been taking weekly shots of vitamin B12 to treat her anemia, and she'd left a bag of needles in her bedroom closet before she'd headed off to school six months earlier. But when she went looking for the supply, it was gone. She sat down on the carpet and stared up at the holes in the wall, punched by Asher in a fit of rage; her dad had patched over them, but you could still see where his fist had smashed through the plaster. She did not want to believe that Asher had stolen her needles, because that would mean not only that Asher was a thief and a liar but that he was an IV drug user too.

All the way down the hallway to Asher's room, she prayed that it wasn't true. When she found the bag, nearly empty and crammed inside his sock drawer, her heart dropped into her feet, because she knew that this was the moment where she had to draw the line. She knew that it wasn't really Asher who stole the needles—it was his disease, his addiction—but even though she cared about him as a sister, she couldn't continue protecting him.

When Asher came home to the confrontation awaiting him, he was furious. He started screaming and slamming his head against the wall, and the cops were called. But Bailey knew she had done the right thing for Asher, and she refused to let herself feel bad about it.

She recalled a scripture: "I will not cause pain without allowing something new to be born." All she could do was hope that something good would come of her decision, that Asher would somehow turn away from the darkness and toward the light.

Sometimes Bailey thinks Asher has a chance of making it. A few months ago, when he was in rehab, he wrote a letter to himself, trying to convince the addict part of him to stay sober in order to avoid the hellish withdrawals he endured every time he tried to stop using heroin. "I will get severe anxiety attacks, not being able to feel my legs, thinking everyone is looking at me and get unbearably hot," he wrote.

> I will get the chills at random times in the day, my teeth will chatter and I will have no control over it. I will not be able to think straight and I will think I'm doing everything wrong. I will get very depressed and watch the day pass while I'm just sitting on the couch. My muscles will twitch in my

arms, legs, everywhere and I will become tired and sore. I will have terrible, very weird thoughts and feelings of suicide. I will get night sweats and dreams of me dying: drowning or falling off a building. I will spit up black gunk. I will be hurting my family and friends and they will think I do not care about my health or future, which I think about every fucking day and just want to get past it and I haven't lost my mind fully yet but will if I don't stay sober and eventually I will die. For once I'm admitting I need help to get through this and I can't do it myself. The sun is always shining, make the right decision. You have to! There are no more chances this time.

Three weeks after he wrote the letter, Asher relapsed again.

Bailey has lost count of Asher's relapses. She can't allow herself to get wrapped up in them anymore; she is only twenty years old, and she's already sick of the roller coaster—first with her oldest brother, Kai, age twenty-four, although thankfully he's been able to stay clean; then for the last few years with twenty-one-year-old Asher. Although she's the baby of the family, she's taken on a maternal role with both her brothers and her parents, setting clear boundaries and sticking to them.

It helps that she has learned more about addiction in her classes; she'd always had compassion for her brothers, but she didn't really understand the way addiction had affected their brains. Bailey herself had never been drawn to drugs: she'd witnessed firsthand that her brothers' curiosity had taken them to places they'd never imagined—terrible places she had no desire to go to. But for years, she took on their struggle as her own, because she loved them so much and hated to see them suffering.

Her deep faith in God has also helped, though Bailey doesn't really know where it came from. Their parents hadn't raised them in a particularly religious household, so she wasn't primed to turn to God when things started to fall apart. Call it a survival mechanism, or call it a miracle, but at some point Bailey decided that living in fear was going to get her nowhere and that she was going to give it all up to a higher being.

She won't let herself sit around anymore, living her life in limbo, waiting for a tragedy to happen before finding peace; that would just mean that the drugs were winning. By admitting she was powerless, she was releasing herself from the crushing responsibility she felt to save Asher's life—and a feeling of comfort replaced her anxiety.

"I needed help, so I surrendered to God," she says simply. "And if I didn't have God, I'd probably be doing drugs too right now."

So Bailey goes on with her life, knowing she might bury Asher, moving forward with the understanding that, any day, he might die, and that there is nothing she can do about it except pray that it won't happen. She doesn't proselytize to her brother exactly, but she does try to show him that if he could just do the same thing—admit that he is powerless—he might have a fighting chance at sobriety.

On the good days, Bailey feels like he's hearing the message, even if it takes awhile to get through. A few weeks ago, she convinced Asher to come hang out at the beach with her and Kai—a rare opportunity for the three siblings to spend time together, since Kai didn't like hanging around when Asher was using. Under the 90-degree sun, Kai confronted Asher, asking him what he was trying to hide with his long-sleeved shirt.

"Just take it off," Kai said. "You need to fix yourself now, or here's your reality: go to prison, become homeless, commit suicide, go psycho, or die." The assault angered Asher, who fumed in the front seat next to Bailey after they dropped Kai off at his sober living house.

"When was the last time you did heroin?" she asked tentatively as he stared stone-faced out the passenger window.

"A couple of days ago," he said first.

"Last night," he said next.

Finally, "Fine, I did it this morning."

"It's okay Asher, I'm not mad at you," Bailey said. "I just want to know why you're doing this to yourself."

Asher's face suddenly went slack, as if all the weight of the world were on his shoulders.

"I'm like a dog, and heroin is my owner," he said. "It keeps me on a leash, makes me heel and sit, chokes me. I'm heroin's bitch."

Bailey slammed on the brakes, the tires screaming in protest as their heads jerked forward and then backward with the force of her stop. Asher was freaking out, grabbing his hair and digging his fists into his face.

"Look at me in the eyes," Bailey said, laying her hand on her brother's shoulder. She felt a divine strength coursing through her veins.

Asher looked.

"You can beat this thing, Asher," she said. "Don't make your sister plan your funeral. You are digging your own grave."

"Maybe we can hang out again sometime," she added. "Thank you for spending time with me today. I'm so glad you wanted to see me. I love you."

Asher glared into the distance, silent. Then, softly, he said, "I love you too."

Bailey considered that a good day.

On the bad days, Bailey prays for peace for Asher. Sometimes she thinks peace looks like sobriety; other times she thinks peace looks like death.

On those days, she prays for God to take him home.

41 | ROSES AND WEEDS

THROUGH MY BEDROOM window, the plum tree shimmers in the cautious warmth of April. Thousands of cobweb petals dance through the air, a relentless waterfall of tiny white spirals. They fall to the damp earth like snowflakes, smelling of sugar, reminding me of home.

We had a plum tree there too. Every other year it bloomed at Easter time, heralding the arrival of spring. I don't remember any white petals, though, only the tart amethyst-colored fruits we hunted like lost treasure. Their sun-roasted skins snapping as we bit into them, their juices spraying outward and down.

I remember Pat as a little boy, climbing to the top of the plum tree and hopping over the neighbor's fence. The warm, tangy-sweet liquid at the back of our throats. The smell of spring, like a promise: the promise of Easter-basket delights, rainbow-colored plastic eggs filled with jelly beans hidden among the periwinkles and ivy, a rabbit made of solid chocolate at the center of the dining room table.

Sour grass has begun to bloom along the hill near my house, blinking along the slopes like tiny yellow lighthouses. I run my hands through the tall grass and let my fingers linger on its velvety petals. I force myself to think: What is the promise I hope for now?

Pat, running through the shadows of the pine trees in the forest by our cabin. His hair catches the flickers of light and he laughs. I conjure this image, a mixture of memory and dream. Little by little, I have been letting him fade away.

The promise I hope for is peace. To see Pat, scaling the plum tree, ascending among the tufts of cotton-soft petals, surrounded by sweetness and sun. If some part of him still exists, I hope it is the child part of him: the innocence of our youth, before the dark crept in.

I hope he is settling there in the petal-clouds, falling asleep, dreaming of whatever it is he wished for as a boy.

✖

UNDERNEATH THE VEIL of the cottonwood tree, the roses in my mother's garden bloom. The wind shakes sticky pods from branches, petite half moons that wander past the petals and thorns before nesting on the ground next to the old playhouse, vines blanketing its petrified walls. The roses are just beginning to open toward the sky, each bush representing a member of our family. There is the red Mister Lincoln for Mom and Dad, a deep, velvety bloom that smells of tea and damask. For me, there is the John F. Kennedy, heady and white. Cait's is the musky Midas Touch, a regal bloom with golden petal crowns that gleam in the sun; Bri's is the Rio Samba, with blossoms that take on a reddish-orange halo as they mature. And for Pat, there is, of course, the St. Patrick, its yellow inner sanctum cradled by a halo of petals of shamrock green.

There are other roses blooming in the garden too: the fragrant Perfume Delight, symbolizing our family's strength; the delicate Blue Moon for our friends; the classic Chrysler Imperial to remind us of our many blessings; and the majestic Peace rose, representing our hopes and dreams.

My mother tends the garden, coaxing life from the gnarled branches. She stays up late at night, reading about roses and how to grow and nurture them.

"Choose a sunny area of the garden that gets at least four to five hours of sun," she learns. "Do not crowd your rose with other trees and plants. Some roses, such as climbers and shrubs, don't mind company, but most like to mix with other roses or other non-invasive plants. A newly planted rose doesn't like to grow in the same soil that an older rose bush has been in."

She is focusing her energy on the roses, but she has always loved weeds. The weeds that grow through the asphalt on the patio, through the slats of the wooden fence, through the winding bricks of the stairs that lead to the backyard. They are testimonies to the ability to endure, she has explained to me: the urge to survive so fervid that they succeed at defying life-stopping challenges.

I want to grab her by her garden-gloved hands, the warm soil dusting the canvas roughness, and say, *Look at yourself. You are the weeds, making the roses grow.*

I am staying up late at night reading too. By now, the smudge on the ultrasound screen has turned into a recognizable form, a tiny figure with hands, feet, a round belly, the slope of a nose, and two lips. I am trying to assuage my fears of loving so much, and losing; there is love, building inside me, uncontrollable and unbidden, and as it multiplies, so do my fears. But I am being moved forward. "Bonding is a continuation of the relationship that began during pregnancy," I am told. "Now you can see, feel, and talk to the little person whom you knew only as the 'bulge' or from the movements and the heartbeat you heard through medical instruments. Inside, you gave your blood; outside, you give your milk, eyes, hands, and voice—your entire self."

I do want to give my entire self to this new being, despite my fears. I want to teach her to be like my mother, to be like the weeds. I think of my mother's newly planted roses, the ones that don't like to grow in the same soil as their predecessors, and talk softly to my little unborn rose as she somersaults around inside of me: *I cannot imagine our lives without you. We love you already, more than you know.* It is hard for me to reconcile this new life with the loss of my brother.

I think of bowing three times at Pat's grave: We loved you then, we love you now, we love you always. I hold a picture of him as a baby in my hands, marveling at his tranquility. In a fuzzy blue sleep sack, he dreams on my father's chest, his nose buried, his hand on my father's heart, his eyes shuttered and serene. I will show my daughter this picture one day, so she will know Pat, so she will know that everyone was once a baby: pure, perfect, at peace.

✖

A CLOSE FRIEND calls me one night, panicked and tearful. Her twenty-three-year-old brother, the baby of the family, has just admitted that he is a heroin addict. The revelation isn't completely out of the blue—for a long time, it's been clear that he was troubled—but no one suspected anything like this: needles, track marks, the family's jewelry pawned, their cash stolen. He has been holed up in their parents' house for two days, white-knuckling his way through the first stages of withdrawal, and she wants to know what she should do. He doesn't seem all that sick, and claims he doesn't need to go to rehab.

The call thrusts me back in time. Four years ago, I'd called this friend as I drove from San Francisco to the Cedar Street house. It was in the days following Pat's overdose in San Diego, when everything was just beginning to fall apart. Mom's computer had crashed, and she was frantic; she needed to be able to research treatment centers for Pat. I was rushing to her house in the middle of the day to get her back online. I remembered telling my friend how frustrated I was that everything always revolved around Pat, how once again my whole day would be taken up with flurrying to find help for someone who didn't even want to be helped.

Now my friend's brother is the one who needs help, and I feel momentarily at a loss. What suggestions can I possibly offer when clearly I did everything so wrong in the past? I remember my mother in the weeks after Pat died, hesitant to return to her job teaching preschool. "How can I presume to teach parents how to parent, when I failed so miserably?" she had asked. "If I'm such a great mom, then why did I raise a drug addict? Look at me, and you see failure as a mother." I had begged her to believe that it wasn't her fault, but inside I understood how she felt, because that was how I felt too: *Look at me, and you see failure as a sister.*

How then, now, can I presume to tell my friend what to do?

But today I know that I didn't fail Pat as a sister any more than Mom failed him as a mother. We did what we were capable of; we did the best that we could. I also know that my friend knows there isn't one clear path that will save her brother. There is just what I know from my own experience, and the good thing is that this is her brother's story, not Pat's. The ending is yet undetermined, so it is also full of possibility.

I don't soften my thoughts: if he's not super sick, he's probably not clean—you don't go from being an IV drug user for a year to sobering up in two days. "I hate to tell you not to believe your brother, but doubt everything that comes out of his mouth," I say. I'm guessing he's still using, whether it's heroin or pills or something else, and I advise getting him into a detox facility as soon as possible and then into an inpatient treatment center, preferably something long-term. As I talk, I am aware of how ruthless my words are; I sound cynical and severe. Though I don't say it, my heart is breaking for her: of course, I am hoping for the best for my friend and her brother, but I know how quickly it can all disintegrate. And even if he makes it, which I hope desperately he does, there is so much struggle in store for him, for her, for their whole family.

I think of Pat, crying in my arms as I held him on the way home from the airport after his overdose, his wet tears on my fingers, his hot breath on my knees.

"Tell your brother how much you love him," I say to my friend, choking a little on the heat that rises in my throat in the face of this rising storm.

✖

THERE ARE STONES left unturned in the bitter earth where the roses and weeds grow. Hiding places that catch the sunlight, their secrecy illuminated only when stumbled upon. Where once I reached down into these shadowed places, hoping to know the truth about what they obscured, now I find myself turning away.

Late one night, Brian sits on my couch with his feet propped up on the coffee table. He's here for the weekend, taking a break from law school exams, and we've just escaped the evening fog that had rolled in as we were walking up the hill. In these moments, time and space collapse, and we ramble on, the shared memories serving as our vessel. He is a young man now: self-deprecating, whip smart, sensitive. He's a brother to be proud of, to cherish. Sometimes it makes me sad to look at him. To remember two tousled blond heads peeking over the top rail of the bunk bed; to think of the closeness he shared with his only brother, a bond that has now been severed perfunctorily, a simple snip of scissors cut through rope.

Except for those first few months, Brian has rarely spoken to me about what it felt like for him to lose Pat. I have never known what he said to our mother that cold February morning, after rising from the front steps to meet her at the edge of the driveway as Caitlin and I watched from inside the house. That memory—Brian walking toward

Mom, the fear in her face, the sound of her scream, my sister and I running out of the house to catch her as she fell—is deeply traumatic for me. I have spent years facing it, breaking it down into more manageable parts, attempting to make peace with it. But I have never talked to either my sister or my brother about it. I have wondered about it often: how did Brian bear it, shivering there on the stairs alone, waiting for Mom's car to pull up and the terrible spiral to begin? Did he plan out what to say to her, or did it just happen? Which words did he choose? How explicitly did he spell it out? "Pat didn't make it," or "Something bad has happened to Pat," or was it simply, "Pat is dead"?

I have found myself wondering too how Brian felt earlier that day: answering the call from Pat's girlfriend after the locked bedroom door was broken down, being informed by the paramedics that Pat couldn't be resuscitated, calling me with the news we had all dreaded for months. And later, knocking on our relatives' doors, the bearer of words that would break their hearts. And later still, as the months went on and our lives marched necessarily onward. How did he feel then, I want to know?

But as we sit here tonight, we are warm and full. The electric glow of the city skyline blinks through the mist in the distance. The dog makes a whimpering chirp in his sleep and we laugh. I find that for some reason, it is okay not to know the answers to these particular questions, not to probe into the depths of my brother's private pain. Not tonight—maybe not ever.

"Addiction can show us what is deeply suspect about nostalgia," Ann Marlowe writes. "That drive to return to the past isn't an innocent one. It's about stopping your passage to the future, it's a symptom of fear of death, and the love of predictable experience." If I refuse to leave the past behind, I will be stuck there perpetually in its grip. Though it feels safer there somehow because it is familiar, because I have gone over and over its crevices and cracks, I cannot stay there forever. Or rather I could, but I find that choosing to close that door—not all the way, maybe leaving it open just a crack in case I need to return—feels okay. Frightening, but possible.

Later, Brian tells a story about Pat and cries a little. I do too. We are remembering a time playing Animal Rescue Patrol in the backyard, a convoluted game that involved us pretending to be lifeguards who flew around the world saving animals who were in distress at the hands of unknown aggressors. We were all choosing names for ourselves: I was Jenny (my best friend that year), Cait was Sara (her best friend that year), and Bri was Bill (one of our uncles, who drove a really cool Jeep). We asked three-year-old Pat what he wanted his name to be. He pondered this opportunity thoughtfully, folding his hands across his lap in a way he sometimes did that was hilarious because it was so prim, so un-Pat-like.

"Cup," he said emphatically. "My name is Cup," and there was a pause before the rest of us dissolved into laughter because it made no sense.

"I just miss him so much," Bri says finally. "I just wish he was here, to keep going through life with us. That would have been nice."

I agree. There is a void in our lives that can never be filled by anyone else, and we will always miss him. But I also realize that there is an undeclared bond that has emerged between us—me, Mom, Cait, and Bri—building its layers slowly over the course of the years: we are the survivors. Only we know what it was like to grow up alongside Pat. Only we know what it was like to love him, and lose him.

Only we can find a way forward for ourselves.

Mostly, we must forge our own path alone, each finding our own new way of being without Pat. But sometimes, like now, we make progress together. And although there is still a sense of bewilderment that the world hasn't collapsed—and even a trace of guilt—we are able to move forward, sustained by the memories of our lives before, when Pat was here.

42 | WALKING WITH THE DEVIL

ANDREW HAS BEEN searching for happiness his entire life. He tells his mother, Diana, that he finally feels like he has found it: "I tried drugs, I tried everything to make me happy," he says. "But now I finally realize that the happiness I was seeking was inside myself all along."

Diana has waited so long to hear these words. Despite all his problems, she truly believes Andrew is a good person who, given the chance, will make a difference in this world. Her son is brilliant, polite, respectful, and charming, with a tender soul and an ardent desire to help others—that is, when he isn't high. But Andrew has two personalities now: his using self and his clean self, Andrew the addict and Andrew her son. To Diana, it is like walking with an angel or walking with the devil, and she does not know which one will ultimately be by her side.

Diana used to walk in shame, hoping no one could see her secret— the secret of her son's addiction. She remembered so clearly the day he was born, six weeks before her due date, his angelic baby face not yet marred by the complications of life. She often wondered how such innocence descended into such darkness. *Andrew's addiction is my fault*, she would think to herself in those moments. *I'm his mother, so his mistakes are a reflection on me.*

But Diana has come a long way since then. She's not sure when the transformation happened, the exact point at which she reached her limit. Was it when she finally kicked Andrew out onto the streets of Orange County last year, telling him, "If I continue to put a roof over your head, you'll die in my home"? Was it later, after he'd been homeless for months, when she realized that she was clenching her teeth every time the phone or doorbell rang, thinking he'd been found dead? Or was it still later, when the extended family had gathered at a local photo studio to do a family portrait for her in-laws' fiftieth wedding anniversary and she could barely keep herself from crying because without Andrew, her family wasn't complete?

All Diana knows is that at some point, she made the decision to choose peace for herself. She would support her son in his journey, holding his hand along the way as long as they were both walking on a healthy path, but she could not walk it for him, just as he could not walk hers for her. And she had to know when to let go of his hand and accept it when he let go of hers.

Diana knows that each day, Andrew must make the choice to stay clean. She loves that her son is sober right now, but she hates that he has a disease that requires him to make that choice each day. She knows that like other chronic diseases that may cycle through periods of improvement and regression, such as diabetes, hypertension, and asthma, addiction carries with it the very real possibility of relapse—between 40 and 60 percent of drug users do.[65] And so each day, Andrew and Diana must make a choice in their separate journeys. Andrew's is whether to stay clean or whether to use; Diana's is whether to allow her son's addiction to creep into her life and destroy her peace, or to hold tightly to what she has learned and keep her hope alive. Whether to walk with the angel or with the devil.

For both of them, right now, the angel is winning. Diana is walking in hope, not in shame, and she is holding her son's hand.

She only wishes her son wasn't behind bars.

✖

ANDREW DOESN'T REALLY remember breaking into the woman's house—just that he was strung out and brutally sick from all the pills and heroin. He remembers the scabs on his face, the shakiness that rattled his bones. And most of all, he remembers the exhaustion. He was so tired of the chase: he'd run out of cash, no one was taking his phone calls, and he knew that once again, he'd managed to alienate everyone in his life. He needed to either get clean or get high, and fast.

That night, Andrew chose to get high, hence the break-in that resulted in the cops picking him up and charging him with residential burglary. Andrew knows that if he had been in his right mind, he never would have tried to rob someone. But once he crossed the threshold into opiate withdrawal, he'd do anything to get his hands on drugs. He was walking with the devil, going against everything he believed in just to quiet the madness inside him.

The arrest that night was actually a good thing, Andrew thinks, because he ended up getting into a six-month residential treatment program after serving out seven months of his sentence. But less than a week before he was set to graduate, the cops had decided to arrest him for another robbery he'd committed. Since it was the second time he'd been charged with residential burglary, the case carried an automatic five-year enhancement on his original prison sentence, meaning that Andrew is now facing the possibility of seven more years behind bars.

He is twenty-three now; he could be thirty by the time he gets out.

Andrew tries not to fixate on this. Instead, he remembers that he has been clean since the day he was thrown in jail for the second robbery, and that every day sober is a victory.

Sobriety is still very new to Andrew: addiction has always been part of his life, even before he got hooked on opiates. Growing up, he and his brothers watched their father numb his pain with alcohol, pot, and prescription drugs, and several times almost die. They were there for everything: the ambulance rides, the medevac transports, the hospital-izations during which their dad's liver failed or he was in a coma. Even after Diana divorced the boys' father, and a judge ordered him not to use for twenty-four hours prior to or during his scheduled visits, things didn't improve: they were constantly witnessing their dad being wheeled out of the house on a gurney or handcuffed and loaded into a patrol car for violating the judge's order. And Andrew learned two things as he witnessed his father drink and drug himself nearly to death: first, that life is hard, and second, that you can block out the pain of life by numbing yourself out with substances.

So that's what Andrew did, beginning with his dad's drugs of choice, since they were easily found around the house. The painkillers were his favorites—Vicodin, Valium, Norcos, Ativan, Roxies. He just ate them at first, but then he started smoking them, and pretty soon his daily quota was up to fifteen pills. Eventually he began adding other drugs to the mix, including meth and heroin. Pretty soon he found that he needed about a gram of heroin a day, usually with a couple of Klonopin or Xanax bars thrown in, just to feel normal. He was like every other opi-ate addict he'd ever met: a kid from the tree-lined suburbs who swore he'd never be an IV drug user who ended up scouring the alleys of South Gate or the streets of Huntington Park to score heroin, which he shot with dirty needles.

It all happened so fast that Andrew could barely believe it. All of a sudden, it seemed, he had cycled through seven different rehabs in the span of three years. He'd been diagnosed with major depressive disorder, and the counselors and psychiatrists had thrown every medication in the world at him to try and fix him: Remeron, Depakote, Seroquel, Prozac, Saphrise, Pristiq. He'd been thrown in jail a bunch of times too, but none of it seemed to help. He always found a way to go back to drugs, even though he hated them and everything they entailed. He hated wandering the streets covered in dirt, his face pockmarked with sores; he hated hallucinating that he was being chased; he hated feeling afraid for his life all the time and at the same time being numb to everything, all the anguish he was causing his whole family—especially his mom. But he just loved getting high so much, and once he made the decision to get high, there was no stopping him.

When Andrew thinks of those days now, he feels ashamed. He drums his freckled fingers on the graffiti-covered ledge of the prison visiting booth and tells me it feels like another time, another person.

"The guilt was terrible," he says, smoothing his short red hair self-consciously. "It was a never-ending cycle of self-sabotage. It was absolute hell."

I ask him why he used if the guilt was so bad.

"I really don't know why I would choose to get high, but I do," he says. "I don't know what normal is."

Recently, though, Andrew feels like he has reached a positive mental place; with a solid chunk of clean time, his conviction to stay sober has strengthened. From what he sees of the kids coming into the jail, things aren't getting much better on the outside, so he tries to talk to them— and their parents—about what he has been through. Though he thinks all the money in the surrounding suburbs plays a part in enabling kids to buy copious amounts of expensive pills, and later heroin, he's quick to point out the undercurrent of emotional neglect he sees running through many of their lives.

"I wish parents would take the time to really listen to their kids," he says. "Forget about dinner. Forget about soccer practice. Your kid might be going through something, and they might really need to talk about it."

At the same time, he's seen too many parents become consumed with guilt over their actions or inactions—especially the parents of some of his addict friends who have passed away of overdoses. Many of the addicts he's known always felt that something was missing for much of their lives—not anything that anyone else could have filled, but somehow the drugs filled it. It wasn't anything their parents did or didn't do; they did not cause the addiction, he tells them.

You did what you could to help your child, he says to them. *You loved him; he knows you loved him. It is not your fault.*

Diana, for her part, knows that she did her best as a parent. Her choice to take the "tough love" route and kick Andrew out of her home ended up facilitating his fall to rock bottom, and her son ended up in rehab and then in jail, where he has stayed clean. She has to live with that choice and find her peace with it, just as Andrew must make his choices and find his peace every day. His choice equals her peace, because if he chooses to go back to using, his hell—and hers—will start all over again. She will once again be living with the constant fear that today will be the day her son dies.

But right now, Andrew is in recovery, and that is Diana's peace for today.

"He is in jail, his freedom taken away, but in all this he found his happiness and knows that if he stays clean he can continue to live in happiness with himself," she says. "There is hope, even in the darkest hours."

43 | WHEN YOU WERE FREE

ALL ALONG THE shoreline, tiny white waves dissolve into foam as they meet the hardened sand. We walk along the breaking point, cooling our bare feet, the Pacific Ocean to our left, the cliffs to our right. Swarms of sand flies rise up from parched piles of seaweed as we pass them by, and they absorb into the wind.

It is Brian and Elise's wedding day. The ceremony is being held on a remote stretch of beach that borders the rural ranch area where she grew up. As we walk toward the spot where the wedding guests are gathering, her long blond hair twists in the breeze, tethered by a halo of flowers, and she grasps Brian's hand. He has rolled up the legs of his suit pants, giving him a boyish look. They are glowing against the horizon, incandescent, ethereal in their youth and happiness. Their happiness spreads outward and around them, filling me, filling us, filling everyone here. I want to bottle this feeling so that I can come back to it later; it feels so precious and fleeting, like something that should be carefully preserved. It is sweet, and heavy, and as we walk along the beach, I feel a twinge of longing for the way we all used to be. Maybe it is the way Bri has rolled up his pants, or the way my sister and I had cuddled on the bed earlier this morning, giggling as we decided on the most embarrassing childhood memories to include in our speech tonight. Maybe it is the way poor old Romeo lopes goofily in the sand behind us, his hardened legs like spindles, his tongue hanging out sideways with his earnest efforts to keep up.

Back at the house where our family is staying for the weekend, there is a Charleston Chew in the freezer. One of Pat's best childhood friends brought it to symbolize him, because she was missing him. I think of the Charleston Chew as we walk now, remembering Pat, his jaw working the icy candy, his brown smooth legs dangling into the clear waters of the lake by our cabin. I wish that he were here now, older, dirty or clean, broken or not. I would take him any way he came.

We all would.

I know that over the course of my life, there will be so many more of these moments in which I wish that Pat were here. In these moments, I still haven't figured out what to do. I'm not sure there really is anything to do, beyond acknowledging this wish that can never be fulfilled. Sometimes, as now, I send a little thought to the sky for him, as if he lives there now and can hear me. What else can I do? There will always be this absence, this hole that should be filled, a pause in the chatter.

The imaginary Pat walks beside us in the sand. He is healthy and laughing, and he has also rolled up his pant legs. We smile at the memory of some forgotten joke and head toward the bend in the cliffs ahead.

The ceremony is beautiful, filled with laughter and tears and the crash of the breaking waves. Overhead, a gull's cries echo against the ocean, and I look at my brother, at the fullness in his eyes, and I am so grateful for the love he has found, despite all the sorrow.

Afterward, the wedding party walks back down the beach and up a small hill to a wooded clearing. The sun sinks westward, filling the trees with amber light. During the speeches, I am stunned when, in the midst of praising Brian, one of our uncles suddenly mentions Pat.

"There was once another Daly kid too, who was just as great," he says.

Though he moves on, I clench inward, reeling at the reminder. A part of me feels assaulted by the insertion of tragedy during this moment, which should be filled with only joy and warmth. When I look up at Bri, he is crying, as Elise wraps her arms around his shoulders.

I fidget for a few minutes after the speeches have ended. Our uncle's honesty has left me feeling torn: would I prefer that Pat had been left unmentioned, when sometimes—especially when we are all together without him—all I want to do is scream his name? Or am I grateful to my uncle for speaking the uncomfortable truth?

The party has moved on; knives clink against champagne glasses, urging the couple to kiss. I see Brian and Elise, their heads thrown back in laughter, reflecting the rising moon. I see Cait, joining hands with Mom, pulling her out onto the dance floor. I see Ben coming up behind them, all silliness, and Grandma and Kathy smiling from the sidelines. I see the little girl inside me as she turns, and I even see Dad, who watches us from a distance, as if peering in at us from the other side of a sliding glass door. The only one I cannot see is Pat, and I am reminded of a poem Mom used to read to us when we were children:

> I see the moon and the moon sees me,
> And the moon sees the one that I can't see.
> God bless the moon and God bless me,
> And God bless the one that I can't see.

✖

THE SWIPE OF crayon against paper makes a frantic *swish-swish-swish* sound, and Pat chomps down on his lower lip in concentration. He pauses to cram a handful of Nerds into his mouth, then resumes his coloring. Fluorescent polka dots smudge the edges of the picture where his hands, caked in candy sugar, steady the paper for its final assault.

"Look!" he says to me then, holding the picture up to face me where I sit across the kitchen table, reading a book. His open-mouthed grin is framed by bright lime and pink streaks of candy or crayon. I'm not sure which.

I kick him lightly under the table and say bossily, "Don't interrupt." Whatever I'm reading is very important, though I can't see the words on the page. He shrugs and giggles and goes back to his artwork.

"Silly Ern," he says.

When I wake up, I feel bad. I try to return to the dream to tell him I'll look at the drawing and tack it up on the fridge. But Pat isn't at the kitchen table anymore. I sit back down and play with the cardboard opening of the Nerds box, inhaling its sweet fruity scent. I reach my hand across the table to where he was sitting, feeling the sticky saccharine threads, the remnants he left behind.

Though he's gone, I say the words anyway, to the empty chair across from me: "I'm sorry, Pat." And I know—or compel myself to believe that I know—that he is okay. After all, he has reverted back into a child. His world is much simpler: he knows only laughter and joy. His life is uncomplicated by things that carry heavy weight. He is light, unrestrained.

This is where I choose to hold him, not in the place he was in at the end, not as the wrecked person he became. I choose to hold him in the time when he was happiest.

When he was free.

44 | THE PROMISE

KRISTA REMEMBERS THE night she felt herself drifting away. Everything inside her was numb, silenced by the painkillers' seductive poison. She had no fear, no happiness: all of her feelings had vanished. She felt untouchable, apart from the world. That night, she watched her soul float out of her body and hover over her head. She realized that she was waiting to die.

"God, please, whoever is out there, please help me," she had whispered.

Today she looks at the beautiful baby on her lap and the strong young man beside her at their home in Marin County. The baby brings her fist, glistening with drool, to her rosebud mouth and looks back at her mother with saucerlike eyes. Krista thinks, *Everything makes sense now. It was always meant to be.*

Life is happening so quickly these days, like watching a movie in fast-forward. It is completely different from her life before, when she was using: back then, everything was so slow and dark. Sometimes, now that the world is bright and full of promise, beckoning her forward, she forgets the smallness of the world she thought was possible for herself.

Krista has come to believe that her story has already been written, each part of her life a necessary conduit to the next: if she hadn't started drinking, she wouldn't have gone to AA, where she met the guy who introduced her to OxyContin, and then she wouldn't have gotten so hooked on the pills that she almost died, and then she wouldn't have gotten sober, and then she never would have met Max or become pregnant with their daughter. She wouldn't be sitting here now in this life full of light and love, with her future shining in the distance like a beacon, guiding her home.

"Everything happened the way that it did so that the three of us could all be here together like this," she says, eyes shining as Max takes the baby and throws her up into the air, laughing.

✖

THE WEDDING WILL be held at the end of the summer, in a Napa Valley barn overlooking a wide expanse of hillside vineyards and gardens overflowing with roses, dahlias, and lavender. The baby has started to crawl, so if she's walking by then, she'll be the flower girl. Krista and her bridesmaids will wear cowgirl boots, and Max will pull the baby around in a little red wagon.

It will be the official beginning to their new life together—a life that by many counts was never supposed to happen. They met in recovery three years ago, when Max, then twenty-three, had six months clean, and twenty-one-year-old Krista about twice that. Dating other recovering addicts in the early, fragile stages of sobriety is taboo in some circles; the thinking is that the focus should be on learning to take care of yourself rather than potentially forming a new addiction to another person. But there was an indescribable pull, something magnetic that drew them together, something that felt so right. So at the beginning of their relationship, Max and Krista made a promise to each other: no matter what happened between them, their sobriety would come first. If one person was in danger of relapsing, that person would leave rather than drag the other person down.

That promise still stands, though it has become more complicated. There is the baby, and their upcoming marriage, so walking away would be a lot more difficult. But the promise forms the bedrock of their union, giving them each the motivation to stay sober while ensuring that they will be protected if the other one goes down.

They take the promise seriously, just like they take their daughter and their marriage seriously—they have to, to preserve this new life. It takes effort to remember what it was like when they were using, even though it was only a few short years ago, because it was so terrible that they have let it fade into the past—and that is dangerous. They don't want to constantly relive it, but they must remind themselves of the importance of what's at stake. So they try to keep at least some of it alive: they frequently speak with high school students about their stories of addiction, and Max is working as a sober companion for a local recovery organization, helping addicts from treatment facilities into long-term sobriety.

Sometimes Max feels like it's all too good to be true—the addict inside him telling him he's not worthy of this. He knows that if he hadn't called his mom that day in March 2010, begging for help, he'd be dead right now. So he gives himself a reality check, remembering the hellish path that brought him down.

He was a good kid growing up, energetic and athletic. His dream was to be a professional baseball player, and he was even picked to play on the varsity team as a freshman in high school. But after two games, he got caught smoking weed and was kicked off the team. After that, Max began failing out of his classes and was sent to a continuation high school. It was like a training ground for drug addicts, and his downfall was quick: first Darvocet and Percocet, then OxyContin. After a month he couldn't afford the Oxys anymore, so he started doing heroin. All of a sudden, he was shooting up to 5 grams of heroin a day and also doing cocaine and pills, as well as methadone.

Max went to his first treatment center when he was twenty years old, but he didn't get sober. He kept thinking that a geographical change would help, so he moved around a lot, started living on the streets, sleeping on couches—and using. In 2008 he decided to get a fresh start by moving from California to New York City to go to acting school. He brought just four 80-milligram Oxys with him, thinking to himself, *This is the end.* Within three days the pills were gone and Max was up in Spanish Harlem hunting for heroin. Seven months in, he'd caught pneumonia, was failing all his classes, and had sold all his possessions for drugs. He overdosed multiple times and became terrified of death, but even that fear didn't stop him from using.

"I would nod out and hear myself stop breathing, feel myself turning blue," he says. "Not everyone makes it back, but I did. And I don't know why."

When Max's dad was in a motorcycle accident and fell into a coma, Max flew home and sat beside his father in the hospital, unsure of whether he would live or die. Despite that, Max stole his dad's credit cards and flew back to New York as if nothing had ever happened. The realization of what he had done brought him to his knees.

That was when he called his mom for help, and his new life began. It still seems dreamlike: his sobriety, meeting Krista. From the beginning, she was different than the girls he'd had relationships with in the past—and not just because she was sober. Krista was solid, focused: she wanted her life to be the opposite of what it was when she was using, but she also understood the darkness inside Max, because it lived inside her too. Krista's parents didn't have the best marriage, and early on she had taken on the role of the hero, hoping that if she was the perfect child, maybe her home life would get better. The summer before she started high school, she had her first drink while sleeping over at a friend's house: tequila and orange juice. Her friend hated it, but Krista loved it. She started drinking more, and the way she drank was embarrassing and shameful.

"I never had a 'that's enough' button," she says. "I was waking up in the ER and being told that I had almost died. It didn't faze me."

Krista had ruined so many relationships that she transferred schools, promising herself it would be different. Her mom had split up with her dad and had joined Al-Anon, and Krista had started going to meetings. But she kind of felt like her life was over: how do you be sober at age seventeen and still have a social life? That was when she met a guy in AA who talked about Oxy and was shocked that Krista had never done drugs. His dad always had a bunch of Oxys lying around his apartment, and one day Krista's friend snorted them in front of her. Krista was curious: she thought she'd try Oxy just once, and it would be no big deal; after all, her problem was drinking, not drugs.

"But it was instant love," she says. "It was so much better than alcohol. Nothing could touch me. I wanted to feel that way all the time."

The painkiller fulfilled its promise: it killed all the pain. But it also killed all the good. It stole Krista's soul. The blond Catholic schoolgirl from the suburbs was suddenly so hell-bent on getting her hands on more pills that she had no problem venturing into the inner city—she was so high that she had no fear. It was two more years before the little girl she had once been, the one who had grown up carefree and hopeful with nothing but dreams for the life ahead, finally screamed out: *We're not going up from here.* She was so broken down that she was willing to do whatever it took to get sober. At the time, she could never have imagined a life beyond addiction. The life she has now, with Max and with their child.

Someday, when she's old enough to understand, Max and Krista will tell their daughter about the past, about the nightmares that brought them together, somehow resulting in this future that was once unimaginable.

Max will say to her, *My desperation was a gift. I have the life I used to lie about.*

Krista will say to her, *I got a second chance, and now all my dreams are coming true.*

Then they will remind themselves of their promise to each other.

45 | AWAKE

THE DIRT ROAD stretches before us, the softly cooling light of the dusk collecting in the crevices of its borders, surrounded by vines. We are all there, walking down the path together: me, Cait, Bri, Mom. There are birds all around us: plump little ones with sapphire feathers and yellow stick-legs, pigeons with bodies brown as dust, and, because it is a dream, scarlet macaws, the rainbow parrots we saw soaring through the rain forests of Costa Rica all those years ago. They sit in the trees lining the road, murmuring as we travel there beneath them.

A spot appears on the horizon. As we make our way down the winding path, the spot grows wider: it is a clearing at the end of the road, where people mill about, so many of them that they are like a whole ocean, their hair the waves, the occasional hat like a drifting sailboat.

The sun sets, wistful, and the moon rises, wise. Just before we reach the clearing, a man separates himself from the group and approaches us. He wears a pair of moccasins, just like Dad used to put on when he came home from work, shuffling around the house with us kids wrapped around his legs, giggling.

"Pat is okay," the man says to us, though we hadn't asked. "He isn't here, but he's okay."

I scan the faces around us, searching anxiously for Pat.

"No, not here," says the man. "Look over there," and he points to a tree to our right.

From behind it, Pat emerges, shirtless and grinning. He is wearing board shorts, and on his wrists are the rubber bands and shoelaces he'd worn as bracelets. He runs around the tree and disappears behind it again.

I call out to him, "Bunny, please come back. I love you!"

After a few seconds he pokes his head out again and he comes out from behind the tree, only this time he isn't skipping, he's floating, and he drifts closer to us as I reach out to him, saying, "Oh Bunny, I love you I love you I love you," and he doesn't speak but he reaches out his hand to me too, and he is smiling, and as our hands touch he doesn't say it but I feel him think, *I love you. It's okay. I'm okay*, and I am awake.

NOTES

THE REPORTING FOR this book took place over the course of almost five years, from March 2009 to September 2013. With the launch of my blog, Oxy Watchdog (www.oxywatchdog.com), in October 2009, many people from around the country began to reach out to me, wanting to share their experiences. These people included parents whose children had struggled with painkiller and heroin addiction; current and former addicts; law enforcement officials, including an FBI agent and a special agent with the DEA whose daughter was addicted to opiates; addiction professionals; grief counselors; emergency room doctors and nurses; pain-management specialists; lawyers; lawmakers, including state representatives and members of the U.S. Congress; state officials; social workers; activists; and a host of others whose lives had been touched in some way—personally, professionally, or in some cases both—by the prescription painkiller and heroin epidemic. Though I didn't formally interview all these people, my conversations with them informed my reporting and helped paint the larger picture of opiate abuse in America today.

At various points during this time, I traveled around the country to conduct in-depth reporting in areas that had been disproportionately affected by addiction to pills and heroin. These reporting trips included stints in Boston, Massachusetts, and its surrounding suburbs; Miami-Dade, Broward, Palm Beach, and Pinellas counties in Florida; Los Angeles, San Diego, and cities in Orange County in southern California; and various cities and suburbs of the San Francisco Bay Area in northern

California. Together, these trips resulted in more than one hundred formal interviews, as well as dozens of off-the-record conversations that contributed to my reporting.

The following is an accounting of where the information in this book comes from, though in many cases my sources requested anonymity due to the sensitive nature of their stories. In these instances, I have provided as much attribution as possible without compromising their understandable desire to use pseudonyms.

I am grateful to my family and friends for supporting my decision to make Pat's story public and for allowing me to identify them by their real names.

All titles and workplace attributions reflect the time during which the interviews were conducted.

INTRODUCTION

The description of Lance Fiske's embalming was provided by George Fiske of the Funerarias Multi Culturel funeral home in Brockton, Massachusetts, in an interview on August 2, 2010.

Conversations with numerous other parents of opiate-addicted children—specifically at a series of meetings in August 2010 of the Massachusetts-based support group Learn to Cope, as well as at the Northeast Alliance for Addiction Recovery/Massachusetts Organization for Addiction Recovery parent group—contributed to the description of teens and young adults becoming hooked on heroin after starting with pills. Informal interviews with anonymous addicts at several rehab centers in Boston and surrounding areas also informed this discussion.

The information regarding the opiate addiction epidemic comes from interviews in the Boston area in August 2010, including with Nic Tenaglia of the Men's Addiction Treatment Center in Brockton, William Ostiguy and John McGahan of the Gavin Foundation in Boston, Professor David Rosenbloom of Boston University's School of Public Health, Massachusetts state senator Steven Tolman, and Vic Degravio of the Mental Health and Substance Abuse Corporation of Massachusetts.

Fred Newton, administrative director of Hope House in Boston, provided the quote about the lack of older opiate addicts due to the high death toll among young addicts.

PART I: DENIAL

The quote at the beginning of this section is from David Sheff's book *Beautiful Boy: A Father's Journey through His Son's Addiction*, Mariner Books, 2009, page 177.

1 | WAITING

The content in this chapter is based on my personal recollections and experiences, and those of certain family members.

2 | JUST LET ME FORGET

Luke is a pseudonym. The description of my time with Luke stems from a two-day period in April 2012 at Serenity House in San Juan Capistrano, California. I met Luke through Annalisa Capozzoli, one of my sources for a multimedia investigative series reported in conjunction with the Center for Investigative Reporting/California Watch (published in July 2012 and available at http://californiawatch.org/health-and-welfare/rise-young-painkiller-abusers-officials-see-more-heroin-overdoses-17550); see the notes for chapter 4 for more details. Luke agreed to be interviewed by me as a part of that series on condition of anonymity.

Jack is also a pseudonym. Anna agreed to use her real name; see notes for chapter 4.

3 | TWO SATURDAYS

The content in this chapter is based on my personal recollections and experiences, and those of certain family members.

4 | REMEMBERING

Annalisa Capozzoli's story is based on interviews in March and April 2012 conducted at her home in Dana Point, California, as part of the Center for Investigative Reporting/California Watch series. On May 16, 2013, I interviewed her again in Dana Point independently as part of my research for this book.

The description of the recovery meeting is based on observations of a meeting I attended with Anna in San Juan Capistrano, California, on May 20, 2013. The quotes from that meeting are from anonymous attendees.

Anna's story was corroborated by her sponsor, Tori DeGroote, alumni coordinator at Mission Pacific Coast Recovery Center in Laguna Beach, California. Tori also provided information regarding certain principles of addiction and recovery work that are alluded to in this chapter.

As previously mentioned, Luke is a pseudonym; see notes for chapter 2.

5 | THE FALL

The content in this chapter is based on my personal recollections and experiences.

6 | RUN LIKE HELL

The description of the prescription painkiller sting operation and subsequent arrests come from my ride-along in Largo and Pinellas Park, Florida, with the Narcotics Division of the Pinellas County Sheriff's Office on June 24, 2011.

Captain Robert Alfonso provided much of the background information on the narcotics team's strategy and the prescription drug addiction issue in general.

Most of the quotes in the chapter come from Detective Ryan Kornacki, drug diversion investigator of the Strategic Diversion Unit, who coordinated my ride-along and provided additional information on Florida's opiate epidemic. The comments of other narcotics officers on the team contributed to my description of the suspects' arrest and interrogation.

The description of Florida's days as the national epicenter for illegal pill sales comes from the above sources, as well as from an interview and ride-along on June 21, 2011, with Sergeant Richard Pisanti of the Special Investigations Unit of the Broward Sheriff's Office in Oakland Park, Florida.

Interviews with James Hall, executive director at Up Front Drug Information Center in Miami, Florida, on June 20, 2011; Karen Perry, executive director of the Narcotics Overdose Prevention and Intervention (NOPE) Task Force in West Palm Beach, Florida, on June 20, 2011; and Pat Castillo, vice president of the United Way of Broward County Commission on Substance Abuse in Fort Lauderdale, Florida, on June 22, 2011, also contributed to this description. Claude Shipley, strategic planner for the Florida Governor's Office of Drug Control, also provided numerous studies and statistics regarding Florida's painkiller problem.

7 | CHOOSING TO BELIEVE

The content in this chapter is based on my personal recollections and experiences, and those of certain family members.

The letter from Pat was written on December 6, 2004, and contains minor grammatical and spelling edits for clarity.

The names Victor, Brandon, Ross, and Jasper are pseudonyms used to protect these individuals' identities.

8 | BUYING TIME

Ethan is a pseudonym, but the rest of the individuals in this section are identified by their real names. Ethan's story is based on a number of interviews, both in person in Irvine and Santa Ana, California, by phone, and by mail, beginning in April 2012 and continuing through July 2013. I first interviewed him as part of the Center for Investigative Reporting/California Watch series and subsequently interviewed him independently as part of my research for this book.

The descriptions of Ethan's overdose, his time in the hospital, and his experience with his probation officer were provided by Ethan himself and were corroborated by several of his acquaintances, including Joey Whynaught's mother, Alice Whynaught; see notes for chapter 10.

The description of the criminal history typical of many young opiate addicts is based on an interview with Lieutenant Douglas Doyle of the Orange County Sheriff's Department, Special Investigations Bureau, in Santa Ana, California, on April 6, 2012. That interview was also conducted as part of the Center for Investigative Reporting/California Watch series.

The description of Ethan on the beach is based on our phone and mail conversations while he was incarcerated at the Orange County Men's Jail in Santa Ana, as well as in an in-person interview at the jail on May 17, 2013.

9 | SAYING NOTHING

The content in this chapter is based on my personal recollections and experiences, and those of certain family members.

The email from Pat to his girlfriend was first observed during our family trip to Costa Rica in July 2008 and later accessed via Pat's email account. It was shortened to preserve his girlfriend's anonymity but is otherwise quoted without edits.

10 | COME BACK

Joey Whynaught's story comes from his mother, Alice Whynaught, whom I first interviewed in April 2012 as part of the Center for Investigative Reporting/California Watch series. As a part of that project, I attended Joey's memorial service on April 17, 2012, at Saddleback Church in Lake Forest, California. The description of Ethan (a pseudonym) during the service comes from my own observations, as well as from Ethan's recounting of the event during our May 17, 2013, interview; see notes for chapter 8.

Alice's husband, Ted Whynaught, also agreed to use his real name.

I subsequently interviewed Alice independently as part of my research for this book, first in a series of phone calls and letters during the remainder of 2012 and the beginning of 2013 and later in a formal interview on May 18, 2013, at her home in San Juan Capistrano, California.

Alice also provided numerous personal documents from Joey's childhood, adolescence, and adult years that contributed to the telling of his story.

The description of Ethan in jail comes from our May 17, 2013 interview.

11 | LOSING FAITH

The content in this chapter is based on my personal recollections and experiences, and those of certain family members. Documents retrieved from the San Diego County Jail corroborate the details of Pat's arrest.

PART II: ANGER

The quote at the beginning of this section is from Bill Clegg's book *Ninety Days: A Memoir of Recovery*, Little, Brown and Company, 2012, page 49.

12 | UNTRUE

The content in this chapter is based on my personal recollections and experiences, and those of certain family members.

LifeGem offers to synthesize diamonds from the carbonized remains of humans or their pets; the quotes regarding the company's products were taken from one of its brochures and can also be found at www.lifegem.com.

13 | STRANGER THAN FICTION

The description of the mortuary and information on cremation is based on an interview and on-site visit with Christopher J. Iverson, general manager of the O'Connor Mortuary in Laguna Hills, California, on May 23, 2013, and a phone interview with Neil P. O'Connor, the mortuary's president and CEO, on May 24, 2013.

The continuation of Joey Whynaught's story comes from my interview with his mother, Alice Whynaught, on May 18, 2013, at her home in San Juan Capistrano; see notes for chapter 10.

The description of Alice learning about addiction comes from our discussions regarding her Internet research and reading on the subject, including David Sheff's *Clean* and *Staying Sober: A Guide for Relapse Prevention* by Terence T. Gorski and Merlene Miller, Herald House/Independent Press, 1987.

The quote regarding shame is excerpted from a handout Alice received at a May 22, 2013, meeting of SOLACE (Surviving Our Loss with Awareness, Compassion and Empathy) in Mission Viejo, California. The handout, titled "Guilt & Shame: Understanding the Difference," was written by Peter Salerno, a marriage and family therapist who was also in attendance at the meeting, and is reprinted with his permission.

The description of Alice at the SOLACE meeting and the quotes from other anonymous attendees, as well as the quote from SOLACE coordinator Elaine Werner-Hudson, were based on my observations at that event.

14 | WAX

The content in this chapter is based on my personal recollections and experiences, and those of certain family members.

15 | SIGNS

Josh Werner's story comes from a phone interview with his mother, Elaine Werner-Hudson, on March 14, 2013, as well as two in-person interviews in Mission Viejo, California, on May 15, 2013, and May 22, 2013, and was corroborated by Elaine's other son, Zach Werner.

Elaine and Zach also provided numerous personal documents from Josh's childhood, adolescence, and adult years that contributed to the telling of Josh's story. These documents include Josh's own description of his addiction to painkillers, which was condensed and lightly edited for clarity. Josh's full description can be viewed on the website of Project JOSH at http://www.projectjosh.org/about/.

The email excerpt from Josh's former girlfriend was provided by Elaine and was lightly edited for clarity and to protect the individual's identity.

16 | DIGGING FOR BONES

The content in this chapter is based on my personal recollections and experiences, and those of certain family members.

Pat's autopsy was retrieved from the Los Angeles County Coroner's Office on June 8, 2009, and is quoted without edits.

17 | OVERTAKEN

The description of Jodi Barber's testimony before the Medical Board of California stems from my attendance at a legislative hearing on March 11, 2013, in Sacramento, California, during which Jodi and other activists spoke about the prescription drug abuse epidemic.

The line "I hope the Pacific . . ." is from the 1994 movie *The Shawshank Redemption*.

Jarrod Barber's story comes from a series of phone interviews with Jodi throughout 2011 and 2012, as well as from in-person interviews at her home in Mission Viejo, California, on April 6, 2012 and May 21, 2012. Jodi's husband, Bill, and other son, Blake, also agreed to use their real names.

The description of Jodi's presentation comes from my attendance at the assembly at Fountain Valley High School in Fountain Valley, California, on May 21, 2012. The grieving mother and young recovering heroin addict who spoke at that event requested anonymity; Connor is a pseudonym.

Jodi also provided numerous personal documents from Jarrod's childhood, adolescence, and adult years that contributed to the telling of his story.

18 | WHERE ARE YOU?

The content in this chapter is based on my personal recollections and experiences, and those of certain family members. The email from Pat dated January 27, 2009, was lightly edited to protect his girlfriend's anonymity, and for clarity.

19 | SIXTEEN DAYS

Dale and Ellie are pseudonyms. Dale provided me with his story during an in-person interview at his rehab center, Full Circle Outreach, in Norco, California, on May 20, 2013. Jodi Barber was also present at this interview. I re-created his account of his overdoses based on his descriptions, which were corroborated by his mother, Ellie, in a series of phone interviews between June 2013 and August 2013; see notes for chapter 22.

Alyson, Noah, Mike, and Brady are also pseudonyms.

20 | *TRANQUILIDAD*

The content in this chapter is based on my personal recollections and experiences, and those of certain family members.

The quote, "What is death, but a negligible accident?" is from a sermon titled "Death the King of Terrors" by Henry Scott Holland, a professor of divinity at the University of Oxford, given in May 1910.

PART III: BARGAINING

The quote at the beginning of this section is from Joan Didion's book *The Year of Magical Thinking*, Alfred A. Knopf, 2005, page 146.

21 | THE TALISMAN

The content in this chapter is based on my trip to southern California, including various residential locations in Burbank and San Diego, in April 2010. I interviewed several of Pat's friends during this trip on condition of anonymity; their descriptions of his addiction contributed to my retelling of Pat's story. In San Diego I also visited the motel room where Pat overdosed, the hospital where he was brought following the overdose, and the courthouse where his legal proceedings were conducted. I retrieved court documents and medical records from these locations that contributed to my retelling of his story.

On April 12, 2010, I conducted an in-person interview with Evan Raycraft, whose relationship with Pat is described in this chapter. That interview was followed by a series of phone and email conversations that also contributed to Pat's story.

22 | LETTING GO

Dale and Ellie are pseudonyms. I interviewed Ellie at her home in Mission Viejo, California, on May 16, 2013. In addition to providing her own perspective regarding her son Dale, she corroborated the details of his overdoses and history of addiction, which was provided to me by Dale in a separate interview; see notes for chapter 19.

23 | BROKEN

The content in this chapter is based on my personal recollections and experiences, and those of certain family members.

24 | SECRETS

Julie and Trey are pseudonyms. Julie provided the story about her son Trey's addiction in an in-person interview at her home in Laguna Niguel, California, on May 23, 2013.

Brady, Abby, and Sam are also pseudonyms; see notes for chapter 26.

25 | MAKE IT NOT SO

The content in this chapter is based on my personal recollections and experiences, and those of certain family members.

The quote by Thomas Lynch is from his book *Bodies in Motion and at Rest: On Metaphor and Mortality*, W.W. Norton & Co., 2001, page 111.

26 | TOO LATE

The description of opiate overdoses among teens and young adults comes from Dr. Robert H. Winokur, M.D., emergency room physician and medical director at Mission

Hospital in Mission Viejo, California. I interviewed Dr. Winokur at his home in Laguna Niguel on May 17, 2013, and again at the hospital on May 22, 2013. The statistics regarding opiate overdoses in Orange County are based on data compiled by Dr. Winokur, which he provided to me during our interviews, and were also reported in my August 15, 2012, article on CaliforniaWatch.org, "With rise in young painkiller abusers, officials see more heroin overdoses," http://californiawatch.org/health-and-welfare/rise-young-painkiller-abusers-officials-see-more-heroin-overdoses-17550.

The section about Abby contains pseudonyms at the request of the interviewee. Abby provided the story of her son, Brady, in a phone interview on June 6, 2013. Brady's story was corroborated by his girlfriend Catherine in two in-person interviews on May 16, 2013, and May 23, 2013, as well as in a series of phone interviews in July 2013; see notes for chapter 29. Jeff is also a pseudonym.

27 | THE GOD STORY

The content in this chapter is based on my personal recollections and experiences, and those of certain family members.

The note from Pat, which is undated, was lightly edited for clarity.

The quote "Perhaps our lives spread out around us like a fan and we can only know one life, but by mistake sense others," is from Jeanette Winterson's book *The Passion*, Grove Press, 1987, page 144.

The text of Pat's eulogy was provided by Jennifer Kraushaar, whose siblings, Justin Perkins and Juliann Perkins, also agreed to use their real names.

The quote, "Love is stronger than death . . ." is by an unknown author.

PART IV: DEPRESSION

The quote at the beginning of this section is from Nicholas Wolterstorff's book *Lament for a Son*, Eerdmans Publishing Company, 1987, page 42.

28 | BLACK TEARS

The content in this chapter is based on my personal recollections and experiences, and those of certain family members.

"Black Tears" is a poem by Pat, found in his personal journals, date unknown. The verses included are an excerpt of the full poem.

29 | YOU WITHOUT ME

The names in this section are pseudonyms at the request of the interviewee. The continuation of Brady's story was provided to me by Catherine in two in-person interviews on May 16, 2013, and May 23, 2013, at various locations in Mission Viejo, California, including Florence Joyner Park, as well as in a series of phone interviews in July 2013. Catherine also shared portions of Brady's journals, parts of which are quoted in this chapter and were lightly edited for clarity.

30 | LITTLE BIRD

The content in this chapter is based on my personal recollections and experiences, and those of certain family members.

"In the midst of life, we are in death" is the title and first line of a Latin text, "Media Vita in Morte Sumus," translated into the vernacular by Thomas Cranmer for use in *The Book of Common Prayer for the Episcopal Church*.

The quote from Elisabeth Kubler-Ross is from her book *On Grief and Grieving: Finding the Meaning of Grief through the Five Stages of Loss*, Scribner, 2005, page 39.

31 | IMPRISONED

The names in this section are pseudonyms at the request of the interviewee. The story of Bryce and his addiction comes from an in-person interview with his mother, Leigh, at her home in Huntington Beach, California, on May 21, 2013, as well as from a series of phone interviews in July 2013.

32 | HAUNTED

The content in this chapter is based on my personal recollections and experiences, and those of certain family members.

33 | ATONEMENT

Joel is a pseudonym. His story comes from an in-person interview with him at Henry Ohlhoff House in San Francisco, California, in June 2010, as well as from conversations via email and text message between July 2010 and March 2013.

Eddie Bridgett, program director of the men's residential treatment center, provided information about the demographics of Ohlhoff House's clients.

Joel's text messages, and my own, were lightly edited for grammar and clarity.

Nate is also a pseudonym.

34 | DESPAIR WITHOUT HOPE

The content in this chapter is based on my personal recollections and experiences, and those of certain family members. It also includes information from my interview with Kerry and Kenny Washburn of Swampscott, Massachusetts, at their home on July 28, 2010, regarding their son Casey Washburn.

35 | BLINDSIDED

Mark Melkonian's story stems from an interview with his friend Brianne Costa at her home in Laguna Niguel, California, on May 17, 2013, as well as with his mother, Sylvia Melkonian, in interviews on April 6, 2012, in Laguna Niguel, California, and May 18, 2013, in Sunset Beach, California.

The description of Mark's grave comes from my visit to the Good Shepherd Cemetery in Huntington Beach, California, on May 22, 2013.

36 | FALLING APART

The content in this chapter is based on my personal recollections and experiences, and those of certain family members.

The quote "There has never been a tunnel so long . . ." is from Harold S. Kushner's book *The Lord Is My Shepherd: Healing Wisdom of the Twenty-Third Psalm*, Anchor Books, 2003, page 99.

PART V: ACCEPTANCE

The quote at the beginning of this section is excerpted from *Four Quartets,* a series of poems written by T.S. Eliot, published individually over a six-year period in the 1940s. The excerpt is from "Part II: East Coker."

37 | A TERRIBLE TRUTH

The content in this chapter is based on my personal recollections and experiences, and those of certain family members.

The quote from Anne Lamott is from her book *Help Thanks Wow: The Three Essential Prayers*, Riverhead Books, 2012, page 27.

38 | I SEE YOU

Alex (a pseudonym), a project manager at the unnamed harm-reduction nonprofit in Oakland, California, provided the information about naloxone statistics and use in an interview at her office on April 25, 2013, and at a training workshop on May 10, 2013, at the same location, as well as in a series of phone and email conversations during 2012 and 2013.

The description of Alex's work at the unnamed drop-in center for homeless drug users in San Francisco stems from my own observations at an event held at the center on April 11, 2013.

Brendan, Emily, Corey, and Tim are also pseudonyms.

39 | ANOTHER LIFE

The content in this chapter is based on my personal recollections and experiences, and those of certain family members.

The quote about phantom limbs is from *The Perception of Phantom Limbs: The D.O. Hebb Lecture,* by V.S. Ramachandran and William Hirstein, Oxford University Press, 1998, available online at http://www.dgp.toronto.edu/~elf/199/content/Phantom%20Limbs.pdf.

My interview with the young heroin addict, who asked that his name be withheld, was conducted on May 9, 2013, in Concord, California.

The information regarding risk factors for a drug overdose was provided by the DOPE (Drug Overdose Prevention and Education) Project, a project of the Harm Reduction Coalition.

40 | TAKE HIM HOME

Bailey, Asher, and Kai are pseudonyms. Bailey provided the story of her brother Asher in two interviews in San Clemente, California, on May 20, 2013, and May 23, 2013, as well as in additional conversations via phone, text message, and email between June 2013 and July 2013.

Bailey also provided numerous personal documents from Asher's childhood, adolescence, and adult years that contributed to the telling of his story. The quotes from Asher's letter to himself, written during his treatment in April 2013, were lightly edited for clarity.

The scripture "I will not cause pain without allowing something new to be born" is from Isaiah 66:9, New International Version (http://www.biblica.com/niv/).

41 | ROSES AND WEEDS

The content in this chapter is based on my personal recollections and experiences, and those of certain family members.

The quote about growing roses is from the website of the nonprofit All-American Rose Selections and can be viewed at http://www.rose.org/planting-roses/.

The quote about bonding with your newborn is by William Sears, M.D., as cited by the website of Attachment Parenting International at http://www.attachmentparenting.org/support/articles/artbonding.php.

The quote about addiction and nostalgia is from Ann Marlowe's book *How to Stop Time: Heroin from A to Z*, Perseus Books, 1999, page 10.

42 | WALKING WITH THE DEVIL

Andrew Presta's story comes from an interview with his mother, Diana Presta, in Mission Viejo on May 19, 2013. On May 24, 2013, I conducted an interview with Andrew while he was incarcerated at the Lamoreaux Justice Center in Orange, California, and he corroborated his mother's version of the story.

Diana also provided numerous personal documents from Andrew's adolescence and adult years, as well as her own personal writing, which contributed to the telling of his story.

43 | WHEN YOU WERE FREE

The content in this chapter is based on my personal recollections and experiences, and those of certain family members.

44 | THE PROMISE

Krista and Max are pseudonyms. Krista and Max provided their story during in-person interviews in San Rafael, California, on November 9, 2011, and May 6, 2013.

45 | AWAKE

The content in this chapter is based on my personal recollections and experiences.

ACKNOWLEDGMENTS

THANKS TO MY agent, Penny Nelson, for fighting to bring this story into the light. My editor, Liz Parker, provided invaluable guidance with honesty and sensitivity in equal measure.

Over the course of my writing career, I have had the privilege of working with many excellent journalists. They have provided advice and mentorship, both professionally and personally, and I am lucky to count many of them as friends. In particular, my former editor at Law360, Marius Meland, has my deep gratitude for encouraging me on my path.

To my sources, named and nameless, thank you for trusting me and for making the difficult decision to share your stories with the world. You are courageous and admirable and beyond brave, and you have my heartfelt respect.

To those who work in the field of addiction, thank you for everything you do to help people like my brother.

To my many dear friends, you have carried me over mountains on your shoulders. Thank you. This book would not exist without you.

To my family and those who are like family, thank you: to Mom and Dad for raising me to believe I could be anything I wanted to be; to Cait and Bri for being the most amazing siblings, confidantes, and cheerleaders; to Elise for loving us; to Kathy for your unending love and lightness; to Betty and Tom for your steady presence and wise counsel over the years; and to everyone else who has supported and cared for me.

To Ben, thank you for making it possible for me to chase my dreams. Thank you for being the rock to my kite. I promise not to write another book for at least ten years. Maybe five.

And thank you, Pat. Thank you for being you.

RESOURCES

THE FOLLOWING WEBSITES and organizations can provide more information
on prescription drug and heroin addiction.

Advocates for the Reform of Prescription Opioids
http://www.rxreform.org

American Society of Addiction Medicine
http://www.asam.org

The Courage to Speak Foundation
http://www.couragetospeak.org

Harm Reduction Coalition
http://www.harmreduction.org

Faces and Voices of Recovery
http://www.facesandvoicesofrecovery.org

GRASP (Grief Recovery after a Substance Passing)
http://grasphelp.org

Learn to Cope
http://www.learn2cope.org/index.php

The Medicine Abuse Project
http://medicineabuseproject.org

NaloxoneInfo.org
http://www.naloxoneinfo.org

Nar-Anon
http://www.nar-anon.org/naranon/

Narcotics Anonymous
http://www.na.org

National Coalition against Prescription Drug Abuse
http://ncapda.org

National Council on Patient Information and Education
http://www.talkaboutrx.org

National Institute on Drug Abuse
http://www.drugabuse.gov

Oxy Watchdog
http://www.oxywatchdog.com

The Partnership at Drugfree.org
http://www.drugfree.org

Physicians for Responsible Opioid Prescribing
http://www.supportprop.org

Recovery.org
http://www.recovery.org

Substance Abuse and Mental Health Services Administration
http://www.samhsa.gov

U.S. Centers for Disease Control and Prevention Injury Center
http://www.cdc.gov/injury/about/focus-rx.html

SOURCES

1   Jana Burson, M.D., Pain Pill Addiction: A Prescription for Hope (Indianapolis: Dog Ear Publishing, 2010), 54.

2   "How Aspirin Turned Hero," Sunday Times, September 13, 1998, reproduced at http://opioids.com/heroin/heroinhistory.html.

3   Barry Meier, Pain Killer: A "Wonder" Drug's Trail of Addiction and Death (Emmaus, PA: Rodale, 2003), 57.

4   Burson, Pain Pill Addiction, 54.

5   Meier, Pain Killer, 58–59.

6   Burson, Pain Pill Addiction, 70.

7   Burson, Pain Killer, 74.

8   Thomas Catan and Evan Perez, "A Pain-Drug Champion Has Second Thoughts," Wall Street Journal, December 17, 2012, http://online.wsj.com/article/SB1000142412 78873244783045781733426570446 04.html.

9   Barry Meier, "Profiting from Pain," New York Times, June 22, 2013, http://www.nytimes.com/2013/06/23/sunday-review/profiting-from-pain.html?_r=0.

10 Burson, Pain Pill Addiction, 74–75; Meier, Pain Killer, 72–73.

11 Ibid., 77–78.

12 Andrea Trescott, Stanford Helm, et al. "Opioids in the Management of Chronic Non-Cancer Pain: An Update of American Society of the Interventional Pain Physicians' Guidelines," Special issue, Pain Physician 11 (2008): S5–S62.

13 Burson, Pain Pill Addiction, 82–83.

14 Steven Passik, Journal of Pain and Symptom Management 21, no. 5 (May 2001) 359–60.

15 OxyContin Abuse and Diversion, Report GAO-04-11 (Washington, D.C.: U.S. General Accounting Office, 2003).

16   Melody Petersen, Our Daily Meds: How the Pharmaceutical Companies Transformed
      Themselves into Slick Marketing Machines and Hooked the Nation on Prescription
      Drugs (New York: Farrar, Straus and Giroux, 2008), 9–10.

17   Burson, Pain Pill Addiction, 83.

18   Barry Meier, "Narcotic Maker Guilty of Deceit over Marketing," New York
      Times, May 11, 2007, http://www.nytimes.com/2007/05/11/business/11drug.
      html?pagewanted=all.

19   "Prescription for Peril," Coalition against Insurance Fraud, 2007, http://www
      .insurancefraud.org/downloads/drugDiversion.pdf.

20   Greg Allen, "The 'Oxy Express': Florida's Drug Abuse Epidemic," National
      Public Radio, March 2, 2011, http://www.npr.org/2011/03/02/134143813/
      the-oxy-express-floridas-drug-abuse-epidemic.

21   Timothy W. Martin, "Painkiller Abuse Hits New States," Wall Street Journal, March
      10, 2013, http://online.wsj.com/article/SB10001424127887324281004578352243321
      1552104.html.

22   Donna Leinwand Leger, "OxyContin a Gateway to Heroin for Upper-Income
      Addicts," USA Today, June 28, 2013, http://www.usatoday.com/story/news/
      nation/2013/04/15/heroin-crackdown-oxycodone-hydrocodone/1963123/.

23   "National Drug Threat Assessment 2010," U.S. Department of Justice, http://www.
      justice.gov/opa/pr/2010/March/10-ag-314.html.

24   "Effect of Abuse-Deterrent Formulation of OxyContin," New England Journal
      of Medicine 367 (2012): 187–89, http://www.nejm.org/doi/full/10.1056/
      NEJMc1204141.

25   "Epidemic: Responding to America's Prescription Drug Crisis," Executive Office
      of the President of the United States, April 2011, http://www.whitehouse.gov/sites/
      default/files/ondcp/issues-content/prescription-drugs/rx_abuse_plan.pdf.

26   Letitia Stein and Meg Laughlin, "The Rise and Fall of Florida's Drug Monitoring,"
      Tampa Bay Times, March 11, 2011, http://www.tampabay.com/news/health/
      the-rise-and-fall-of-floridas-drug-monitoring/1156674.

27   Lisa Girion, Scott Glover, and Doug Smith, "Drug Deaths Now Outnumber
      Traffic Fatalities in U.S., Data Show," Los Angeles Times, September 17, 2011,
      http://articles.latimes.com/2011/sep/17/local/la-me-drugs-epidemic-20110918.

28   "Policy Impact: Prescription Painkiller Overdoses," U.S. Centers for Disease Control
      and Prevention, November 2011, http://www.cdc.gov/homeandrecreationalsafety/
      rxbrief/.

29 "Neonatal Abstinence Syndrome and Associated Health Care Expenditures, United
    States, 2000–2009," Journal of the American Medical Association, May 9, 2012,
    http://jama.jamanetwork.com/article.aspx?articleid=1151530.

30 "Results from the 2011 National Survey on Drug Use and Health: Summary of
    National Findings," U.S. Department of Health and Human Services, September
    2012, http://www.samhsa.gov/data/NSDUH/2k11Results/NSDUHresults2011.htm.

31 Catan and Perez, "Pain-Drug Champion."

32 "Opioids Drive Continued Increase in Drug Overdose Deaths," U.S. Centers for
    Disease Control and Prevention, February 20, 2013, http://www.cdc.gov/media/
    releases/2013/p0220_drug_overdose_deaths.html.

33 Nancy Shute and Audrey Carlsen, "FDA's Rejection of Generic
    OxyContin May Have Side Effects," National Public Radio, April
    18, 2013, http://www.npr.org/blogs/health/2013/04/17/177602393/
    why-fdas-rejection-generic-oxycontin-may-have-side-effects.

34 "FDA Statement: Original Opana ER Relisting Determination," U.S. Food and Drug
    Administration, May 10, 2013, http://www.fda.gov/Drugs/DrugSafety/ucm351357.
    htm.

35 Timothy W. Martin and Jonathan D. Rockoff, "Unmeltable, Uncrushable:
    The Holy Grail in Painkillers," Wall Street Journal, May 5, 2013, http://
    online.wsj.com/article/SB10001424127887323798104578453210799151732.
    html?mod=rss_whats_news_us.

36 Edward Marshall, "W. Va. heroin overdose deaths in 2012 tripled," The Journal,
    July 27, 2013, http://www.journal-news.net/page/content.detail/id/597015/
    W-Va--heroin-overdose-deaths-in----.html.

37 "Drug and Alcohol Intoxication Deaths in Maryland 2007–2012," Maryland
    Department of Health and Mental Hygiene, July 2013, http://adaa.dhmh.maryland.
    gov/Documents/content_documents/OverdosePrevention/2007-2012%20intox%20
    report_final.pdf.

38 Stuart Tomlinson, "Oregon drug deaths: More people in their 20s dying over heroin
    overdoses," Oregonian, May 31, 2013, http://www.oregonlive.com/health/index.
    ssf/2013/05/oregon_drug_deaths_more_people.html.

39 "SAMHSA: Pain Medication Abuse a Common Path to Heroin," Journal of the
    American Medical Association, October 9, 2013, http://jama.jamanetwork.com/
    article.aspx?articleID=1750124.

40 Barry Meier, "F.D.A. Urging a Tighter Rein on Painkillers," New York Times,
    October 24, 2013, http://www.nytimes.com/2013/10/25/business/fda-seeks-tighter-
    control-on-prescriptions-for-class-of-painkillers.html.

41   "FDA approves extended-release, single-entity hydrocodone product," U.S. Food
      and Drug Administration, October 15, 2013, http://www.fda.gov/NewsEvents/
      Newsroom/PressAnnouncements/ucm372287.htm.

42   Barry Meier, "Addiction Specialists Wary of a New Painkiller," New York Times,
      November 15, 2013, http://www.nytimes.com/2013/11/16/business/addiction-
      specialists-wary-of-a-new-painkiller.html.

43   "Abuse of Prescription (Rx) Drugs Affects Young Adults Most," National Institute
      on Drug Abuse, June 2013, http://www.drugabuse.gov/related-topics/trends-statistics/
      infographics/abuse-prescription-rx-drugs-affects-young-adults-most, citing data from
      the U.S. Centers for Disease Control and Prevention.

44   "DrugFacts: Heroin," National Institute on Drug Abuse, April 2013, http://www.
      drugabuse.gov/publications/drugfacts/heroin.

45   "Attorney General Holder, Calling Rise in Heroin Overdoses 'Urgent Public Health
      Crisis,' Vows Mix of Enforcement, Treatment," U.S. Department of Justice, March
      14, 2014, http://www.justice.gov/opa/pr/2014/March/14-ag-246.html.

46   "Prescription Painkiller Overdoses in the U.S.," U.S. Centers for Disease Control
      and Prevention, February 15, 2012, http://www.cdc.gov/features/vitalsigns/
      painkilleroverdoses/.

47   "Policy Impact: Prescription Painkiller Overdoses," U.S. Centers for Disease Control
      and Prevention, November 2011, http://www.cdc.gov/homeandrecreationalsafety/
      rxbrief/.

48   Singh A. Manchikanti L., "Therapeutic opioids: a ten-year perspective on the
      complexities and complications of the escalating use, abuse, and nonmedical
      use of opioids," Pain Physician, March 11, 2008, http://www.ncbi.nlm.nih.gov/
      pubmed/18443641.

49   "Drugs, Brains, and Behavior: The Science of Addiction," National Institute
      on Drug Abuse, August 2010, http://www.drugabuse.gov/publications/
      drugs-brains-behavior-science-addiction/drug-abuse-addiction.

50   David Sheff, Clean: Overcoming Addiction and Ending America's Greatest Tragedy
      (New York: Houghton Mifflin Harcourt Publishing Co., 2013), 101.

51   "Florida Doctors No Longer among the Top Oxycodone Purchasers in the United
      States," U.S. Department of Justice, April 5, 2013, http://www.justice.gov/dea/divisions/
      mia/2013/mia040513.shtml, citing the U.S. Drug Enforcement Administration's
      Automation of Reports and Consolidated Orders System (ARCOS).

52   Thomas R. Collins, "Invasion of the Pill Mills in South Florida," Time, April 13,
      2010, http://content.time.com/time/nation/article/0,8599,1981582,00.html.

53 Michael Montgomery, "Majority of third-strike inmates are addicts, records show," CaliforniaWatch.org, September 30, 2012, http://californiawatch.org/public-safety/majority-third-strike-inmates-are-addicts-records-show-18132. California's three-strikes law was revised in 2012 to impose a life sentence only when the third felony offense is serious or violent and to authorize courts to resentence prisoners convicted of low-level third offenses; see Brent Staples, "California Horror Stories and the 3-Strikes Law," New York Times, November 24, 2012, http://www.nytimes.com/2012/11/25/opinion/sunday/california-horror-stories-and-the-3-strikes-law.html?_r=0.

54 NIDA, "Drugs, Brains, and "Behavior."

55 David Whiting, "Prescription meds kill in O.C. every two minutes," Orange County Register, January 23, 2013, http://www.ocregister.com/articles/deaths-408993-year-drugs.html; Erin Marie Daly, "With rise in young painkiller abusers, officials see more heroin overdoses," CaliforniaWatch.org, August 15, 2012, http://californiawatch.org/health-and-welfare/rise-young-painkiller-abusers-officials-see-more-heroin-overdoses-17550.

56 "Brain Maturity Extends Well beyond Teen Years," National Public Radio, October 10, 2011, http://www.npr.org/templates/story/story.php?storyId=141164708.

57 David Sack, "Why Relapse Isn't a Sign of Failure," Psychology Today, October 19, 2012, http://www.psychologytoday.com/blog/where-science-meets-the-steps/201210/why-relapse-isnt-sign-failure.

58 Sheff, Clean, 95, 99–101.

59 Ibid., 100.

60 NIDA, "Abuse of Prescription (Rx) Drugs."

61 Daly, "With rise"; see also notes for chapter 26.

62 The numbers regarding overdose reversals in San Francisco due use of naloxone were provided by the DOPE (Drug Overdose Prevention and Education) Project, a project of the Harm Reduction Coalition; the national statistic comes from U.S. Centers for Disease Control and Prevention, "Community-Based Opioid Overdose Prevention Programs Providing Naloxone—United States, 2010," Morbidity and Mortality Weekly Report 61, no. 6 (February 17, 2012), http://www.cdc.gov/mmwr/pdf/wk/mm6106.pdf.

63 Tessie Castillo, "Big Pharma Jacks up Price of Overdose Life Saver by 1100%: Now, More People Will Die," AlterNet.com, April 8, 2013, http://www.alternet.org/big-pharma-company-jacks-price-overdose-life-saver-1100-now-more-people-will-die?page=0%2C0.

64 Sheff, Clean, 92, 253–55.

65   "Relapse rates for drug addiction are similar to those of other well-
     characterized chronic diseases," National Institute on Drug Abuse, July
     2008, http://www.drugabuse.gov/publications/addiction-science/relapse/
     relapse-rates-drug-addiction-are-similar-to-those-other-well-characterized-chronic-ill.